MAEVE BINCHY

MAEVE BINCHY

THE BIOGRAPHY

PIERS DUDGEON

The Robson Press

This edition published in Great Britain in 2014 by
The Robson Press (an imprint of Biteback Publishing Ltd)
Westminster Tower
3 Albert Embankment
London SE1 7SP
Copyright © Piers Dudgeon 2013

ISBN 978-1-84954-695-9

10 9 8 7 6 5 4 3 2

A CIP catalogue record for this book is available from the British Library.

Set in Caslon and Perpetua

Printed and bound in Great Britain by
CPI Group (UK) Ltd, Croydon, CR0 4YY

For Deirdre

'I still think, as I did when I was twenty, that I could run everybody else's life. Not my own of course, as my own is deep confusion to me.'

– Maeve Binchy[1]

CONTENTS

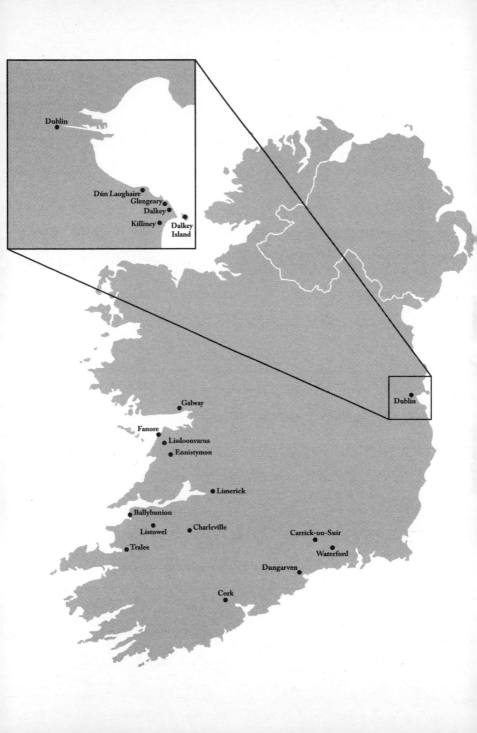

ONE

BEGINNINGS

The morning of Wednesday 15 August 1956 saw the sun rise full and bright over Killiney Bay, creating a perfect backdrop to the image of a tall teenage girl hurtling down the Knocknacree Road in a blur of bicycle wheels towards the little town of Dalkey.

On a day as glorious as this the deep blue sky and sea, sun-soaked white buildings, occasional palm trees and distant shadowy aspect of the Wicklow mountains to the south beg comparison with the fabulous view over the Bay of Naples, to which the roads surrounding – Vico, Sorrento, Monte Alverno, San Elmo and Capri – seem also to bear testimony.

But you won't find a road in the whole of Italy called Knocknacree. And the town of Dalkey, inscribed more or less on three sides by the sea, is inescapably Ireland. Old Dubliners used to say of it, 'For God's sake, sure that's the end of the line; sure, it must have been the last place God made and left His tools behind Him.' Up to 1876 there was no road beyond it along the coast, and it was literally the end of the line for the Dublin tram.

Stables for the old horse-drawn version were constructed here in the 1880s, before it gave way to the motorised vehicle, but that disappeared in 1949. 'It's strange,' said Patricia Hamilton, who lives there now, 'but Dalkey is still a little like a cul-de-sac. You're not going through it *to* anywhere.' Why would you? As Flann O'Brien described it in his novel *The Dalkey Archive* (1964), it's the perfect antidote to Ireland's capital city.

Dalkey is a little town maybe twelve miles south of Dublin, on the shore. It is an unlikely town, huddled, quiet, pretending to be asleep. Its streets are narrow, not quite self-evident as streets and with meetings which seem accidental. Small shops look closed but are open. Dalkey looks like an humble settlement which must, a traveller feels, be next door to some place of the first importance and distinction...

In 1956, untroubled by traffic, this southern outpost of Ireland's capital city was not among the towns and villages of the Gaeltacht (traditional, Gaelic-speaking Ireland), but its closed-in nature fostered just as strong a sense of belonging among its people. The family values which lie at the heart of Irish tradition imbued life here: the girl on a bicycle had spent her first seventeen years surrounded by more love than anyone could hope for.

As she careered, less perilously now, down Railway Road into Castle Street in the centre of town, Findlater's, the grocery and provision merchant at No. 37, with its sacks of dried peas and porridge oats on the old wooden floor, was opening its doors. Searson's Wines & Spirits, Dartry Dye Works and Felton the Draper at No. 47 lined the way as she glided into the old Dalkey lands – the seventh-century ruins of St Begnet, the original parish church, the two medieval castles standing sentry on either side of the road, and the nineteenth-century Church of the Assumption, where she brought her bicycle to a halt.

Leaning it against the wall of the church she glanced respectfully at the figure of Our Lady in the churchyard, for it was indeed *Her* day, 15 August, Feast Day of the Assumption, the day reserved by Catholics to celebrate the Virgin Mary's ascension into heaven.

Making her way inside, she saw with relief that she was alone and walked silently down the nave towards the east end of the church where stood a rack of candles and a collection box covered in hard white wax.

Put a penny in the box and you could light a candle for someone ailing, or for their soul if they were dead. She and her friends generally did it to make a wish come true, and today the girl would need all the help she could get. She was expecting the results of her Certificate of Matriculation, which would decide whether she could go to university. It was a day that could change her life forever.[2]

With the candle lit she knelt in one of the long pews in the main body of the church. The carving of the Last Supper on the face of the High Altar and the white plaster sculptures depicting the Stations of the Cross on the walls above her were scenes she knew intimately, quite as well as the furniture in any of the rooms at home.

Raising her head she looked up at the three magnificent

3

stained glass panels of the east window, framed like a triptych over the High Altar. The one in the centre commanded her attention in particular. It showed the very moment the Mother of God was taken into Heaven, her earthly life over.

She held the vision in her mind as she covered her eyes with her hands and told God exactly why it was that she was there, that she was sure He would understand that it was time now for her to leave Dalkey and put all the tortures He had seen fit to heap upon her to good use.

She had a very special relationship with God, frank and open. She regarded him as a friend, an Irish friend of course. He knew her innermost thoughts, both good and sinful. He also knew her innermost problems, or 'tortures' as she referred to them. He knew them because it was He who had given them to her, to challenge her and make a saint of her, which she fully intended to be. In later years she would be reticent about her spiritual beliefs. But now, though seventeen years of age, she was still an innocent child and was clearer, freer and more content with her inner life than she ever would be again.

Hers had been the best start any girl could want. She was born Anne Maeve Binchy, in a maternity unit at 26 Upper Pembroke Road in Dublin, on 29 May 1939, the eldest daughter of a young barrister, William Francis Binchy, and his wife, Maureen.[3]

Her father was a studious, intellectual and gentle man. As a barrister he wasn't especially high-achieving, but he had a deep and serious interest in the law and was clearly something of a workaholic. Whether at home in his study, or sitting in the garden in the summer, or on holiday with his wife and children, William always had a bundle of solicitors' briefs with him.

Maeve's upbringing might have been a thoroughly ordinary middle-class Catholic one had it not been for her mother. Maureen Blackmore was completely different to William. She was an extrovert, with an irrepressible personality grounded in an unquenchable interest in people, whoever they might be and wherever she might find them. If she and Maeve were on the bus together Maureen would not only talk to the person next to her but to the whole bus, making her daughter more self-conscious with every passing moment. Often Maureen could be found down in the open-air market in Dublin's Moore Street, sitting in a fur coat on an upturned box, furiously smoking her Gold Flake cigarettes and engaging with the traders, famous for their banter and thick Dublin accent. What was important to Maureen was what went on between people – her world was made up not so much of things as of people, and in particular of the resonances between them.

Very much an authentic free spirit, caring, socially conscious but unaffected, a natural socialist, she brought compassion to people's lives and had an intuitive way of always saying what turned out to be right. This wasn't a learned skill nor did she have to try to find the words. They were 'just there', as Maeve put it. It seems that Maureen was something of a seer, and Maeve felt that her mother's marriage to her father was definitely touched by fate.

Maureen and William were both working in Dublin around the time that they met, William as a lawyer, Maureen as a nurse at St Vincent's, a major academic teaching hospital in Ireland's capital city. But they actually came together for the first time elsewhere, under extraordinary circumstances.

Regularly each summer Maureen booked in to a seaside resort called Ballybunion, far to the west of Ireland on the beautiful Kerry coast, for the final two weeks of July. And every year, with the same regularity, William went to the same place for the first two weeks of August. For years they missed one another by a few days or hours. Then one summer, on the last day of July, Maureen happened to miss the bus home and decided to go back to the hotel and see if she could stay on a while longer.

Bursting into reception, she explained what had happened and asked if she could keep her room. Unfortunately not, she was told, it had just that minute been taken. The receptionist had nodded towards a young man still hanging around in the foyer looking rather perplexed at any difficulty he may inadvertently have caused.

Being a gentleman, William insisted that Maureen should have the room, and then surprised himself by saying that perhaps they'd see each other at the dance that evening.

Ballybunion was a popular rendezvous for hundreds of families, singles and gangs of young people from all over Ireland and farther afield. At that time the Pavilion was the place to go dancing in the evening. Sure enough, William and Maureen did meet at the dance – a meeting of chance which they made much of with their children over the years. Perhaps it takes fate to step in for two young people so completely different to one another, to make as loving a relationship as theirs turned out to be.

William and Maureen wed on 29 March 1938, at the Catholic church of St Michael in the ancient port of Dún Laoghaire (pronounced Dunleary), a couple of miles north-west of Dalkey.

Maureen recorded no rank or profession on the marriage certificate, but Maeve was always told that she was a nurse training to be a physiotherapist at the time. She gave her address as Piltown, County Kilkenny. She had been born further west, on a rural estate called Cregg, a few miles to the north of Carrick-on-Suir on the border of Tipperary with Kilkenny. Her father, Thomas, was a farmer on the estate and her mother, Bridget, kept two servants, one a domestic, the other a farm servant. The Blackmores lived at 'House No. 14' on the estate but, according to Maeve, Thomas and Bridget died when Maureen was a child and she'd been 'brought up by step-relations', probably in nearby Piltown.

William and Maureen's first home together was at Beechgrove, a house at the south end of the Lower Glenageary Road, on the border of Dalkey and Dún Laoghaire, not far from where William had been renting a room on Summerhill Terrace.

Everyone gives the year of the birth of the couple's first-born as 1940, as Maeve herself did. But the child's birth certificate states plainly and unequivocally that she was born on 29 May 1939. Her sister Joan was born in 1942; Irene (known as Renie) followed in 1944 and her brother William in 1947.

Maureen made both Beechgrove and, later, Eastmount (the house on Knocknacree Road to which the Binchys moved in 1952) warm and happy homes. The family was a complete and significant entity in the lives of the children and they would live at home during and after university, and return to live nearby as mature adults.

'My childhood was a joy,' Maeve confirmed. She remembered no arguments between her parents during the entire course of her childhood and only one difference of opinion. It had begun as a discussion about the precise structure of a horse-drawn cart, a subject Maureen, being a farmer's daughter, might be expected to know something about, but evidently also one that a pedantic legal mind might want to examine in minuscule detail. Pretty soon voices were raised and it developed into a row, one that other families probably wouldn't even have noticed. But so harmonious was life usually in the Binchy household that to the children it seemed that their parents were one step away from divorce. Maeve remembered sitting on the stairs with her three siblings, taking her role as the eldest seriously and organising who would go to live with whom.

Religion was an integral part of life, for the Binchys were a practising Roman Catholic family and Maeve attended church from when she was a baby. On Sundays in the 1940s and 1950s the shops closed and *everyone* went to church. It was very much a family event, as well as a cultural and spiritual one, a freshening of the spirit of the community.

The two sacred institutions around which life turned when Maeve was a girl, family and religion, both came together at Christmas, which she always associated with the best moments in her childhood.

One year Maeve asked Santa for a doll's house, but it was too late for her father to get hold of one. William and Maureen stayed up all night trying unsuccessfully to make one, in desperation writing a note from Santa saying that it was too big for the chimney and would come the following year.

But while nothing was too much for her parents, Maeve was not spoiled materially. She said that she and her three siblings were dressed by Maureen in hand-me-downs from their cousins. Money was lavished neither on the children nor on the house, the interior of which Maeve described as 'shabby'. Eastmount was comfortable but not self-consciously so. Life was for living, not a 'permanent examination where women would be found wanting'.[4] Maureen had a horror of pretension of any sort and this transferred to Maeve along with much else of her mother's qualities and temperament.

It was a feature of Christmas that Maureen would invite people to lunch who had no family of their own. Maeve doesn't appear to have liked this custom very much, but Maureen was not interested in any grouse from the children about wanting Christmas for them alone. Her children were her priority for the other 364 days of the year, beginning on St Stephen's Day – Boxing Day – when Maureen would take them on the bus to Leopardstown races in Foxrock, a little to the west of Dalkey. William had no interest in racing but Maureen loved it, especially meeting all the people. Maeve remembered it as marvellous.

At home there was an open-door policy for the children and Eastmount became a centre for all their friends. It was a sea of affection and laughter, a swelling tide of squealing and giggling and wriggling excitement when they were young, which surely inspired the atmosphere in Maeve's first novel, *Light a Penny Candle* (1982), of the O'Connors' home at 14 The Square, Kilgarret, a small town in County Wicklow, also just south of Dublin, 'where there was constant companionship and apparently half the town passing through on some errand or other'.

Light a Penny Candle, set in Ireland and England during and after the Second World War, is a tale of friendship between Aisling O'Connor (generally pronounced Ash-leen) and an English evacuee to Ireland, Elizabeth White, who arrives in Kilgarret at the start of the Second World War. Elizabeth's mother Violet knows Aisling's mother Eileen because they went to school together at a convent in England. At the beginning of the novel both girls are just ten, but their friendship continues to survive against all odds, long into the future.

There are many reasons to return to this novel, one being the affecting picture Maeve draws of life at home in the O'Connor household, a wonderful testimony to the happy and supportive childhood William and Maureen gave its author.

In the beginning the White family is the yardstick against which the O'Connors' happy family scene is measured. Elizabeth, her mother Violet and father George live a drab, grey life in suburban London. George has a dreary job in a bank and has been rejected as unsuitable for war. His rejection seems less to do with his deafness, varicose veins, flat feet and whistling chest than with his utter dullness and inadequacy. George seems to invite rejection from every quarter.

Elizabeth's mother, Violet, has been ground down by marriage to George. Her features are flat; all sparkle has disappeared.

Elizabeth longs for her parents to be happy, and escapes upstairs pretending to do her homework when in fact she is sitting on her bed crying and unpicking the stitching of a favourite doll.

This is in vivid contrast to the tumbling humanity of the O'Connor family in Kilgarret – Sean O'Connor, his wife Eileen, young Sean, Maureen, ten-year-old Aisling, truculent Eamonn, consumptive Donal and baby Niamh.

The O'Connors are passionate, fun, lively creatures. On arrival, the evacuee Elizabeth is overcome by the sheer boisterousness and confusion and extravagant emotion of this, a traditional Irish family.

It is then that Aisling, with her wild red hair and intuitive ways – the person Maeve said she would most like to have been of all her fictional characters (and in many ways actually was) – takes control, initiating and encoding the friendship she will have with Elizabeth in a sign that she draws up for the door of the bedroom they will share. It reads, 'Aisling and Elizabeth. Please Knock. No Admittance.'

Elizabeth's integration is just one of the many joys of this novel. We know it is complete when the English girl catches the rhythms of the language of the O'Connor family, adopting the music of their speech patterns, learning the emotional resonances, and discovering their potential to heal. Leaning over to the distressed Mrs Moriarty one day, Elizabeth engages her with a sure and motherly warmth, of which only a few months earlier she would have been incapable. It is a wonderful and significant moment. When it happens, everything stops and everyone looks at her. You feel she has apprehended something unique at the very heart of the family, which cannot be put into words but is signalled by the rhythms of the Irish language. 'You talk like us now,' says Aisling, laughing. 'God help us, we'll have to get that out of you fast before the war is over,' says Eileen.

When, five years later, Elizabeth returns to cold, suburban Clarence Gardens in London and her parents' ailing marriage, we know that a part of her will always remain in the lap of Ireland. Their parting and coming together again, and Elizabeth's final return when Aisling's mother Eileen is dying, are emotional high points that go unchallenged elsewhere in Maeve's stories.

Eileen O'Connor is the mother in the novel, the homemaker. Everything about her is spontaneous and natural. She is a passionate wife even after giving birth to six children, responding wholeheartedly to her husband Sean as he turns to her in bed. Eileen has a heart big enough to include far more children than those she has already. She is the mother-of-all-things, intuitive, always capable of saying the right thing.

So it was with Maeve's real mother. The whole novel has its roots in Maureen's non-intellectual, emotional, intuitive and loving nature. One not insignificant difference between Maureen Binchy and Eileen O'Connor, however, is that Maureen was almost obsessively protective of her children. She was so fussy and protective of Maeve that her husband was driven almost to distraction over it. There was a running joke that when Maeve was made by her school to swim in the sea on cold days it wasn't beyond possibility that her mother would pack her off with an electric fire to make sure she got properly dry afterwards, because it would be terrible if she put on damp clothes and caught rheumatic fever. Maureen's protective instinct, Maeve said, even lay behind the 'open house' policy at home. Behind her insistence that she should have all her friends come to the house lay the thought that Maureen would then know where her own child was, and that she was safe.

There was also a culture of praise which Maeve discovered later, much to her confusion, went beyond the bounds of reality. As far as Maureen was concerned Maeve was the brightest, most beautiful and best, and she never stopped telling her so.

By the time she commented on her childhood Maeve had already made the discovery that rather than confinement, real love offers freedom. But she understood why it was ever thus with her mother, because of the deep sorrow Maureen felt at the loss of her own parents, whose premature death had taken the beauty of her own childhood away.

Maeve wrote that Maureen compensated for her lost childhood by making her own family such a definite and important entity. Though Maeve and her siblings looked back at their childhood with 'laughter and affection' as well as a sense of how lucky they were, Maeve was shielded from life – not only as a child but also as a young adult – and she would feel the need for release eventually.

The first outside influence to impinge on Maeve's life came in the shape of nursery school at the age of five. She was sent to St Anne's, an imposing three-storey terraced building at No. 36 Clarinda Park East, a short walk from Beechgrove, off the northern end of Lower Glenageary Road.

St Anne's was founded by Gertrude Russell in 1912, who, when Maeve arrived, was assisted by Gertrude's two nieces, Peggy and Eileen Bath, known to the children as 'Hot Bath' and 'Cold Bath'. There was no school uniform, but there seems to have been a practice of tying ribbons in big bows on the top of the girls' heads, or at least on Maeve's. The bow was ironed for Maeve every morning by her mother and she went off proudly to school with a little bottle of milk with a cork in it and two Marietta biscuits, looking like a cockatoo.

While Maureen, the farm girl from Tipperary with no higher education at all, thought that Maeve was the best girl in the world and took every opportunity to tell her that she would be able to do whatever she wanted in life, her father, aware that academic success is not a matter of wish fulfilment, took her education seriously.

He was a scholar of literature and graduated in 1928 not in Law, but with First Class Honours from University College Dublin in English Language and Literature. The following year he was awarded a Master's, again in English Language and Literature, and again with First Class Honours.

During the course of her childhood William read his daughter everything he could, from *Winnie the Pooh* to bits of James Joyce's *Ulysses*. Before he had gone farther than the first few lines of the former she would demand to know her place in it: 'Where am I?' He told her that of course she was there, sitting in a tree or perched on a gate. Once Maeve knew that she was there she was happy and would submit to his telling of the story completely. Journalist Donal Lynch sees this as significant:

'A writer has to believe in themselves as a protagonist of sorts. Maeve must have had that instinctively from the start.'[5]

Certainly it shows a lively imagination and Maeve did have a clear sense of herself at the centre of the world, because for her first three years she was an only child and the focus of her parents' attention. Later, Maeve would 'shiver with embarrassment' when friends of the family related how her parents would get her down from her room and parade her in front of them. Indeed, given Maureen's culture of approbation it is a wonder that Maeve wasn't insufferably self-centred even at this stage. The signs were certainly there. When her sister Joan was born Maeve asked if she could swap her for a rabbit, so put out was she at the diversion of interest in her.

Maureen, though not a great reader herself, did also play an important role in ensuring that there were books in the house. She liked to go to furniture auctions, which in those days often included cheap deals on boxes of second-hand books. William also loved nothing better than combing the second-hand bookstalls which lined Dublin Quays on the river Liffey, and came home laden with the spoils.

Before long the walls of Maeve's bedroom, her private world, were covered with shelves and she had a desire bordering on the obsessive to organise her ever-growing library, which she did by colour rather than author. It was as if they were valuable property to be organised and stored, Crusoe-like, in the lumber room of her head for the purpose of survival on the little island where her childhood was playing out.

In time all the spare wall space throughout the house was

covered with bookshelves and reading was part of a family routine after supper when the homework was done. It wasn't all plain sailing. Later, like any young teenager, Maeve did tend to resist her father's recommendations of some of the classics (notably Carlyle, Trollope and Thackeray). But because reading was never a pressurised activity at home she eventually came around to them.

Between reading *Pooh* and *Pendennis*, she devoured Enid Blyton and afterwards became heavily involved with Peter Cheyney, Agatha Christie and Graham Greene, his *Stamboul Train* occasioning a rare moment of parental censorship after she enquired as to the night-time berthing arrangements of Myatt and Coral Musker on the *Orient Express*.

Books took Maeve out of herself. She remembered at eleven or twelve becoming completely carried away by *Gone with the Wind*, so much so that the day she read it she didn't come down to lunch, which was something that had never happened before.

The experience got her thinking about its author, Margaret Mitchell, and how clever she must have been to write it and the amount of research it must have taken and how interesting it was that she had only written the one book. Maeve concluded that Mitchell was born to it.

Being a writer was an idea that Dalkey itself recommended. Telling his daughter about her home town's high-powered literary history was an inevitable and important part of William's education of her. Samuel Beckett, who, later, Maeve would meet and interview for the *Irish Times*, was born and brought up in nearby Foxrock. Leopardstown racecourse, the Foxrock railway station and Harcourt Street station, the Dublin terminus of the Dalkey line, all feature in his prose and plays.

The playwright, poet, prose writer, travel writer and collector of folklore John Millington Synge was born in nearby Churchtown and later lived at Glendalough House, Adelaide Road, Glenageary, close to where Maeve first lived. Synge was one of the co-founders of the Abbey Theatre in Dublin, along with W. B. Yeats and the dramatist Augusta, Lady Gregory. A key figure in the Irish Literary Revival, he is best known for his play *The Playboy of the Western World*, which caused riots in Dublin during its opening run at the Abbey, led by Irish nationalists who saw the play as an offence to public morals and an insult against Ireland.

Another local was George Bernard Shaw, who had lived in Torca Cottage on Dalkey Hill, very close to Eastmount. And Maeve knew exactly where James Joyce had lived, just a walk away from her.

William introduced her to Joyce's personal history as well as to parts of his landmark novel, *Ulysses*, and she realised from a young age what a touchstone Joyce was to the spirit of Ireland and to that of Dublin and Dalkey in particular. There were a number of points on which, even as a child, she could identify with him. Joyce was born to a Catholic middle-class family like hers. He had been schooled by Jesuits and University College Dublin, where many members of the Binchy family had studied. In 1892 Joyce's family had taken a large semi-detached house at No. 23 Carysfort Avenue in Blackrock, just the other side of Dún Laoghaire from Dalkey. And in 1904 he had actually taught at a school in Dalkey,[6] in that same year staying for the best part of a week with his friends Oliver St John Gogarty and Samuel Chenevix Trench at the Martello tower in Sandycove,[7] a popular bathing place a short walk from the centre of Dalkey.

Martello towers were built to withstand invasion during the Napoleonic Wars (1803–15) and there are two in close proximity here. The story of Joyce's time at the Sandycove tower, rentable then for eight pounds a year payable to Dublin Castle, is riveting and will have appealed strongly to Maeve's young mind. From the top of the tower, accessible by means of a tight internal spiral stone staircase, one can look out across the bay to the Muglins, a group of rocks with a distinctive lighthouse, which get a small mention in *Ulysses*. When the weather was warm the three young men sunbathed up there, moving around the raised sentry platform of the tower to get the best of the sun and to avoid the wind, discussing plans to 'Hellenise' Ireland – to dismantle the Catholic theocracy and return it to the traditions and Platonic values of ancient Greece, birthplace of Western culture.

The principal living area of the tower, where Joyce slept with the other two, occupies the first floor. It was in this room, on the night of 14 September 1904, that the three occupants were asleep when Trench had a nightmare about a black panther, reached for his revolver and fired at the fireplace where he imagined the beast to be crouching. As the others woke in alarm, Trench fell back to sleep and Gogarty took the gun. When Trench stirred again, Gogarty said, 'Leave him to me' and fired a few shots at the saucepans on the shelf over Joyce's bed, bringing them down on the terrified poet. Joyce dressed and left immediately, walking through the night into Dublin, never to return.

Maeve heard of these exciting antics from her father, who then read her the opening scenes of *Ulysses*, which are set the morning after this incident. Gogarty is immortalised as 'stately, plump Buck Mulligan' (the opening words of the novel) and Trench is Haines. Maeve imagined the events of the book happening on her very doorstep.

Maureen's natural way of life was clearly in tune with that of Joyce – both of them eschewed any form of pretension and both celebrated reality as what went on every day between the ordinary people of Dublin. The ability to see the marvellous in the everyday was Maureen's way and Ireland's natural way, and would become Maeve's way too, as a person and a writer.

Meanwhile, radio also played a big part in the growing child's imagination. People born much less than sixty years ago will find it difficult to appreciate how captivating radio was before the more immediate, effort-free, visual stimulus of television. The pictures one conjured while listening to radio plays were somehow so much more fulfilling than the easy option of television. Maeve loved radio and it became a significant part of her development. *Saturday Night Theatre* on the BBC Home Service was her favourite. In the 1940s and 1950s the programme followed shortly after the nine o'clock news and lasted around ninety minutes. Listening to it was an activity she alone could undertake with her parents. Only she, being the eldest child, was allowed to stay up to listen to it. These were entertaining plays, but well written; indeed, writers featured included (among many others) Dorothy Sayers, Edgar Wallace, Peter Cheyney, Somerset Maugham, J. M. Barrie, George Bernard Shaw, Charles Dickens, Eugene O'Neill, Lewis Carroll, J. B. Priestley, Dodie Smith, Agatha Christie, Freddie Lonsdale, A. A. Milne, John Galsworthy and Noël Coward. The programme was successful because of its simple formula: 'good popular entertainment value associated in the minds of Mr & Mrs Everyman with the general idea of Saturday night', as BBC Director of Drama Val Gielgud put it. More than twelve million people listened in each night, though figures declined with the increasing popularity of television in the late 1950s.

Another interest of Maeve's was her father's library of law books, which he kept in his study. This was his territory. William liked nothing better than to deliberate over the rule of law with whoever was to hand, and he would occasionally discuss his case histories with Maeve, always with the enticing proviso that she must keep the details a secret. Maeve loved to be a part of her father's serious other world and became convinced that she wanted to follow in his footsteps, but not just as a lawyer – she wanted to be a judge, because William held judges in awe and they didn't seem to do half as much work as he did.

The idea persisted but was dented by a professor of law who asked her why she thought that a solicitor would choose to give a brief to a young woman when he could give it to an experienced man like her father. At the time Maeve could find no answer to that.

The professor, a man of course, was not alone in his thinking at the time. There was still a culture that women were going to marry and become housewives. In the 1940s and 1950s it wasn't done for a wife to work and in some industries you weren't allowed to work if you were a married woman, because it was taking a job away from a man during a period of serious economic depression. Maureen knew well enough that in her home county of Tipperary thousands were leaving in search of employment abroad, often to England, where they could be held in derision as Paddies and Biddies and where the jokes made about them were humiliating in the extreme. 'Born for Export' was a catchphrase among mothers of the day. During the period 1946 to 1956 alone the number of Irish emigrating from just one county in Ireland (Cavan) exceeded 11,000, as against registered births of 12,481.

What could an Irish girl expect by way of work in Ireland after the Second World War? If you were bright with a few years in secondary education behind you, and your parents had a few pounds set aside, you might be able to buy six months' unpaid work in a clothes shop or hairdresser as an apprentice learning the trade. Or you might train to be a nurse, even chance your arm as a trainee nurse in England, where you could expect to earn your keep initially by scrubbing floors. With women closed out of almost all professions it is not difficult to see why being a housewife seemed the better option.

Such would never be an option for Maeve. As Maureen kept telling her, she could be whatever she wanted to be. But first she would need a higher education.

'To go to university,' said Geraldine MacCarthy, a contemporary of Maeve at school, 'you had to have your Leaving

Certificate, and you had to get Irish and maths, and you had to have Latin, but then of course you had to be able to pay.' And even if you could pay and you did all this you would have to cope with the prejudice shown by that professor of law.

As far as the Binchys were concerned, university was very much on the cards for all the children. Maeve said that her father sacrificed everything for their education. All schools in Ireland charged fees of some sort. It wasn't until 1968 that the free state school system, heralded in England by the Education Act of 1944 and implemented in the six counties of Northern Ireland in 1947, was introduced to Eire.

But some schools cost more than others and Maeve's father was stretched to pay for the ones he chose for the children. His philosophy nevertheless was that, if necessary, all their savings should be spent on education. They splashed out on Eastmount, it is true, the first and only house William and Maureen ever purchased (it cost them £3,000, a great deal of money in Ireland in 1952 and double the average house price in Britain at the time). But the family never had a car or went to restaurants, which Maeve understood to be so that the three children could go to university. She grew up with the sense that money might not always be there; it was one reason her father gave her to study hard and pass all her exams.

Today it sounds like the typical middle-class thing to do: stretch yourself financially for the sake of the next generation. But in the case of the Binchy family, the importance of education was hot-wired into their thinking by their own paternal history.

TWO

THE LINE

Long before the Norman Conquest of Britain in the eleventh century, the Binchys were to be found with their own heraldic coat of arms in Middlesex, an ancient territory and county of England which originally incorporated London but which was abolished in 1965, fragmenting into parts of Hertfordshire, Berkshire, Surrey and a new administrative area known as Greater London.

The Irish branch of the family descended from Cromwellian settlers in County Cork, in the province of the south-west of Ireland known as Munster.[8] The line began with two Binchy brothers who found their way to Charleville, a market town on the original mail coach road between Cork and Limerick, beside a headwater of the river Maigue.

The two young men arrived in the wake of the Ascendancy – the political, economic and social domination of Ireland by the Protestant English/English-Irish – following Oliver Cromwell's merciless brand of mayhem, brought to bear from 1649.

After the execution of King Charles I in that year, Cromwell had turned his attention to Catholic Ireland with relentless savagery, his campaign lasting six years and costing 600,000 lives. By the time he left, only 8 per cent of the country remained in the hands of the indigenous Catholic Irish. His 'final solution' required men, women and children, the sick and the infirm, all classes of people, to be herded into Connacht, the province of the north-west of Ireland, in a small reservation between the river Shannon and the sea, a place where 'there was not wood enough to burn, water enough to drown, nor earth enough to bury a man', as one of the commissioners responsible described it. Anyone found east of the line after 1 May 1654 could expect to be executed and, when there were too many flouting the rule to make this practical, they were sold into slavery to Jamaica in the West Indies, so that even today Jamaican English retains many aspects of Irish intonation.

In order to fill the vacuum left by this unbridled genocide and ethnic cleansing, large-scale plantations of settlers came over from Britain and Europe, creating new communities of Protestants which replaced the older indigenous Catholic ruling class and secured the authority of British Crown government in Ireland.

All this had its seat in the Reformation, the Protestantisation of England by Henry VIII a century earlier, and followed Elizabeth I's 'Act of Uniformity', which made the Protestant liturgy compulsory in Ireland and led to similar atrocities and ethnic cleansing, with large-scale plantations, or settlements, of new Protestant population-stock. The sixteenth and seventeenth centuries marked a devastating period for Ireland, when the country's very identity was threatened with extinction by the English.

The founding of Charleville as a Protestant stronghold by an Englishman called Roger Boyle, from Marston in Somerset, was part of this disastrous development. Boyle, a seasoned and ruthless campaigner, as well as a man who changed his loyalties to suit his ends, was directly responsible for Cromwell's success in overcoming the south of Ireland.

On Cromwell's death in 1658, and now known as Lord Orrery, Boyle returned, resumed his command in Munster and secured Ireland for Charles II by inviting him to land at Cork, confirming his loyalty to the new king by asking his permission to name Charleville after him.

When the Binchy brothers arrived in the late 1700s,[9] Ireland was still subordinate to Britain. The great majority of the population were Roman Catholic, but had no power or say in the governing of the country. Charleville remained very much under the yoke of the Protestant Ascendancy. Boyle's immigration policy was designed to ensure that Catholics never had a look-in. 'I admit,' he said, 'neither presbyter, papist, independent, nor as our proclamation says, any sort of fanatic to plant here, but all good protestants.'

Before his coming it had been a Catholic village with, so he put it, 'the heathenish name of Rathgoggan'. He raised it from 'village insignificance and obscurity' to the position of Borough, and with the king's blessing made it the seat of his court as Lord President of Munster, building in it a church, an endowed school and, on an 800-acre plot, a grandiose mansion with landscaped gardens, fish ponds and pleasure grounds, giving it a reputation for 'much revelling and wine-drinking', but also attracting manufacturers in linen and woollens, and tradesmen to the town. In 1670, Charleville petitioned successfully for a Royal Charter, which gave it the privilege of appointing two Members of Parliament.

But Boyle's uncompromising stance on Catholicism was eventually his family's undoing. In 1690, when no member of the family was present, the Catholic Duke of Berwick, illegitimate son of James II, happened by on his way back from the Siege of Limerick, where his forces had resisted the Protestant William of Orange. He feasted at the family's expense and then razed their mansion to the ground.

It was into this turbulent scene of bigotry and sectarianism that the Binchys sowed their seed. The two brothers, one a grocer, the other a lawyer, at first found no Catholic place of worship in the town. The Constitution of 1782, however, which gave Ireland legislative independence of Britain, began to ease the situation for Catholics generally, and when the Acts of Union were passed in 1800, promising Catholic representation in Parliament (delivered in 1829), the yoke was finally lifted.

For the Binchys, the first outward sign of change in Charleville had been the building of a Mass-house, a sort of hut, with two side walls, a gable and a thatched roof under which the faithful gathered. Then, in 1812, the foundation of a Catholic church was laid in Chapel Street; its construction began the following year. And by the time we find useful records of the family in the first decade of the twentieth century they are living in a completely integrated Irish Catholic township, with names such as Holy Cross Place, The Presbytery and the Convent of

Mercy, and with one of their number, Margaret Binchy, a Sister of Mercy.

Maeve's paternal grandfather, William Patrick Binchy, was born in 1858 and became a successful retail merchant in the town, the family store servicing a large local farming community, many of whom descended on the town on market day.

His immediate family consisted of his wife Annie, a woman seven years his junior (they married in 1896) and five children (a sixth died). In 1911 they lived with Mary, William Patrick's mother, born in 1831, at No. 42 Main Street along with two female servants and a male apprentice.

Charleville is built on a crossroads. Main Street, with Chapel Street and Smith's Street running across it, is as wide and straight a street now as it was then, with substantial three-storey buildings, many of them two-storey residential quarters over a street-level store.

One can easily imagine the noise on market day of the wagons, cattle and horses piling through, and the farmers with their lists, 'busy men who hated having to take any time at all away from their deals and discussions on beasts', clearly drawn upon by Maeve in her wonderful depiction of Sean O'Connor's store near the beginning of *Light a Penny Candle*.

Another branch of the family lived at nearby Gortskagh, still within the official vicinity of Charleville. Head of the family was James Binchy, a solicitor also based on Main Street, born four years before William Patrick. The family firm of James Binchy & Son is today in its fourth generation. In the 1920s, James's son Owen became the first Binchy to own an estate, Knight's Lodge, one of the choice houses of the area, now known as Binchy Park and still owned by the family.

Over the years the Binchy family's commercial interests were quartered in various stores in the town. In 1914 they had a china and glass dealership, a hardware store in Smith's Lane, and at some stage also a timber yard. Then, in or around 1920, they acquired Synan's bread shop and set up Binchy's Bakery at the corner of Smith's Street, which Maeve's favourite cousin, Daniel W. J. Binchy, born in 1940, managed from 1957 right up until it closed in 1982, after which he became a novelist.

Two more Binchys, both farmers, both called James and born within ten years of each other, lived in Ballynoran and in Churchtown respectively, again close to Charleville.

The family was prospering and extensive in the area. Since the two boys' arrival towards the end of the eighteenth century, they had been instrumental in the reversion to power of the indigenous culture, with which they were now integrated.

The pattern is not an unusual one. Time and again, since the very first conquest of Ireland by Henry II in the twelfth century, English settlers were embraced by the indigenous Irish culture, instead of the Irish being converted to English ways, as had been intended.

But that is not to underestimate the effort and application it took for the Binchys to rise in their newfound society, or the character which was formed during this time and which then flowed down the line into the modern generations of the family, all of whom have their roots not only in the indigenous culture of Ireland but also in the energy and frontiersman spirit of the two original brothers.

But the key to their rising beyond Charleville to high political, academic and literary positions in Europe and elsewhere in the world lies in their resolve, incubated in the culture of the Catholic Church. The Irish, fighting for their very identity in those days, lived in a theocracy. The Church brought you into its sphere of operations through baptism, educated you, policed you spiritually and morally, possibly employed you as priest or nun, and sent you out of the world at the end. Critical to the process was the Jesuits' Society of Jesus, and Ireland was top of the list for 'enlightenment' from the moment it was formed. The first Jesuit school was established at Kilmallock in County Limerick in 1565.

In Maeve's second novel *Echoes* (1985), we detect irony in her approbation of Jesuit teachers. The teacher in small-town Castlebay, Angela O'Hara, is said not to compare with Jesuit teachers, who are 'on a different level entirely'. If only Miss O'Hara had been a man then she could have been a priest and taught the children properly, as doctor's son David Power suggests. In fact, Angela O'Hara is the best kind of teacher imaginable.

The 'level' on which Jesuit teachers operated was emotional and psychological as well as academic and spiritual. The writer Catherine Cookson, for whom Maeve reserved no small amount of respect, a Catholic Irish girl who grew up on Tyneside in the north-east of England at the same time as Maeve's father and uncles were growing up in Charleville, was terrified of the Jesuit missioners because they filled her little head with fears of hell and purgatory. The primitive sense of the supernatural which they appealed to, and the punitive schedule of abuse, shame and guilt which they apparently imposed on their charges, put pain and fear on the religious agenda. In the mouths of Jesuit priests the flames of Hell were a reality, everlasting fire a destiny which could be met surprisingly easily.

Certainly a Jesuit education was rigorous and uncompromising, but it was also thorough, and it had need to be if Catholics were to counter the effects of the Protestant Ascendancy and be returned to the position they had once occupied in the land of which so many had been dispossessed.

The Binchys were ambitious: education was therefore a priority and they did what hard-working rising middle-class Catholic families did with their boys. They sent them to a Jesuit boarding school.

In 1911 five Binchy boys between the ages of eleven and seventeen – Michael, James, Joseph, Owen S. and Daniel A. Binchy – were being educated at the Jesuit college, Clongowes Wood, in Balraheen, County Kildare.

Academically brilliant, Clongowes has prepared Catholic pupils to play important roles in the political, economic, social and literary life of Ireland and beyond since its inception in 1814. But like many other Jesuit schools, it was once infamous for its uncompromising approach and tough discipline, as Joyce recalled from personal experience in *A Portrait of the Artist as a Young Man* (1915).

We know that Maeve's uncle, Daniel Anthony Binchy,[10] was there at eleven. Before being sent there he was educated by French nuns, and left a wryly understated note about the difference between the two experiences: his memories of the Jesuit education were not as warm as his recollections of the French nuns.

Daniel was bright and made very good use of the college. He matriculated in 1918, well disciplined, primed for eternity and very well educated for this world, too, to take up a place at University College Dublin, which had been founded as the Catholic University in 1854, and where at the very early age of twenty-four he was appointed Professor of Legal History and Jurisprudence. At twenty-nine he was appointed, 'at British insistence', Irish Minister to Germany. Hitherto Ireland had been represented in Europe only by British ambassadors.

Daniel was the model for the Binchy future and his was the route written in stone for Maeve, even as she prepared to leave St Anne's in 1950. She had been born to a family that had risen against all odds. Its history and the value it attached to a good education lay behind the pressure on her to study hard and pass her exams and, as the eldest, to set the pace for her three siblings. Likewise, the difficulties and uncertainties inherent in such a rise in the world lay behind her father William's anxiety and his warning to her that the money might not always be there. The world had taught the Binchys that nothing should be taken for granted.

In turn, an awareness of the pressure all this heaped on Maeve was almost certainly behind her mother Maureen's constant, anxious reassurance that she was the brightest and the best and would be bound to succeed.

Expectations for Maeve were from the start very high. What was new was that the Binchys were for the first time thinking of educating a *daughter* for professional and possibly international service.

THREE

HER LITTLE WORLD

In the early 1950s one or two secondary schools in Dublin seemed to be gearing up to meet the growing demand among girls for a university education and a career. Pembroke School, a lay Catholic school for girls in an elegant Georgian house in Pembroke Road, Dublin 4, was better known as Miss Meredith's after its founder, Kathleen Meredith. It had a first-class reputation for academic achievement, combined with a friendly, liberal atmosphere and small classes, where dedicated teachers gave personal attention to each pupil.

Maeve's contemporary Geraldine MacCarthy was doing well there when suddenly her parents decided to move her. People had begun talking about a new school for girls called the Society of the Holy Child Jesus, which had started up in Killiney, the next little town along the coast from Dalkey.

I moved to Killiney because some friends of ours, the O'Donnells, met my parents at some dinner and said there's only one school your daughter should be at, and that's the

Holy Child, Killiney! They said what's so special about it? And they said, 'Go out and see. They give you more than a brilliant education, and still get you into university and a future career.' And it changed my life.

Geraldine's father told her that the school, which offered places to both boarding and day girls, would get her to university and help her make her way in life – and that soon became William Binchy's view, too. But the point the O'Donnells made was that while it offered a brilliant education, it also provided more than that. And there were plenty of girls at the Holy Child whose parents wanted that special something for their children who were not cut out for academia. It was perfectly possible to take domestic science instead of maths and Latin, and feel no humiliation in doing so. 'The view at the time was that we who took this route had a lot more fun,' as Adrienne Lavelle, another contemporary of Maeve, recalls. 'We used to go twice a week to the technical college in Dún Laoghaire and come back with all these food dishes. Others used to envy us for that.'

The Society of the Holy Child was founded in 1846 by Philadelphia-born Cornelia Connelly and approved in 1887 by Pope Leo XIII. Its rules and constitutions were confirmed and ratified in 1893 and based on those of Saint Ignatius of Loyola, the founder of the Jesuits, although it was not a Jesuit order.

The Society had initially been turned down by the dioceses in Ireland to which they applied because there were already many religious orders running convent schools there, including the Sacred Heart, the Dominicans, the Mercy Sisters, the Presentations and the Loretos. Only when the Catholic Archbishop of Dublin, John McQuaid, became concerned that too many Irish girls were going to England for their education and marrying Protestants, did he invite the Society of the Holy Child to open up in his diocese.

On 15 September 1947, a century after the founding of the Society, the school at Killiney settled into an old hotel overlooking Killiney Bay, a short walk from the railway station and close to the Archbishop's own house.

McQuaid already knew the Binchys, having attended Clongowes Wood in the early twentieth century alongside Michael, James, Joseph, Owen and Daniel. Maeve became a day girl at the Holy Child Killiney in 1950, travelling the few miles from Dalkey on the little train which even to this day takes the girls to and fro around the bay.

The school was ordered along lines set out by the then headmistress, a one-off who had a huge effect on Maeve, such that she kept in touch with Mother St Dominic, as she was known, until she died in her nineties among the Holy Child community in Harrogate, North Yorkshire.

Mother St Dominic was the hidden factor of excellence at Killiney. As soon as anyone met her they were won over, and the girls trailed after her as if she were the Pied Piper of Hamelin. Past pupils remember a very tall, bespectacled woman with a wonderful smile and great presence, a sense of proportion and above all a sense of humour. Said Susan McNally, 'She *was* Killiney. We all loved her.'

Instead of the Jesuit model of discipline, Mother St Dominic exercised Cornelia Connolly's conviction that girls will never learn unless they are happy, and put the onus of discipline onto the pupils themselves. As Valerie, also a contemporary of Maeve, remembers:

> When it came to discipline the nuns tried to get us to think for ourselves. They tried to develop a sense of *self*-discipline in us and we were frequently put on our honour to act in the right way. They tried to get us to see the bigger picture of life and where our responsibilities lay. We were not compelled to do things. Discipline did not come down on us from above. It was not imposed on us, as it was in other schools. This was something new.

In the 1950s this was indeed new. If a major infraction occurred then it would be pursued. 'Not to steal was a huge thing at school,' remembers Maeve's friend Patricia Hamilton. 'I remember once someone was discovered to have been stealing and the whole school was summoned and the nuns were there. We were kept in there for ages, and people had to go through other people's lockers to see if they were the culprit.'

But day to day, rather than chastisements, Mother St Dominic brought her personal charisma and – most especially – her character and sense of humour to bear. Said Susan,

> We would be in the classroom making an awful noise, and nuns always wore their rosary beads down from the waist and Mother would always come holding her beads so we

didn't hear her coming. Suddenly she would appear and she would just stand at the door with a big smile on her face. That was what she used to do! She would never *say* anything.

Teresa Mee, a nun seconded to Killiney for six months, once saw a young Holy Child girl running furiously down the corridor (not allowed) and as she turned the corner she ploughed into Mother St Dominic. The girl was horrified at what she had done. Mother St Dominic, seeing the extent of the child's mortification, drew herself up to her full height, let loose a great smile across her face and commanded, 'Do it again!'

Maeve liked to say that the nuns, who had only just arrived in Ireland, were utterly unaware of what they had got themselves into. Unable to understand the Irish accent, they were putty in the girls' hands; the girls could tell them anything and they'd believe it.

For her part, the shrewd Mother St Dominic used to play along with this and respond that given the choice between teaching natives on the Gold Coast of Africa (another mission of the Society of the Holy Child) and fulfilling her missionary duty among middle-class Irish girls in County Dublin, the Gold Coast presented itself as distinctly preferable!

There was a happy atmosphere at Killiney and a compassionate one, with attention to the individual a priority. Mother's great strength was to instil self-esteem in her girls by finding something in each one of them to admire. 'She had the most wonderful insight into each of us,' said Susan McNally. 'It had an incredible binding effect on all of us.' It worked like this: 'She had a room downstairs where she would have little chats with you. She always used to say, "Come in Susan, close the door, sit down, now what's on your mind?" You could pour your heart out to her.' Every girl availed herself of these 'chats with Mother'.

As the fathers of Maeve and Geraldine hoped, Mother's regime also prepared the girls for a fast-changing world in which women were already gaining ground. One of Maeve's early articles for the *Irish Times* praises nuns for being at the forefront of career guidance, which at the time barely existed in Ireland. 'They no longer look out on the wicked world from behind cloistered walls and urge their girls to seek similar shelter,' she wrote. 'People would say there was something about the Holy Child girls,' agrees Valerie. 'They would stand up. They were able to express themselves. They were able to have an opinion about things.'

Independent thinking did not extend to religion, however, which was dispensed with Jesuit intensity. From the moment Maeve arrived in 1950 she entered what she later referred to as her 'religious maniac' phase.

At school 'our Catholic faith permeated everything', says Valerie.

Everything we thought about, said or did during the school day. The first class of the day was Christian doctrine. We said a prayer before each lesson and we said grace before meals. The boarders attended daily Mass and evening prayer in the school chapel. We had a yearly retreat and at the end we exchanged holy pictures with something personal inscribed on the back.

In *Light a Penny Candle*, Elizabeth's friend Monica cannot believe that at the convent they pray before every class, even before maths and history. The novel captures beautifully the innocence and unquestioning beliefs of Maeve's younger self and her friends during their time at the Holy Child. As Elizabeth White is a Protestant evacuee from England she knows nothing of Irish or Catholic ways. All must be explained to her, like the concept of 'limbo', for example, which Catholics believe to be a place where dead babies are held; not having been baptised they are in a state of original sin and cannot be admitted to Heaven. The idea of masses of innocent dead babies hanging in some remote space, in endless twilight, would be macabre in any other context, but in the convent with Sister Mary and Sister Bonaventure, Elizabeth is soon prepared to accept it as perfectly natural.

Then, of course, dear sweet innocent Elizabeth is herself perceived to be in danger of everlasting damnation, because she has not been baptised into the Catholic Church. The girls realise that it is up to them to set matters straight. Outside classes it becomes their purpose to save her soul. Elizabeth submits to four baptismal rituals and there is some concern whether any of them has worked. Were the words said at exactly the same moment as the water flowed? Should the service have been conducted in Latin rather than English? Later the class ponder on how they can arrange for her First Communion, because sooner or later she is going to have to make her confession to cast out the sins with which, as a Protestant, they believe she is riddled.

As a child Maeve never had a Protestant friend like Elizabeth. It was a mortal sin at the time for a Catholic even to enter a Protestant church or attend a wedding that was not a Catholic one. A mortal sin meant that you would be consigned to Hell for eternity. As a Catholic child one knew that there was no way back from everlasting Hell. Children sensed the divisiveness of so exclusive a regime.

Though there was a Protestant presence in 1950s Dalkey, and friendships and marriages across denominations did exist, generally there was minimal integration and sometimes a degree of unpleasantness about it when it did occur. 'When my father married my mother, who was a Protestant,' one woman explained, 'there was a huge rift in the family. Honestly, they wouldn't speak to her. When she had her first child, who died, one of her sisters said, "Well that's one Catholic out of the way."'

Utterly convinced of everything she was told, and being a caring person inside, Maeve began to worry about the father of a friend of hers, who was a Protestant while the rest of his family attended the Catholic church. Every Sunday he would drive his family to church but instead of joining them at Mass he would go for a walk on the pier at Dún Laoghaire.

She spent hours with her friend discussing the situation, fearful that he would suffer 'the Devil and the pain that goes on forever' and actually teamed up with her friend, faced her father with the situation and urged him to reconsider!

The compassionate ethos of the Holy Child Killiney was clearly at odds with the Church's wider determination to marginalise and alienate anyone outside the Catholic community, but this only fell clear to Maeve in her late teens when she went to university. And even then, so completely had she lived within an opaque Catholic bubble that when she travelled abroad in her twenties she found it difficult to believe that there were countries where the Angelus bell did not ring at midday.

The Catholic family to which Maeve belonged at Killiney enveloped her completely – not only Mother St Dominic, but other less corporeal figures, like St Patrick, who was always looking out for her, St Anthony, whom she relied on to find things for her, St Peter, who was always dependable, and St Francis, her father's namesake, who was the saint of the poor and of course friend of all the animals and birds.

So closely did she come to belong that Maeve would sometimes rather be at school than at home. Once, for example, she opted to celebrate St Patrick's Day by swelling the ranks of boarders at the school, attending Mass with them in Killiney rather than with her parents and siblings at the Church of the Assumption in Dalkey. She remembered persuading a nun to let her decorate the statues of all the saints, so that St Patrick 'up there' would have a good day and not feel over-adorned in the otherwise stony naked company of St Peter, St Francis and 'the other lads'.

During this time she was determined to become a saint. When this was mentioned by a priest during her funeral Mass sixty years later the congregation actually laughed out loud, but the ambition really wasn't so unusual in the 1950s. Life for everyone in the Catholic community had a spiritual dimension which was wholly real. Even if you were a poor boy living in a village in a rural area, there'd likely be a day or two a week when you'd rise early to serve the priest at Mass before school. And the possibility of seeing a sacred vision, meeting 'in the real world the unsubstantial image which his soul so constantly beheld', as James Joyce described the metaphysical dimension of Catholicism so well, seemed high.

Maeve herself developed a terror of emulating the shepherd children at Fatima and apprehending a vision of Our Lady in a tree – there was a period when to avoid a repetition of the famous visionary experience she kept her eyes firmly on the ground whenever she went outside.

As for becoming a saint, this was no passing childhood ambition. She still planned to be one when she was twenty-three. It wasn't a question of hoping; she was convinced that she would be.

At the Holy Child, recognition of a pupil treading the path of the saints was vested in an award known as 'The Child of Mary'. The award was one all of the girls coveted, but to receive it one would have to partake in daily Mass and receive Communion. A combination of religious intensity and good character was also required and the award demonstrated that one was fit to be a leader as much as a saint. The climax of Maeve's apprenticeship was a one-day retreat early one December, followed by a candle-lit ceremony, for which she wore a white veil and, round her neck, the medal itself on a long blue ribbon, which she continued to wear with great respect and pride every day. Maeve developed her special relationship with God in pursuit of the medal. They spoke to one another like the Italian priest Don Camillo speaks to Christ in Giovannino Guareschi's popular series of books, which first appeared in print in English at this time. God was 'a friend, and Irish, and somebody who knew me well'.

In spite of, or perhaps because of the highly disciplined religious life that the nuns had elected to pursue, tensions were released daily in an abundance of character and humour. Valerie remembers a typical incident.

> We lived up the road here and my dad had his office in St Stephen's Green in Dublin and in those days there was so little traffic that he would come home for lunch, it would take twenty minutes or so. Now, if one of the nuns wanted to go to the dentist or something they would ring my mother and ask for a lift into town after lunch. One day this nun, Mother Immaculata, who was quite elderly and a very tiny person, asked if my father could give her a lift into town. He called for her in his very smart car – some sort of sporty Jaguar – and she got in beside him – she could barely see over the dashboard. And she asked him, 'May I ask, would you do something for me?' He said, 'Yes, what is it?' She said, 'Would you take me down to the Big Tree – (which was the only bit of motorway; well, there were two lanes rather than one) – and will you drive me at 100 miles an hour?'

Maeve's readers may remember Mother Immaculata in her novel *Echoes*. But her fictional Immaculata is quite unlike the person Valerie describes – she has 'a face like the nib of a pen' and is a thoroughly difficult woman, concerned to impress on plucky young Clare O'Brien the importance of everything she does for 'the good name of the school'.

Maeve was always at pains to make clear that she never took a whole person from the real world into her fiction, only parts of them. But this story about Mother Immaculata reminds us how influential the convent became on her work. When the film of *Echoes* was shot at Dunmore East, an idyllic seaside resort in County Waterford, not far from where Maeve's mother Maureen was born, Maeve saw to it that a lot of the nuns got parts as extras. It takes a nun to walk like a nun, apparently. Real nuns don't so much walk as glide!

Mother Immaculata's phrase, 'the good name of the school', was one used relentlessly to motivate the girls at Killiney, notably in sport, which also accorded great popularity if you were any good. Maeve said she was hopeless at games and even refused to vault the horse in the gym for fear of some injury. She also ducked out of hockey whenever she could, generally in the company of another girl. Together they used to hide in the toilets rather than go onto the hockey field, and then make a quick getaway. Otherwise, as Maeve wrote with winning caricature, it was a question of standing around on the pitch, looking like a sack of potatoes in her green uniform tied in the middle, legs blue with cold, hoping that the action would remain at the far end of the pitch.[11]

The games mistress was at a loss as to how to get her to participate in anything at all until she hit on the idea that her height could be put to use on the netball pitch. Maeve was unusually tall, six foot or more as a teenager. All she had to do was hang around the net, wait for a pass and dunk the ball in – easier for her to do than not. She became a lethal striker and for two years actually made the school's 1st VII netball team.

There were protests, however. Some schools refused to believe that so tall a girl was young enough to be playing for the team. They may have had a point: there is a discrepancy of one year between Maeve's declared age and the one indicated on her birth certificate. No one will say for sure when the change was implemented, or why. Was it an attempt by Maureen to give Maeve the best chance of success in life following a long absence from school? Did she miss a year due to an extended bout of glandular fever, as one of her friends suggests? Whatever was the case, Maeve remained a year younger than her officially recorded age for the rest of her life.

More significant to Maeve than sporting success were writing competitions in magazines, which girls were encouraged to enter because here was another opportunity to show the school in a good light. Maeve remembered in particular one Christmas winning a prize in a magazine called *The Pylon*, subscribers to which (for a few pence a year) could proudly call themselves Electrons. To be an Electron and enter a writing competition was terribly important. Like being good at sport, it showed 'school spirit, girls!', while winning meant being fêted by staff and girls alike.

Maeve won this particular competition with a story about a girl called Jane, who wanted to be a missionary and teach the natives in Africa. Jane succeeded by beating the natives out of their own customs and forcing hers upon them. The win stuck in Maeve's mind because of a particularly prescient remark made by her father when he picked her up that day from school. 'When you become a writer, you will always be able to say this was your first work.'[12] When Maeve did become a writer she thanked God that the story had not survived!

Maeve had begun to subscribe to activities that promised a certain amount of status and popularity in the school, and to show less interest in those activities that didn't – like academic work, for example. When she first arrived she had been expected to go the academic route and not, like some of the others, substitute domestic science for Latin and maths. She was a bright girl and found it relatively easy to come near the top of the class, but school reports described her as lazy. She grasped things well, but then became bored and soon lapsed into a daydream. In later life she gave the reason that being at the top of the class wasn't a mark of status at school. It wasn't nearly as important as being good at games, for example, or winning a writing competition.

Seeking status is perfectly normal behaviour among children but here it looks like becoming a definitive motivation, and one wonders why. Knowing how irrepressible a personality she was as an adult, and how popular she became, and being aware of the support dispensed by her mother when she was a child, and of how, at home, she'd had a clear sense of herself at the centre of the world, one would expect Maeve to have been confident and popular and even a bit full of herself at school. But this was not the case at all. One fellow pupil recalls:

Maeve wasn't actually very *obvious* at school at all. I think she really blossomed after she left. I would never think of her as a huge character. I'm not sure that Maeve was a very confident person when she was young. She changed a lot. I think for the better.

It is noticeable that Maeve is almost always in the background in photographs taken of her class at this time, and she confessed to having been a nervous child – always worrying that something lay in wait for her around every corner, afraid of the dark, of going upstairs to the box room in case a monster lay in wait for her, of climbing trees in case she fell, of seeing a doctor in case he wanted to vaccinate her, of going to the dentist in case the drill slipped and went through her head, of passing buses and lorries in case they suddenly left the road and ploughed into her, of the sound of an ambulance or fire engine because she was sure they were bound for her house, of being cut, in case, like the royal haemophiliac, she would bleed to death. Any loud noise made her jump 'four feet', the sound of leaves in the wind was surely a burglar. She was always looking at the sky in case a comet was about to career into her, and she thought she saw the Devil on four separate occasions.[13]

It is tempting to put her nervousness down to Maureen's excessive concern for her safety at every point, together with the child's lively imagination, which had her lowering her eyes for fear of seeing a sacred vision. But this nervousness of hers was consistent with an emotional state which Maeve later admitted came to dominate her psychologically from this time – a crippling self-consciousness.

'I think she was very conscious of her height because she used to slouch quite a bit. I do remember the nativity plays we had, because she was tall she invariably played St Joseph. I don't think she had an awful lot of confidence then,' said Susan McNally.

But it wasn't only her height. In later life Maeve put it plainly: 'I was fat, and that was awful because when you're young and sensitive, you think the world is over because you're fat. I was also a bit lame.'[14]

Another of Maeve's friends, the journalist Mary Kenny, who met Maeve a decade later, remembered her saying that as a teenager she always weighed 'around 15 stone'.

Valerie recalled that she had to have her clothes specially made:

She had great difficulty in getting them to fit. I remember there was a dressmaker called Miss Creegan, who lived in an old farmhouse, an ancient, falling-down place called Honeypark, with her sister. She was a very eccentric lady. I remember her wallpaper was upside down on the walls, flowers growing down rather than up. And Maeve used to get her clothes made by this woman, because she couldn't get anything off the peg to fit her.

At home the issue carried no stigma at all. Maureen did everything in her power not to make any concession to the idea that her daughter's weight might be a problem.

'My best friend at school was Jillyann Metcalfe,' said Patricia Hamilton, and she was also a great friend of Maeve's. She lived quite near her so they would play and go to each other's houses – my house was in Carrickmines, considered the back of beyond in those days, so I didn't go to Maeve's house, but I remember Jilly saying to me, 'Oh, you'd love to go to Maeve's house because she has boxes of chocolates in every room and her mother puts them there just in case the children are hungry.'

'At home,' Maeve said, 'I never felt fat. At home I felt very loved and very special.'[15] But outside the house she became so self-conscious about her size that in adolescence she felt lonely and already 'out of the race', convinced that fat people didn't get on.[16] She was also tortured by the idea that everybody was looking at her, and so she stooped or slouched to appear smaller than in fact she was.

Outside the house there was a gradual dawning that people did find fatness an issue, if only because slimness was the prescribed ideal. And less than a leap away from knowing that was the realisation that she was not the centre of attention at school, as she was at home, because she fell short of the prescribed ideal. She was not one of the gang because she was fat, and so gaining status and popularity at school by other means became her principal motivation.

In her conversations with God it fell clear that He had sent these tortures, among which Maeve listed 'not being good at games (until the marvellous netball "discovery") and being fat at school', to try and test her. From this it followed that 'it was bad, very bad, to be fat'. So she began to construct a defence mechanism to deal with it.

Valerie remembered 'a religious studies class when we were all asked what did we most appreciate that didn't cost us money. I said, "Looking into the flames of a fire." Someone else said, "Sunset." And when it came to Maeve, do you know what she said? "Chocolate biscuits!"'

Maeve's comment raised a laugh from her classmates, and it was intended to. Just as Mother St Dominic played up to the girls at Killiney, who responded with laughter and adoration, so Maeve played to the crowd, learning to cover up her anxieties with a self-deprecating brand of humour. She'd forever be telling stories at her own expense. As an adult it became her trademark. There was always irony behind it, and wit, but sadness too, because it was often designed to disengage her from some pain.

Maeve used her fiction sometimes to dispense her hard-won philosophy through characters whose problems were hers in real life. In *Echoes* we meet Josie Dillon, the 'big white slug ... so fat she's disgusting', as Chrissie O'Brien puts it cruelly. Josie is lonely and doesn't seem to get enthusiastic about anything.

Later comes Benny in *Circle of Friends* (1990), real name Mary Bernadette. If you watched Minnie Driver play Benny in the movie but have not read the novel, you'd fail to appreciate just how unfashionably fat Benny was in the mind of her original creator.

In *Echoes*, Josie is supported by Clare O'Brien, and makes strides on her own account, taking hold of her life and discovering the power within herself to do so. In *Circle of Friends* we always know that Benny is beautiful inside and we suffer with her when her friends betray her, and cheer with her at the end when she realises she is over Jack Foley, the boy who cheats on her with her friend, the shapely Nan Mahon.

As a mature adult, who had put her adolescent tortures behind her and become a confident writer of world renown, the issue of Maeve's weight emerged as the scratching mat against which she developed so much of the great wisdom delivered in her stories. Both Josie and Benny win out in the end *not* by conceding to the fashionable stereotype, *not* by slimming, *not* by moping, nor yet by being transformed into princesses by their creator, but by taking control of their lives and becoming confident in who they are.

But one of her short stories cuts deeper and suggests that there was more to the weight issue. 'Warren Street', from Maeve's *Victoria Line* collection (1980), is a sensitive and imaginative story inspired by Maeve's dressmaker, Miss Creegan. Nan has a dress shop. Shirley is a large woman with a sunny personality and has for years come to Nan for her clothes. Shirley is one of Nan's best customers and Nan tends to dress her in bright colours (as Maeve often chose to be dressed), and it is tacitly understood that there is a close bond of sisterly love between the two women.

The story kicks off with Colin, Nan's boyfriend, catching sight of Shirley for the first time and likening her to a beach ball bouncing out of the door. Nan informs Colin that that was Shirley, whom she's talked about before. Colin says that she never mentioned that Shirley looked like a 'technicoloured Moby Dick'. Nan is furious with him.

Later Shirley spots an envelope on which Colin has scribbled 'Green eye-shadow for burly Shirley', and is so hurt that, in Maeve's words, 'she was almost bleeding'.

Nan gets herself in a terrible twist trying to make things right with Shirley, but her attempts only deepen Shirley's wound, exposing the fact that their friendship is built on Nan's pity for her for being fat.

For Shirley, Nan's hypocrisy is a betrayal of their friendship, and it hurts badly. Things are imagined and said so hurtfully that their friendship is destroyed. What Maeve is asking is, where is truth in a relationship between soulmates when one is not wholly honest with the other?

Whether love or even true friendship should involve always telling the truth preoccupied Maeve throughout her life and elsewhere in her books, notably in the novel *Tara Road* (1998).

What did it say of her relationships with her close friends that they couldn't tell her the truth? One of her school friends refused to engage with the subject even today. 'There is too much written about Maeve's weight and her psychological well-being. Maeve was a fun loving, normal, happy girl.' Yet on Maeve's own admission she was not. Another said, 'Actually, if Maeve hadn't had such a loving, wonderful, supporting family who told her all the time that she was wonderful, she could well have had problems.' A third friend, who knew her only from her forties but became just as close, took the issue further:

She would have you believe that she was always the podgy ugly duckling of the family. Yet on the mantelpiece of the spare bedroom at her home was a photograph of the whole family, with a really stunning, tall girl in an academic gown, standing at the front of the group. It took me several goes of looking at it to realise that this was Maeve, aged twenty-one. We had all accepted her word that Joan was the beauty of the family, but on this very vivid evidence, at that age, it was Maeve who knocked spots off the rest.

Was it really her size that led to her unrest, or was it born of a growing awareness of the difference between how she felt about herself at home and at school? Was there a glimpse of the discrepancy between what Maureen was always telling her – that she was the most beautiful and the best – and the reality, which was that she was not the best academically, nor quite the most beautiful, she was tall and big boned and, yes, a little plump?

Fortunately Maeve had Mother St Dominic, who diverted her interest into what she found to admire in the girl, which was plenty, such as her warmth and humanity and the fact that she was good company, one of those unusual girls who never had anything bad to say about anybody else. Remembers Patricia Hamilton, 'You felt good when you were with Maeve because she was not a knocker of people. You felt "built up" perhaps, because Maeve built you up by her attitude towards you.'

Like mother, like daughter.

Under Mother St Dominic's guidance Maeve became 'more of a chum and a friend of everybody' rather than straining to become the popular, beautiful girl her mother promised she was. As a result the friends she made at school remained, she said, the closest she had as an adult too. And she also made at least one special relationship. Her best friend was Philippa O'Keefe, a boarder one year older than her. The O'Keefes lived on a farm in Drinagh, County Wexford. At school Philippa was a quiet, attractive girl, prudent and discreet, and a member of the local pony club.

The demands Maeve made on herself and her close friends to be honest and true were colossal, if not sometimes unreal. But her relationship with Philippa comes down to us as the ideal. Their friendship endured through school, university and right up until Maeve's death, so that even sixty years after they met Maeve had a file of letters marked 'Dear Philippa' in her study. By then, Philippa had long since left Ireland for London. But like Aisling and Elizabeth, and like Benny and Eve in *Circle of Friends*, their bond was never broken.

Maeve's love for Philippa is why she made the blood-tie of friendship the heart and soul of her first novel. The intimacy of the relationship between Aisling and Elizabeth – innocent, touching and truer than anything that passes between boy and girl or man and woman in her books – is what swept sales of the book to the top of bestseller lists around the world. We watch it forming and being ritualised in baptism by Aisling, and later being challenged by all that fate can throw at it. Elizabeth comes to the friendship timid, unsure of herself, a complete novice to love, while Aisling's family embody the emotion and it comes as second nature to Aisling. They seal their love in Ireland because love says something about Ireland; they mesh blood from their arms, 'like Red Indians'.

Later, Elizabeth's English boyfriend, Johnny, recoils from the intensity of it. Friendships between women so close as truly to merit the epithet 'love' abound in the novels, and are the subject too of a number of Maeve's short stories, but none is as deep as this, most movingly so when they say goodbye at the barrier in Euston station in London after Aisling has come over from Ireland to help Elizabeth through an abortion. While Elizabeth fights the feeling that she'll never see Aisling again and fears that Aisling will look back on the visit and be repulsed by all that has happened, Aisling vows that she can never cut Elizabeth out of her life, that she is an inextricable part of it, and 'if it weren't so soppy I'd say I love you'.

'Well I love you too,' says Elizabeth and there is nothing more to be said, as Aisling is swallowed up in the crowds for the train.

Maeve's 'religious maniac' phase at the Holy Child was followed (but wasn't replaced) by the 'utter hysteria about sex' phase. She had learned the facts of life from her mother at quite a young age. Trailing home from Mass with her family on St Patrick's Day, all wearing shamrocks of course, Maeve was thrilled to learn that this is the one day in the Lent calendar when the order of abstinence is lifted – she would be allowed to eat all the sweets she liked. Buoyed by the news, she decided to settle something that had been bothering her and asked her mother where children come from. Unflustered, Maureen told her. Maeve was so astonished that she refused to believe her, confiding in her father that her mother had got things very confused; her father said that he thought Maureen could in fact be quite right.

Like Nessa and Maura Brennan in *The Copper Beech* (1992), Maeve couldn't believe her parents had 'done it'. For a year she put her father's response down to his wonderful loyalty to Maureen, but by the time she arrived at the Holy Child she was prepared to admit that Maureen's explanation probably did hold some water.

Then the nuns added a vital new dimension to the whole thing – passion and desire. Hitherto there'd been no mention of these, which, according to Maeve, were discussed by the nuns in terms of the level of lust that the girls would meet in the big wide world and the need to bridle it within 'a good Catholic marriage'. They were told how difficult it was for boys to restrain themselves. Girls had to take control of them and insist that they only have sex within matrimony. That was society. Sixty years later, the same girls still remember the dictum: 'Any impure thoughts, get out your rosaries! Go to confession!' Said Patricia:

> Maeve's writing will be very valuable for what it shows about how we behaved in the 1950s. We were very naïve. We really were so innocent and in a way our innocence brought us through life ... It was an Age of Innocence, both for men and for women. None of us had sex, as far as I know...

Maeve listened to the nuns' counsel and to the missioners. The sermons on purity she took very seriously indeed, although she could never quite remember whether sex was meant to be the highest expression of love, or love the highest expression of sex. The girls had nearly choked trying to keep a straight face, and it was all confused further by the crucial matter of 'respect', the idea that if you gave yourself to a boy too readily he would lose respect for you.

Interest in the 'utter hysteria about sex' phase was greatly facilitated by what Patricia referred to as the 'age of chilblains', brought about by the Spartan conditions at the convent. 'What you did in your spare time was go to a radiator and talk to your pal ... It was cold so you'd put your feet on the radiator. And you'd put your hands and feet and lift your skirt up to get warm!'

Thus positioned, Maeve and her friends would have endless conversations. It was where female solidarity, the one certainty throughout Maeve's life, was first implemented. Most of the girls said they had boyfriends. Maeve didn't have one, which must have seemed odd to one who had been brought to believe that she was the most beautiful, so she became immersed in other girls' affairs – so much so that she could tell you the names of their boyfriends even half a century later. It was here, often in an advisory capacity, that she discovered her natural *métier*, a sure talent for discussing other people's problems, and soon realised that it made her very popular indeed. There was no aspect of her peers' relationships that went undiscussed. 'We were given to planning the first night as meticulously as the planning of the Normandy landing,' she once said.

She became a go-between, stuffing letters from the boarders to their boyfriends in town down the front of her gymslip and smuggling them out to the post.

Inevitably, one day a nun stopped her on the way out with a hoard of letters. As Maeve squirmed with guilt, the nun asked her whether she felt all right, because she looked as if she was about to have a heart attack. Maeve, feeling like a hooked fish on the nun's line, assured her that she was fine. But then one of the letters fell to the floor and others followed soon after, each tellingly addressed to Master so-and-so. Maeve felt the depths of Hell yawn beneath her.

She had flouted the trust the nuns had placed in her, the trust at the very root of convent discipline. This time there was to be no wide smile of forgiveness or a 'do it again', only the humiliating prospect of the finger of shame pointing at her the following morning at Assembly, when she would have to give her treasured Child of Mary medal back.

It was terribly upsetting. Maeve likened the ritual humiliation in front of the whole school to a court martial, lightened only a little by the credit she received from the girls for refusing to disclose who had enlisted her to post the letters. Maeve was intensely loyal, especially to the sisterhood. She would not have ratted on any of the girls at the Holy Child had the nuns got out the spiked chains in true Jesuit style. But nothing could compensate for the loss of the Child of Mary medal for the would-be saint.

And her humiliation was made doubly worse by it being evident that she, alone among all the girls involved, had no boyfriend. The nuns might see no boyfriend as a good thing, but Maeve was more than a little bit disappointed that, given the emphasis on the amount of lust she would meet in the outside world, there was so little around for her to repel. 'At fifteen the latent stirrings were there all right, although they were stirring a bit in vain for me.'[17]

Passion and anxiety characterised Maeve's life from the start, but it would be some time before she exercised the former in a relationship with a boy.

She once put her lack of success with boys down to an absence of opportunity. She didn't have an older brother who might bring home a boy of suitable age. William, her brother, was eight years her junior.

The first opportunity came her way at fourteen or fifteen. The local answer to Italy's *passeggiata* was a Saturday afternoon stroll in Dún Laoghaire's local 'piazza', a square-cum-thoroughfare off Lower George Street, outside the local cinema. Kids would hang out there before going in to catch the latest film. The cinema was a regular Saturday treat for Maeve and her younger sisters, and she would look enviously at those girls who had boyfriends and who could engage in this parade properly.

Finally, a boy did ask her out, to see a film called *Roman Holiday*, a romantic comedy starring Gregory Peck and Audrey Hepburn released in 1953. Maeve was thrilled. She could talk about nothing else. At last she had joined 'the gang'. But the boy rang the night before to confirm the date and spoiled it all. He said he'd meet her *inside* the cinema. She said he might as well have slapped her face.

At sixteen an alternative solution to her lack of boyfriend arose in the form of Marlon Brando. She fell in love with him. Yes, *love* was what it was, not some adolescent crush, you understand. She really meant it, though later she admitted it was 'pure sex'!

Brando first appeared in *The Wild One*, dressed in leather astride a motorbike in 1953, and swept aside 'old smoothie Hollywood', welcoming in mean, 'brooding, smouldering Hollywood', with James Dean upping the tempo mid-decade with *East of Eden* and *Rebel Without a Cause*. Brando's *On the Waterfront* followed *The Wild One* in 1954, the heart of waterfront culture being not Dún Laoghaire but Hoboken, New Jersey, across the Hudson River from New York, somewhere deep within a little docksider.

The feelings Brando stirred were a new experience for Maeve and she didn't know what to make of them. She responded by telling herself that he looked lonely and sad and needed someone to look after him. So she wrote to him, she said, and told him that his woman, Movita (the Mexican actress Maria Castaneda), was 'doing him no good'. He should leave her and come to Ireland and marry Maeve instead. At one stage she wrote to him weekly, deeply concerned about the effect on him of some bad reviews and his marital problems, telling him not to worry too much about custody of his son, Christian, by his first wife Anna Kashfi. She was especially concerned that he was letting the role he played in *On the Waterfront* get 'in on his mind too much', which was quite an insight.

William can remember his sister's room covered with hundreds of photographs of Brando. She had expected to hear back from Brando personally but, alas, every time Maeve wrote to him she received yet another photograph with a letter written by some lackey thanking her for being part of Brando's fan club. She was devastated that anyone should have thought her so crass as to want to join anybody's fan club. Her feelings for Brando were true, her invitation to him genuine. Maeve even remembered 'whinging and whining' to Philippa that when Brando agreed to meet her she'd have to bring him to Dalkey, a place too sleepy for anyone their age to be. She recalled Philippa saying, 'It's a pity you don't live somewhere nicer!'

There were, however, other opportunities to meet real boys. Every summer for twelve years, William and Maureen took the family back to where it all began: Ballybunion. The children would be hugely excited, for Ballybunion in the 1950s was a joyous place, full of friends who would meet up every year. Here at last they could run free without their mother worrying about where they were.

The Binchys would start preparing three weeks or more in advance, Maeve being sure to pack a bottle of St Blonde shampoo and another of peroxide, on the basis that blondes have all the fun. Having no car, they would travel down to Tralee by train, the first stage of the journey a taxi ride for Maureen, one child and the family's luggage to what was then Kingsbridge station in Dublin (now Heuston). The rest of the family travelled by tram or rail, and every single year without fail, when everyone was gathered and settled in the compartment at Kingsbridge, Maureen would rise and announce that there were ten minutes to spare, time enough to go and get a magazine. They would moan and watch her browse the stall with ever heightened anxiety lest she would not get back on the train in time for it to sound its steam whistle and draw out of the station.

Ballybunion is the inspiration for Castlebay in *Echoes*, so named because a ruined castle stands central to the cliff-top scene. When, in the novel, the Nolans arrive at Tralee on the train from Dublin, Castlebay's Dr Power picks them up in his car and takes them the twenty miles into the town, while the young people of the party, Caroline Nolan and her school friend Hilary, are taken with the Nolans' maid in a taxi under the guidance of Dr Power's son, David.

The route they take is worth mentioning, because it is the same one that the Binchys took every year, even though it wasn't the most direct route to their regular lodging house in the Sandhill Road. The Binchys would always make a detour so that they could take in the whole scene, the shops and the holiday-makers and the beach paraphernalia and all the sights, sounds and smells that they'd looked forward to so much all year.

In the novel, the girls are silenced by their first sight of the beach, the vast expanse of wet sand spreading 'like a huge silver carpet' between the two headlands. The waters of the Atlantic are warmed by the Gulf Stream, and the spirit of the place seems affected that way too.

As they come down Church Street – Church Road in reality – people are recognising one another from last season, waving and talking animatedly on their way down to the beach. Turning right into Main Street, the girls look excitedly at the big dance hall by the entrance of Dillon's Hotel, which in reality, in Maeve's time, was the Central Hotel. The taxi then turns right again onto Cliff Road and they find themselves at the top of Church Street again, where the doctor's house is situated and the Power family have tea prepared on the lawn. It is a lovely scene, and we get a real sense of Maeve's anticipation as a child of a holiday about to begin.

Dr Power's house, the big house on the cliff which Maeve describes, is in reality Ballybunion House. When Maeve holidayed there it was the residence of Dr Hannan, like his fictional counterpart the only doctor in the town. It is indeed still the home of Dr Hannan's son Tim today.

The Binchys came to know the Hannans, and for her novel Maeve drew on the interior of the house and the garden as it was in the 1950s. Perhaps she first came upon it like Clare O'Brien, who cuts her leg on a piece of machinery and goes to Dr Power's surgery for stitches.

The Pavilion, where Maeve's parents had danced in the 1930s, closed in the early 1950s. The opening of the Central Ballroom in the Central Hotel, which replaced it, was quite an affair. There were over 3,000 people there the night it opened. The line-up featured Josef Locke, a tenor in the mould of Mario Lanza, a real pro hardened by working men's clubs in the north of England and by nineteen seasons in Blackpool, Lancashire. Locke's greatest hit was 'Hear My Song, Violetta', but mostly he performed Irish songs like 'I'll Take You Home Again, Kathleen', 'Dear Old Donegal', 'Galway Bay' and 'The Isle of Innisfree'.

As well as the Central there was another hotel in Maeve's day, the Castle, both establishments owned by the McCarthy brothers, William and Paddy, whose father had managed the Lartigue Railway in the town – a little eccentricity in this far outpost of Eire, which somehow doesn't surprise. The Lartigue Railway, named after the French engineer Charles Lartigue, who invented it, was a monorail system that ran to and from Listowel, little more than ten miles to the east. There were only two ever made, one in Africa and the other in Ballybunion.

The house on the Sandhill Road which the Binchys used to rent from a dentist in Listowel is located on the bend in the road as it leads out of town towards the town's famous 'pro' golf club. Maeve used to say that it was so close to the sea it was like having your own private bathing place. As soon as they arrived, the children would leave everything and rush down to the beach to see who else had arrived. It was at that point that summer officially started.

There are two main beaches in Ballybunion, the Men's Strand and the Ladies' Strand, to the north of which the large cliff is scarred with caves reminiscent of Brigid's Cave, the 'echo cave' of Maeve's novel, where if you wanted to know whether you'd get a fella, you'd call out and wait for the reply. The castle ruin stands on the cliff between them.

Back in the late 1930s, Ballybunion had a parish priest called Father Behan who on a Sunday, when there were a lot of visitors about, used to stand by the castle ruin and insist upon the segregation of the women on the one strand and the men on the other. Few took much notice and he would retire in the end to his own section of the men's beach where the rocks are known as the Priest's Rocks. In the evening, after Father Behan's party had left, children would scamper down and look for any coins that might have fallen out of their pockets.

Times were hard in the '30s, but there seem to have been quite a few children with their eyes glued to the ground looking for a few bob even twenty years later. Aged twelve Maeve had thoughts only for rides on the bumper cars – there was a travelling fairground in summer as well as fixed rides. She was forever scanning the pavement just in case someone had dropped a coin that would pay for the next 'go'.

Gangs of girls and boys hunted in packs at Ballybunion. To Maeve and thousands of others, here was unbridled excitement and anticipation and freedom, unlike anything they'd experienced all year.

At fourteen or fifteen, as her thoughts turned to boys, she would go to her first dance here, and anticipate her first kiss and perhaps have a taste of alcohol at a picnic party down among the sand hills, as she described in *Echoes*.

As she reached adolescence, the big-city teenage rock 'n' roll revolution was just beginning to happen. Chuck Berry's 'Maybellene' was released in 1955. Little Richard charted seven No. 1 hits in less than three years around this time. Theirs was the sound that gave way to white rock 'n' roll – Bill Haley in 1955, Elvis in 1956 with 'Heartbreak Hotel', 'Don't Be Cruel' and 'Blue Suede Shoes'.

At the Central Ballroom, Maurice Mulcahy was the resident orchestra. The band had a line-up of five saxophonists, two trumpets, a guitar, a squeezebox, double bass and drums and was one of the famous Irish show bands of the time. It provided a kind of transition between the big-band sound of the '40s and early '50s and the dawning era of rock 'n' roll. Mulcahy's playlist was pretty conservative but it was quite possible to dance the waltz to 'Tales from the Vienna Woods' one minute and jive to 'See You Later, Alligator' the next.

Except that jiving did have its own set of obstacles at the Central. If you were caught doing it, you were out on your ear. The only chance you had was down on the right-hand corner of the ballroom. The ballroom then had a balcony apparently, and if you met a young lady you had to go up to the balcony for an orange or lemonade and then you took your chances after that.

Maeve remembered that Mulcahy himself used to like to gee up his audience with clichéd innuendo that would set the dance floor alight in a riot of laughter and whistling. He would come to the microphone and ask for silence and make a serious 'lost or found' announcement that a certain girl had gone down to the sand hills last night and lost her ... And then he would pause suggestively, and the audience would corpse themselves laughing. Boys' minds were centred on lost virginity from about 8 p.m. on, when they were getting well oiled in the pubs.

There were no great decisions to be made about what to wear. 'For girls it was summer frocks, somewhere down to between the knee and the ankle and maybe a couple of layers of petticoats. A lot of the boys would have worn suits to the dances,' Tim Hannan says. The great thing was not to look as if you were trying too hard. 'They had a resident photographer in the old days and there was always a rush in the morning to see who you were taken with last night.'

For Maeve's first dance she wore a sixteen-shilling dress in turquoise and white from Clerys, the Dublin department store. She chose the colour, she said, because while red was reckoned by most people to attract more attention, girls prone to red face would be advised against it.

In search of a tan she made up a mixture of Nivea and Brown Nugget boot polish (the cheapest you could get, so cheap, she said, that most people thought twice about putting it on their shoes). She applied this concoction to her face, which set off her white cardigan nicely but made her, as she put it, 'very danger-ous to dance with'.

Generally, her apprehension added considerably to her prob-lems. Expectations were high. Her younger sisters, Joan and Renie, would crane their necks around the main door to see how she was getting on, expecting her to emerge later that night at the very least engaged to a future husband.

Inevitably, the reality turned out to be quite different. The dances started about 8 p.m. and the pubs didn't close till ten, which meant that to begin with there were many more girls than boys in attendance. So crowded was the cloakroom that Maeve couldn't even get a sixpenny spray of Evening in Paris which was available there. The few young fellas who didn't drink and were out for a dance appeared to have been snapped up by girls a good deal older and more experienced than her.

No one asked her to dance, and when she saw the eager faces of her sisters and their friends she was so desperate not to show how completely unsuccessful she was that she made a few passes, twirling by the half-open door in front of them as if her partner was just out of view. This was undertaken, Maeve recalled, during a rendition by Mulcahy of a jive number, which at least would have accounted for the absence of a partner in her arms.

Maeve was actually a very good dancer. The girls at the Holy Child were taught dancing at school by a fine teacher, and before long she would have a whale of a time dancing the night away in Ballybunion. 'If you could manage to get someone to dance with you,' she once admitted, 'then you were there for the night.'

A school friend remembers Maeve coming back from Ballybunion one year saying that she had fallen in love with a fellow called Matt. Maeve showed her a photo of a big hulk of a guy six or seven years older than her and said that she spent the whole summer hovering around and standing at corners hoping to bump into him. 'He featured for many years and it was always her hope that he would fall in love with her.' That was Ballybunion, a harmless '50s fantasy land in which everyone had fun at no one else's expense. It seems likely that Maeve's crush was none other than Dr Hannan's oldest son by the same name, who sadly died in early middle age.

Life may have been simpler back in the '50s, but for Maeve occasionally it was so hurtful that even her sense of humour was not enough to protect her sensitive soul.

In 1956, the year of her Leaving Certificate, she turned seventeen. She was approaching the end of her time at the convent and was nervously awaiting the results on which her passage into university depended when she was invited to a dance at the

Royal Marine Hotel. It was to be a big 'do', a dance given by the parents of two of her school friends.

The Royal Marine has been an elegant fixture in Dún Laoghaire since 1865, with its bandstand out front and stories abounding of guests as various as Queen Victoria, Frank Sinatra and Michael Collins, the Irish freedom fighter who took Room 210 with Kitty Kiernan in November 1920.

Maeve borrowed a dress from a cousin and had a big velvet band let into the front. Diamante earrings were found to complete the outfit, but with frequent practice earlier in the day they had bitten into her ears, so that by the time of the dance she'd had to put patches of plaster on her lobes. Maeve painted the plaster blue to match her dress, though wasn't quite certain she had done the right thing.

But then, as she was leaving the house, Maureen yet again came to the rescue. She looked at her daughter proudly and said, 'You look so beautiful you'll take the sight out of their eyes.'

Alas, it was a cataclysmic failure of a night, one that would inspire what her editor years later described as 'one of the most powerful scenes she ever wrote – the party scene in *Circle of Friends*'. Nobody – not one single person – danced with her, and this was a private party. She was there with her friends and she couldn't hide her utter failure. Her parents waited up for her until she came home, wanting to know not only that she was safe, but about every heartbeat of every dance. Maeve told them that she had been danced off her feet all night long.

Long afterwards she admitted this was a very black time. If earlier she had not dared admit a discrepancy between what

Maureen was always telling her about her beauty and the reality, she surely did now and what did it say of her mother's love that she had duped her all her young life? For days Maeve persecuted herself by imagining people were gossiping behind her back in the tight little Dalkey community. The memory of it still stung on the day her Leaving Certificate results came through. But it was only one of many feelings that were running through her core that day.

Today she would hear whether she had passed – and she was worried sick. The nuns had given their opinion that she was not, after all, of a scholarly frame of mind. If she tried, she could be top at anything, but she had continued to dream and when all was said and done she liked laughing better than working.

She no longer had a particular ambition. She was down to read Law at university, but had no desire to be a lawyer. She didn't at this point want to be a writer nor was she thinking about becoming a teacher. She wanted to enjoy life and with the results hanging over her she had been uncharacteristically moody and difficult at home, flaring up on any subject. Maureen realised that she was worried about her results and wondered if, like herself, Maeve would be more successful in work where no great further study was required.

At the same time, Maeve had not forgotten what had been sacrificed to get her this far. She was aware of her father's expectations of all the children to pass their exams, and remembered his warning that money might not always be there. As the eldest child she felt a duty to prove that they, the children of 'these great people', as she referred to her parents, were indeed swans and not ducks.

Dalkey was such a small town and however familiar and friendly on the surface, it was, like every other small town, full of small-town gossips. Everyone knew where everyone was and what you were doing all day and night. It was like being in a goldfish bowl. It was even suspected that telephone calls – all of which were routed through the local telephone exchange in those days – were listened into by the local postmistress. Imagine the buzz if she failed!

Well, whatever happened, there was at least change in the air. Whether or not she got the results she needed for university, nothing would be the same any more. She was about to make a break with the past, and about time!

Even at twelve, when she first came to live in Dalkey, she sensed she was in the wrong place. Everything seemed to point in the opposite direction, to the bright lights of Dún Laoghaire and the very bright lights of Dublin – the city in striking distance and yet off the map for her. She was never allowed to go there, except with her mother to shop.

Now that Maeve was seventeen, Dalkey seemed just about the dullest place on earth. Walking with Philippa past the pitch of Dalkey United they could appreciate the leggy fellows play-ing football, but they'd never get to know them. There was no cinema, no place for young people to dance, or even to meet. On Castle Street, the main street, there was the Queen's bar, the St Laurence Club at No. 17 – neither of which they could possi-bly go into, or would want to. They went to McKenna's or Hill Stores for sweets, and there were a couple of cafés, one called The Matassa, but that was it. Most of the shops would close for lunch and everywhere was shut by 6 p.m. Apart from a sortie for fish and chips there was nothing for Maeve and her friends to do.

The feeling of being trapped here had been gradual, but Maeve had become acutely aware of it after an exchange trip to France. A letter from a family in Compiègne, in northern France, had been passed to the Binchys by a friend. They were looking, they said, for an Irish family of a certain social status to take their daughter, Odile, for a few weeks in exchange for a child from England. The Binchys assumed that the snobbish element of the letter had been down to the family's poor understanding of the English language, but it transpired that this was not the case at all.

When Maeve arrived in Compiègne she was dreadfully nervous – she had never been out of Ireland before. She said '*très bien*' to everything, committing herself to she knew not what. The mother turned out to be a religious maniac. An impossibly rich aunt stamped around prodding people with her walking stick. The father took delight in penalising Maeve for her poor pronunciation of French by refusing to allow her to eat anything until she had got it right. This was a master stroke – Maeve learned good French very quickly after that.

When Odile's letters started arriving from Ireland, however, things changed for the better. Odile was able to report that although the Binchys didn't appear to be very wealthy they actually had two homes, one in the town close to Dublin and another on the far west coast by the sea at a place called Ballybunion. She had mistaken the house on Sandhill Road for a second home! More important, Odile let slip that the Binchys had paid for everything, even her ice creams.

This had an immediate effect on the French household. A quick calculation showed that they owed Maeve more than £30 in hospitality and suddenly she was being taken to Chartres, to châteaux in the Loire, even to Brussels. The trip was completely transformed. They taught her to ride a horse and to hunt and insisted that she kept a diary of everything they had paid for her to do.

Maeve had got the travel bug; she enjoyed observing the doings and habits of people outside her little bubble of Dalkey.

Before Compiègne she had had no inkling that anyone thought at all differently to the way she had been brought up to think. She was so completely *of* Dalkey, and had so little experience *beyond* Dalkey, that she had no reason to think that her home *in* Dalkey was singular in any way at all. It was while she was in France that she became determined to see more of the wider world.

And now that was once more at the forefront of her mind. What did it matter that no boy wanted to dance with her? She had decided that she was going to see the world before she'd let herself fall for any of them.

But first things first, she did not want to suffer the indignity of failing to matriculate. Today she had decided not to go to school with everyone else to get their results, but to cycle down to the Church of the Assumption – her church – and envelop herself in its comforting silence instead.

Maeve fell to her knees, praying that she would get the exam, telling God that she would be good for the rest of her life if she passed.[18] Like Niamh in *Light a Penny Candle* – the first of the O'Connor siblings to go to university – if she had prayed any harder she would have 'prayed herself into a near coma'.

Fortunately, rescue was at hand.

When Maeve's sister heard the news for which Maeve was waiting, she mounted her bicycle and flew through the town to tell her. When she appeared through the doors at the west end of the church and shouted the good news, there was great satisfaction, not just that Maeve had got the 'Matric', but that all four children were now on their way. For being the eldest of four it was Maeve who was setting the pace.

The two girls got back on their bikes and headed for home, acknowledging Maeve's triumph to everyone on the street as they passed, and then to the shopkeepers who came to their doors to see what all the fuss was about.

It was the end of an era, and no one could begin to imagine just what a new era was about to begin.

FOUR

WATERSHED

My life changed in October 1956 the day I went into University College Dublin, aged seventeen. UCD was like a big light turning on in my life.[19]

No more travelling to and from the convent on the little train around the bay. It was life in the big city – Dublin – a city like no other, as James Joyce has his *alter ego* Stephen Dedalus exclaim to his friend Frank Budgen: 'What a town Dublin is! … I wonder if there is another like it. Everybody has time to hail a friend and start a conversation…'[20]

In 1956, University College Dublin was located in a huge, classically designed building (now the National Concert Hall) situated in Earlsfort Terrace on the southern edge of St Stephen's Green in the heart of the city, only a short way from the maternity unit where Maeve was born.

Initially she had signed up for BA Law and for King's Inns with the intention of becoming a barrister, but soon realised that the law wasn't for her and transferred to English, French and History, with Latin her fourth subject. A year later she sat what they call First Arts in these subjects and then concentrated on French and History for her honours degree, which she took in 1959.

The novelty of university was immediately upon her. New sensations bombarded her on all sides. The noise and bustle were a hundred times bigger than at the Holy Child. Everyone seemed so much more grown up than her, with a confidence and spirit of independence unlike anything she'd encountered before.

Student social life, like that for millions of other young people in the 1950s whether or not they were at university, began in the coffee bar. The burgeoning coffee bar scene was the defining mark of the decade. From Dublin to Liverpool to London's Soho, coffee bars were the new gathering places for the young, and youth was what the late '50s and '60s were all about.

At UCD the student coffee bar was known as the Annexe, as Maeve recalls faithfully in her novel *Circle of Friends* – the novel that owes so much to her experience at UCD in the pre-pill, pre-sexual revolution era, 'when a Catholic culture's threat of damnation was making its last stand against the forces of temptation'.[21]

The Annexe was located in Newman House, the student centre named after the Catholic theologian and scholar Dr John Henry Newman, first rector of the university. The building had been St Patrick's House of the original Catholic University, founded a century earlier.

Located on St Stephen's Green South, it was readily accessible via Earlsfort Terrace or through Iveagh Gardens at the rear of the main university building. St Stephen's Green itself and Iveagh Gardens are public parks, but were always reckoned by everyone in those days to be campus territory. Together with Newman University church, a stunning little building in blue-grey and red brick, next door to Newman House, the area made an impressive inner-city university site.

For Maeve the Annexe was a huge challenge. There were boys everywhere. Suddenly, from a small single-sex school and a single life, she found herself in an almost all-male environment. In the 1950s the vast majority of students at UCD were male, a species she knew nothing about even if she had discussed them with her friends in minute detail.

She had had so little contact with boys before and no boyfriends at all, other than Matt in Ballybunion, who hadn't even been hooked, let alone landed. In the last year at school there'd been a lot of talk of her friends being taken by boys in cars up into the Dublin mountains, but she was never invited. She had met fellows at parties, but that was all. Boys were, as far as she was concerned, a species apart. And she was innocent not only of sex but of talking to boys in the first place.

In the Annexe it was inevitable that something would happen. In *Circle of Friends* Maeve is Benny in this very situation, sitting at a table with her friend, the shapely Nan. A small group of boys come over and their leader asks whether the girls would like to come down Grafton Street for some real coffee. He has eyes only for Nan, who puts him off lightly and with practised ease. But then to Benny's alarm Nan offers her instead. To cover her blushes, Benny surprises herself by issuing an invitation of her own: 'Why don't you bring a chair over and have a coffee here with us?'

And so it began, in reality for Maeve as in the fiction for Benny. Communication was easier than she had anticipated. The boys seemed almost normal – human beings with names and faculties. She managed the initial conversation with a lively charm and wit. There never was even a moment of silence (much dreaded), and soon she had quite forgotten her anxieties.

In the novel the boys accept Benny at once. One of them says that he's heard that the Debating Society on a Saturday night is a lot of fun. We know that Maeve did become a force in the UCD Debating Society and it is easy to believe that her interest did start like this.

The society had a fine reputation for getting in promi- nent speakers, 'like Seán Lemass[22] and James Dillon.[23] And it was a most enjoyable night, well attended,' Tim Hannan, also a UCD student at this time, told me. 'There'd always be a few hecklers in the audience.' But it was also very much the preliminary to socialising. 'Afterwards everyone went to the dance at the Gresham Hotel, next door to the Savoy cinema in O'Connell Street.'

In the novel, attending the dance is suggested but Benny cannot go because she is living at home and cannot be in Dublin at weekends. Poor Benny, what a dampener that must have been, and poor Maeve, for that was her situation too. At first, her parents insisted she spend the weekend at home in Dalkey, and every night during the week she would have to make her dark and lonely way home by bus or train – dark because after the bus passed Booterstown Bird Sanctuary there was no street lighting at all.

Maeve used to long to have a room a few minutes' walk from the university in Baggot Street, for many years home to the world's most famous pub crawl, although pubs were not an attraction to her. In the 1950s few girls went into them, and Maeve didn't drink alcohol at all until she was twenty-two. She had never been tempted to drink. Toothache as a child had always been treated by Maureen with a piece of cotton wool soaked in whiskey and Maeve hadn't liked the taste. On another occasion she had added gin to the trifle at home when they'd run out of sherry and it hadn't worked at all.

Maeve's ideal in those days was to have a boyfriend who wore an Arran sweater, to dance to Dave Brubeck and to sip small cups of black coffee with him. That was the scene in the late 1950s.

William and Maureen were obviously concerned about how Maeve would handle her newfound independence. They must have been aware of just how vulnerable she was. In the fiction, Benny's family want to give her the opportunity of a higher education but are determined not to let her grow out of the middle-class Catholic culture in which she has been brought up. Benny accuses her father of taking her to the top of the mountain, showing her what's available and then refusing her a part of it.

For Maeve, the weekend ban lasted only the first term, but she returned home every night throughout her time at UCD. In reality the two sacred institutions around which life had turned when she was a schoolgirl – family and religion – still dominated her life at university.

The start of the year left new students in no doubt of the heavy Catholic ethos at UCD. There was an opening Mass at which all students had to dress up and troop around in procession, and the front row of the lecture hall was always packed with novice nuns and black-suited students from religious seminaries bound for the pious life, looking notably neater than the main student body. Geraldine, who did History and French with Maeve, remembers, 'It was still all very Catholic, the '50s and the '60s.'

Maeve recalled how she would think nothing of it when, at Friday-night dances at the Gresham Hotel, with the dance band in full swing, there'd be an announcement that a special dispensation had been arranged to allow the party-goers to eat meat, normally banned to Catholics on Fridays.

She and her friends still lived under the shadow of the Church and were full of the notion of sin. But Catholicism at UCD was in one way different to what they were used to. There was a serious political edge to it.

UCD was itself a Catholic institution. If you were a Catholic going to university in Ireland there was no option *but* to go to UCD. It was the university for Catholics, and founded as such. Trinity College on the far side of the green was for Protestants and even after they let Catholics into Trinity, the Catholic Archbishop regarded it as a sin to go there, as Eve Malone tells us in *Circle of Friends*, where the sense is also that Trinity undergraduates were intellectual snobs. With great irony, given the intellectual track record of the Catholic Binchys, Maeve has students at a rugby match against Trinity at Lansdowne Road chant, 'Come on Collidge – C-O-L-L-I-D-G-E', as if Catholics are so thick they can't even spell.

Beneath the Trinity–UCD rivalry lay a thick layer of serious history. During the Second World War, Catholic Ireland elected not to fight alongside Britain (not surprisingly, given the history between the two countries), even though many individuals did fight of their own volition, as Aisling's older brother Sean does in the fiction. To mark the politics, on VE Day the pro-British, Protestant Trinity (whose students obviously did fight for Britain) raised the flags of some of the victorious nations, and lowered the Irish tricolour. Famously, Charles Haughey, who later served three terms as Taoiseach (Prime Minister) of Eire, was among a group of UCD students who burned a Union Jack outside Trinity in protest at their action.

The religious–political edge at UCD was far keener even than that, however. Earlier in the century, when Maeve's uncle Daniel Binchy was a student there, two students actually became martyrs to the Catholic cause.

On Easter Monday 1916, the Irish Volunteers, from which the IRA (the Irish Republican Army) descended, with various other revolutionary republican bodies[24] seized certain locations in Dublin, and at a key moment the Catholic Patrick Pearse read the famous 'Proclamation of the Republic' outside the Post Office on Sackville Street (now O'Connell Street), boldly proclaiming Ireland's independence of Britain.[25]

It was an impressive manifesto, more enlightened than that of any other country in Europe at that time. 'Civil liberty, equal rights and equal opportunities'– women were to have equal rights with men and everyone was going to be able to vote. Pearse and the other leaders of the Easter Rising were summarily arrested and executed by the British. But their work had been done. In the 1918 general election the Republicans won 73 out of 105 seats, and declared independence from Britain the following January.

When Britain did not accept the vote, guerrilla warfare broke out on the streets of Dublin, just as Daniel Binchy took up his place at the university. Earlsfort Terrace became a fortress. It is hard to convey the intensity of feeling on campus at this time. Some students were actually founder members of the Irish Volunteers – passionate, idealistic boys like Frank Flood, who had won a scholarship to read Engineering at UCD, and his school friend Kevin Barry, who was studying Medicine there.

Flood was active in the Literary and Historical Society, which had begun as the Historical, Literary and Aesthetical Society, functioned as a debating society and later became the student union at UCD.[26] Daniel Binchy would shortly become Auditor or President of the L&H, as it was known. He knew Flood and his friends, among them Tom Kissane and Mick Robinson, were all impassioned Republicans. Todd Andrews, another Republican student, noted in his memoirs, 'There were a number of students who were known to be IRA, but unless they were in the same Company or Battalion they never spoke or associated with one another on the basis of their common allegiance.'

No one publicised their involvement with the IRA for obvious reasons, but a cryptic note in the Binchy Archive at UCD observes that Daniel Binchy arrived in 1918, 'when political commitments were hard to avoid'.

The scale of the madness that was to follow was as yet unimagined. With justification people can still talk about heroic ideals and courageous boys believing they were righting the wrongs of 800 years of history, during which successive British forces had robbed them of the traditions and customs that went to make up what being Irish means.

Flood, who was nineteen, was arrested while attacking the Dublin Metropolitan Police at Drumcondra. No police were killed, but he was charged with high treason and executed by hanging at Mountjoy Prison.

He requested to be buried next to his friend and comrade, Kevin Barry, also nineteen, who'd been captured while taking part in a raid on a military lorry collecting bread in Church Street, during which a young British soldier was shot dead. Barry was court-martialled and executed, again by hanging, the expectation of a common criminal – not honourably despatched by firing squad.

The hanging of Kevin Barry outraged public opinion not only in Ireland but throughout the world, particularly because of his youth. 'The Ballad of Kevin Barry' appeared soon afterwards. No one knows who wrote it, but it remains a part of Irish folk tradition and has been covered by Leonard Cohen and by Paul Robeson in his *Songs of Struggle*.[27]

In the wake of these terrible events the Irish Free State was established, and in December of that same year talks began which led to the Anglo-Irish Treaty, which ended British rule in Ireland, except in six northern counties of Northern Ireland. The North–South divide, soon marked by civil war and leading eventually to the Troubles which spilled over onto the streets of London from the 1970s, had begun.[28]

None of UCD's place in the history of this had been forgotten by the time Maeve arrived. On the contrary, annual marches of hundreds of students were organised to the General Post Office and to the graves of Frank Flood and Kevin Barry in the grounds of Mountjoy Prison. Wreaths were laid by the Students' Representative Council to mark the fortieth anniversary of the boys' martyrdom. A Kevin Barry window was even unveiled as a campus memorial and was recently transferred to UCD's new campus at Belfield in the southern reaches of the city.

Catholicism was, therefore, part of UCD's identity, and sectarianism found its way into daily life. Your religion determined everything, even what newspaper you read and which radio station you listened to. A Catholic would listen only to Radio Athlone and take the *Irish Press*, the newspaper controlled by Éamon de Valera and his family in support of Fianna Fáil, the Republican Party, which de Valera founded. The first editor of the *Press*, Frank Gallagher, had fought for old Ireland alongside de Valera during the Irish War of Independence, in which Kevin Barry and Frank Flood were executed. The *Irish Times*, on the other hand, was the Protestant paper. The trust which owned the paper was made up of Protestants. The *Irish Independent*, the third Dublin-based national newspaper, was somewhere in between the two.

Maeve, an insecure fresher from the safe haven of Dalkey

who still had ideas of becoming a saint, was definitely not political martyr material and there was no likelihood of her joining a subversive group or participating in any political heroics at all. But at UCD she became aware for the first time of Catholicism, this religion that had dominated her life as a child and still dominated it, not as a way of life to which everyone subscribed, but as a political force.

How different this all was to the Catholicism of the Holy Child Killiney, the teaching of which had always been based on the love of God for each one of the girls and appeared to carry no political baggage at all. As an undergraduate she remained a Catholic, but her beliefs did not inspire her to action on behalf of the Republican Party. Rather, the movement of the following years was away from received dogma and institutions that would dictate what she should be thinking. Liberation was to be the theme.

'Free love' was part of the liberation movement, a 1950s phrase not free of fear until the pill became available in 1961, and a constant topic of conversation. Of course 'free love' in Ireland in the 1950s was a much more revolutionary proposition than in Britain or America. It was, after all, along with contraception, divorce and abortion, forbidden by the Catholic Church on pain of everlasting damnation. And the government was at one with the Church on this, so that if you bought an English newspaper in Dublin in those days, it would invariably have a blank space where an advertisement for condoms had been erased from the printing plate. The edition would otherwise have been impounded at Customs.

Yet when Maeve wrote in her novels about the conversation of student girls at this time, it was invariably about sex.
In *The Glass Lake* (1994), Clio asks her girlfriend Kit whether
she should sleep with Michael O'Connor, a fairly unattractive
student from a well-off family who has told Clio that everyone
is doing it and that she is provincial and out of step with the
way the world is moving for not agreeing to do it with him.
Clio is afraid that she will lose Michael if she holds out any
longer. Kit tells her that he will hang around if he really likes
her. Clio, who is convent educated, says she sounds like Mother
Bernard. Kit tries to find out what Clio likes about Michael. Is
there a special understanding between them? Does he surprise
her and make her laugh? No, Clio just likes being his girl. It's a
style thing, she likes the Clio and Michael scenario; so typical
of student relationships. It then emerges that Michael will leave
Clio if she doesn't acquiesce. And Kit uses the word 'blackmail'.

At UCD the romantic focus in Maeve's circle seems to have
been on the men in the university's rugby club, as in the novels:
in *Echoes*, Clare O'Brien tells Valerie and other friends about her
near-miss experience with Ian and compares it to rugby tackles
she'd seen earlier in a student rugby game. Valerie produces
vermouth to calm them all down and Mary Catherine wonders
how far you can go before it is deemed unfair to boys not to go
the whole way. Later Clare will have sex with David Power and
rue the day, because she becomes pregnant and the baby comes
early, causing Clare, a scholarship girl, to miss taking her finals,
which had been the purpose of her life since a very young girl.

Suddenly, in the 1950s and '60s, talk between young people

was *all* about feelings, as were films, music and women's magazines. Before the 1940s nobody spoke much about any of their feelings. Brothers and sisters used to talk sometimes. But generally it was thought unseemly to say how you felt, 'like selling yourself'. You would lose respect if you did.

The new science of psychology had opened the door. With the advent of psychology, what was done quietly before was done openly now. Psychiatrists made people talk. In the clinical context in the 1930s, for example, psychiatrists for the first time encouraged workhouse inmates to talk to one another and tell each other how they felt – they became much more difficult to handle afterwards, apparently. In 1939, when Freud died, his daughter Anna took over the world psychoanalytical movement and set up psychological guidance centres all over America to encourage people to discuss their sensibilities.

But the really big change happened earlier, when psychology was harnessed by big business actually to *trade* in people's feelings. Edward Bernays, having devised America's propaganda machine in the First World War, took the teachings of his uncle Sigmund Freud to advise businessmen how to link mass-produced goods to people's unconscious feelings and make them buy things that would make them feel good, whether or not they needed them. For the first time sexual imagery was used by the automobile industry to advertise cars, for example. The policy kick-started the consumer society, became the key to economic progress and became the cornerstone of the American Dream.

In 1946 the feelings of women were for the first time researched in 'focus groups' by the psychiatrist Ernest Dichter, as it was realised that women were the principal target for the new consumerism.

By the 1950s psychiatrists and psychologists were operating in every corner of society, sometimes aggressively in marketing, but also therapeutically, a development that influenced relationships and in particular discipline within the family and elsewhere. It was a change consistent with the enlightened approach of Mother St Dominic at the Holy Child, her little chats in the room downstairs so different to the harsh dictatorial approach of the religious institution of the Catholic Church which had produced the Jesuit schools that Maeve's father and uncles knew.

It is clear how this development also influenced the working lives of Maeve, and her sister Renie, who became a psychiatrist. Ultimately, the change made it possible for Maeve to write whole books about people sharing their feelings, particularly women, who had only recently begun to talk openly about how they felt. It was on this tsunami of emotion that Maeve's novels rode to international success from the early 1980s.

In the meantime, in 1957, Maeve was a nervous undergraduate about to undertake her own personal revolution which would place her mid-current in this sea change. She was nervous because everything was new. But there was much that was new in the late 1950s for all undergraduates everywhere.

The consumer revolution was discovering teenagers. Style was now the official idiom of the marketplace. 'Look at the style,' Benny says wistfully in *Circle of Friends*, scanning the UCD campus. Hairstyles for college girls were 'ponytails, little beat fringes, devil horns on the forehead, kiss curls in front of the ears or little chignons on the back of the head, possibly French pleats'. Daywear was jeans and baggy sweaters, previously made as shapeless as possible by your boyfriend, or brightly coloured skirts over suspender belts and nylon stockings (if you could afford the 18 shillings a pair).[29]

Of great interest to the mass media, particularly to magazines aimed at women, style was what the consumer society was all about, but Maeve was finding keeping up with anyone else's style extremely problematic.

Seeing the mass of students milling about St Stephen's Green, the confidence of the girls with their little ponytails and college scarves laughing and talking with boys as they walked up and down the paths to Earlsfort Terrace, made her feel hopelessly inadequate. Life had begun to seem like a beauty contest she could never win. On campus she felt more desperate than ever before. Since adolescence, she said later, she had been a foot taller than Napoleon and twice the weight of Twiggy. 'There I was, a fat, insecure young woman who thought that the race was won by the small, the pretty and the slim.'[30]

She clung to her childhood culture for support, stopping off at Westland Row church on the way up to campus from the train each morning and lighting a penny candle. Here she had recourse to Sermon-on-the-Mount theology, which taught that those who are dealt a poor hand in this world will be blessed in the world to come. At Killiney she had embraced this, but it was hard, very hard, to embrace it in the cosmopolitan atmosphere of UCD.

Daywear for Maeve was 'dreadful Fair Isle jumpers' not made

roomy by boyfriends, owing to the fact that she didn't have any, and a beige coat with a brown velvet collar, which was really her old school coat from the Holy Child.

The really cool thing to be in those days was a beatnik – one of that section of the young who had come out against the power-mad consumer ideology. In some quarters a certain cynicism was brewing as to the political motivation and purpose of consumerism. Bernays, it seems, had won government support for his project by persuading politicians that by satisfying the deepest longings of the masses they would have them in the palms of their hands, happy and docile. The vision had evolved of a lobotomised society, tranquil, content, under control, conforming to a model dictated by an elite political body using consumerism as the palliative, the feel-good medication – a vision which came to be satirised in the film *The Stepford Wives* and Ken Kesey's book *One Flew Over the Cuckoo's Nest*. Even as consumerism was discovering the new teenage market, the call was out to liberate people from what the playwright Arthur Miller was referring to as 'the whole ideology of this Age, which is power mad'.

'Beatnik' was a word that followed the phrase 'Beat Generation', which spoke of the syncopated rhythms of jazz that was so popular then, and which was a reaction against the Establishment and its consumer ideology. It was a word coined by the American writer and spiritual adventurer Jack Kerouac (*On the Road*, 1957) and Allen Ginsberg (*Howl & Other Poems*, 1956), who defined the offbeat, non-conformist nature of artistic bohemia in the late 1950s. The movement, following two world wars and 150 years of industrial revolution which had brought little but suffering to the working classes, would be one of disenchantment with the political, social and religious institutions which the Establishment had used to control people, and of strides towards individual freedom, emancipation and personal responsibility.

On campus, the duffel coat was the symbol of beatnik dissent, and although as yet she lacked the philosophy that it represented, Maeve knew instinctively that what she wanted more than anything was a duffel coat. And all the time she was worrying about being an also-ran in the game of life, and considering how her chastity would be sorely tested by the blue version of the duffel coat as opposed to the fawn, she was lightly reading a French essay that had to be studied that week for Professor Louis Roche in the hope that he wouldn't somehow single her out in class.

She could remember exactly where she was sitting – on a bench in St Stephen's Green, the big park by the university – self-consciously worrying about what people were thinking about the fact that she was sitting there on her own, about what conclusions they would draw from how she looked, worrying that her coat didn't look scruffy enough. Should she perhaps lie on the grass and roll about on it for a bit? You had to look scruffy if you were a bohemian student in those days.

Then, all of a sudden, something hit her between the eyes. The letters of the sentence she was reading caught fire. The line she was reading was something about a woman who spent her time trying to impress people, and hardly any time actually *living* her life. It was like she was always wishing away the present and living in anticipation of some *dreadful* possibility which rarely, if ever, materialised.

Maeve saw herself, at that moment, for the very first time. It was 'as if I had had a vision, that my whole twenty years had been spent running a futile race'.[31]

She recalled later that it had been a lovely day on the green. The sun was shining. Students were massing. As she put down the book she was reading she said to herself, 'Nobody is looking at me – it does not matter what I'm wearing. All these people walking through St Stephen's Green are not looking at me, they are wondering how *they* look!'[32] Life was not some kind of competition with everyone examining you. She knew she would never worry about what people were thinking ever again. Nor did she.

She described it as an incredible liberation. It was the first step towards taking control of her life and making it her own. 'The secret of the universe is that we do have to take control of our own lives,' she said years later. For years her mother had been saying to her that she was special, unique, that nobody had her personality, her mind, her history. Now she understood the responsibility that conferred: 'My life is up to me alone. No one is going to ride in over the hill and change things for me.'

We do not know the book of French essays she was reading, but the message is that of the existentialists. In the 1950s and 1960s much of the philosophy that was underwriting the great change in attitudes was coming out of France, and from one couple in particular.

Jean-Paul Sartre was the principal exponent of existentialism in France and exercised a considerable influence on the thinking of students and the 'beat' movement after the Second World War, in particular on the student rebellions of the 1960s. In 1953, Sartre's wife, Simone de Beauvoir, kick-started the feminist revolution with *The Second Sex*, the book in which the phrase 'women's liberation' was used for the first time.

If Maeve was reading French at UCD in the late 1950s there is no doubt that she would have been studying existential philosophy. Existentialism was in any case in the ether at this time and Maeve's 'return to self' was precisely what existentialism is all about. Later I would have it confirmed that Sartre was indeed Maeve's mentor and life guide.[33]

His is a philosophy to which she would have taken naturally, for it holds that decisions important to the individual are not solved by painstaking intellectual exploration and dissection of the facts and the laws of thinking about them, but by *action*. It called upon Maeve's passionate, intuitive side. Actions, not words. The motto of the Holy Child, no less!

To become liberated we have to be able to cut ourselves free from the systems that control our thinking, which in her case put Catholicism directly into the target area. There will inevitably be a chaotic period when everything is up in the air (which for Maeve and others of her generation delineated the 1960s), before the pieces of the jigsaw settle down into a true picture of who we are. No one can simply be told how to live; you have to discard what you are born to and find out for yourself; you have to recreate your own essence, and then invent projects to meet your purpose and thereby confer meaning on your existence. This is exactly what Maeve set out to do.

What she referred to as 'my revelation on the park bench' was far more than a moment of recognition that crippling self-consciousness was wasting her life away: it was a statement that she did not intend to be a victim of other people's perceptions or live on the periphery of someone else's idea of what was an acceptable style. The implication was that hers would truly be a meaningful existence, not wasted by being a follower of fashion, nor would she seek reassurance about life's finite nature by worshipping idols such as humanity, science or some divinity. The Sermon on the Mount, which promised her and other woebegone people a great life in Heaven, was not going to be enough. Sartre was about *now*.

Maeve's temple would become her self. Her revelation brought her to *self*-belief, put her on the track to authenticity, wary of affectation, hostile to pretension and fiercely loyal to those who were her friends because of who she was rather than how she measured up to fashionable criteria. The important thing immediately was that she now accepted the hand that Nature had dealt her. It was like she already knew who she was and had suddenly been given permission to *be* that person. Once the veil of self-consciousness fell away she let her real self express itself, intellectually, emotionally, even physically. 'From then onwards I was never afraid. I wore miniskirts in the days when no fat girl should have, and with total delight...'[34] Not being self-conscious opened a door to other things – such as travel and to other cultures and traditions outside the Catholic Church. She became 'more interested in listening to other people talking, and hearing their stories'. Perhaps most important, it gave her the courage eventually not only to be herself but to write about these new principles for others.

Meanwhile, her decision to relinquish the idea of the duffel coat had a surprise piece of irony attached to it. A duffel coat was always reckoned to be highly appropriate attire for the budding 1950s existentialist. A few years later, Jack Kerouac revealed that the syllable 'beat', enshrined in 'beatnik', had in fact been chosen as a shortened form of the Catholic word 'beatitude' and was a hidden reference to the fact that he was a Catholic.

> It is because I am Beat, that is, I believe in beatitude and that God so loved the world that He gave His only begotten son to it ... Who knows, but that the universe is not one vast sea of compassion actually, the veritable holy honey, beneath all this show of personality and cruelty?[35]

Maeve would have very much liked the image of the universe as a vast sea of compassion, but having laid aside the duffel coat she had unwittingly also laid down the apparel of Roman Catholicism, which was the principal institution that controlled her thinking. Eventually, although she didn't realise it yet, her Catholicism would indeed have to go, if she was truly to stand alone.

From this moment, 'Maeve blossomed,' remembers Geraldine MacCarthy. 'She became the centre of a crowd.' Now, lectures took second place and she would be seen more often than not in the Annexe, a smiling bubbly figure amidst her circle of friends, mostly giggling female students, hanging on her every word.

There developed what later came to be identified as Maeve's unique style – a rapid-flow delivery of stories, anecdotes and observations on life. Said Patricia Hamilton, 'She became larger than life, very good sense of humour, a good wit. She was *very* popular. Much more popular than she ever was at school.' From being someone 'not very obvious', she was suddenly noticeable even to people who weren't her friends.

Maeve no longer lived life on anybody else's terms. In particular she stopped worrying about not having a boyfriend. 'It was a freeing thing for her,' Valerie said. 'She could say, I'm not competing with you for men, so I'm free to be myself.' Her crowd now, 'the people who wanted to have coffee and cakes with me, or dance with me, did it because they liked *me*'.[36] She didn't care if a guy had spots, or lank hair falling into his eyes, if he was nice and interested in things.

Her crowning glory was being invited by Myles McSwiney, the President of the Literary and Historical Society (which had, by now, become the UCD student union), to serve on his committee. This was a massive endorsement and made a welcome impact on her social life. Maeve once said that it was the best day of her life until 1976, when her husband asked her to marry him, because L&H organised the dances every Saturday night. There was a huge frisson about who you were going to meet at the Saturday-night dance, even if the Cinderella hour for Maeve was the 11.07 bus to Dalkey.

Subsequently, Maeve did become close to a boy she referred to as the campus hero. She said she didn't fall in love with him, but plenty of her girlfriends did. Perhaps he was the model for Jack

Foley, the UCD campus hero whom Benny falls in love with in *Circle of Friends*. If so, it is instructive to see what becomes of the relationship in the novel. After Foley has cheated on Benny with Nan, her friend, he begs her to come back to him, but Benny refuses because she has become her own woman, and no man has the power to dominate her life any longer.

No man would ever have the power to demean Maeve in this way either.

There was a part of her which actually preferred the company of women to men, and she was as intensely loyal to her women friends at UCD as she had been as a girl in school. Solidarity with women was about as political as Maeve got. And with her newfound self-confidence she could even allow herself a little grown-up viciousness too, as was demonstrated on one occasion with quite terrifying force.

Barbecues at White Rock in Killiney Bay, an open-sea bathing place accessed by a steep path from the Dalkey end of the Vico Road in the lea of Dalkey/Killiney Hill, were great summertime excitements when Maeve was an undergraduate. White Rock has been a popular resort for centuries, with bathhouses even in the eighteenth century, and there's always the possibility that dolphins will be seen at play close to shore.

On this particular occasion – a barbecue to celebrate St Patrick's Day – things began badly and didn't get much better. As they were scrambling down to the beach Maeve, still a non-drinker, dropped her bottle of orange squash, smashing the bottle. 'Thank God it's not the wine!' someone shouted. Maeve was furious as she knew it meant she'd be thirsty all evening.

This little accident turned out to be but a minor preliminary, however, for an act of almost Golding-esque barbarity.

As the wine flowed and inhibitions were relaxed, the sun went down and flames from the fire picked out a girl going off into the shadows with the long-haired boyfriend of Maeve's best friend.

Maeve was incandescent. Her best friend's tears were her business, as she saw it, and there in the dying embers of the evening she came up with the idea that punishment was in order. The boy had by this time fallen asleep, and Maeve's plan was to creep round to him and cut off his long hair while he slept. And she did!

She described the act as 'the most violent thing I did in my youth' and excused it by saying that friends of hers had done far worse things ('or said they did'). Maeve's solidarity with her best friend shines through, but in the symbolism of the act, worthy of Delilah, so does a developing attitude towards the male of the species.

Maeve chose to cut off the boy's hair, not that of the girl, who was possibly guilty to a greater degree than the boy by virtue of her being a girl. Her betrayal of Maeve's best friend flew in the face of the loyalty code of the sisterhood. Perhaps this passed through her mind, for when eventually the episode at White Rock made it into an article in her column in the *Irish Times*, Maeve made some amendments to the story. She didn't admit to doing the hair cutting personally, it was described as a group activity. And it was the girl's ponytail, not the boy's, that was lopped.

FIVE

BECOMING MAEVE

With all the emotional and psychological hiatus and socialising at UCD, Maeve's finals did not go well. 'To my mind,' she said, 'it was a miracle I got any exam at all.'

She will have been sad for her father, the First Class Honours graduate who had such high expectations of her. It was almost Clare O'Brien's humiliation – Clare, the scholarship girl in *Echoes*, misses her finals because her illegitimate baby is born pre-term. There was no pregnancy in Maeve's case but, as in the case of Clare, getting a degree had been the driving purpose of her life thus far.

The result was worse than Maeve was ever prepared to admit. She managed not a first, nor a second, nor yet a third, the so-called 'gentleman's degree' for those who have a good time instead of working. She was awarded only a pass.

It didn't bother her for long, and years later she wrote an article for the *Irish Times* called 'Remembering the Good Times' that explains why. It is, as the title suggests, a joyful reminiscence of her time as an undergraduate, but in it she meets the girl who used to serve her and her fellows coffee in the Annexe and Maeve develops an important point about social discrimination in education.[37] She describes how the waitress had sometimes berated Maeve and her gang for not working harder, for not grasping the privileged opportunity they had been handed. If she had been a student, rather than just a waitress, she'd have forfeited the parties and the fellas, she said, and worked hard to get the best degree she could.

Maeve remembered how she and her friends had laughed at the girl and said that she'd feel differently if she was a student. But the girl had been right; she probably would have got a better degree than Maeve. However, UCD had been utterly significant in Maeve's life for another reason. She had woken up to her potential. It had formed the essential part of her personality and that is ultimately what university should be about.

At UCD she'd found the self-belief that would carry her to the top in whatever she decided to do, the confidence to take control in any situation that presented itself. It was up to her now to find the projects to meet her purpose and confer meaning on her existence.

In her graduation year, 1959, she and her friends had taken jobs, on the grounds that if they got away from the distractions and the barbecues at White Rock there would be more chance of getting work done for their finals. Maeve had accepted an invitation from Mother St Dominic to help out at another Holy Child school, at St Leonards-on-Sea on the south coast of England.[38] Having moved from Killiney, Mother St Dominic was now the school's Mother Superior. The stint returned

Maeve to Mother at a time in her life when she could use her advice.

Geraldine, who followed Maeve as a teacher at the school, remembers, 'Maeve left a huge mark at St Leonards. It gave her the inspiration to go back to UCD and do a Diploma of Education.'

It was the perfect interim solution. Her degree had been so bad that she couldn't have used it for much. She had no money to travel, which she still really wanted to do, and she was expected to begin earning a living. The DipEd would ensure that at least she got a job teaching, and it was clear from her reception at St Leonards – years later, the girls would still remember many fun classes in the open air that summer – that the new Maeve had a talent for getting through to her pupils.

The summer of 1959 also found Maeve studying at a summer school in Wales, along with history students from all over Britain. At the start it had been disappointing; the lessons were all about mining rights and politics – good on facts, but hardly rousing. So instead she began making eyes at a fellow student called Hiram John, who had curly hair and a smile that engulfed his whole face. Hiram's mother was a harpist, his father a preacher, both very Welsh. Hiram took Maeve for walks around Caernarvon, swims in Bangor, on a bus trip to Snowdon, to tea with his family, and she listened to his mother play the harp one night to twenty neighbours, who behaved as if they had known Maeve all her life. Here was the homespun honey of Welsh culture on which, before going to Wales, she had been led by her mother to believe Ireland had a monopoly.

On the last night Hiram had taken her in his arms, kissed her, and told her that she had been the nicest summer-school romance he had ever had (it transpired that she was his third) – and sadly that was that.

Nevertheless, the experience left her with a deep affection for the country and she returned on a notable trip in the mid-1960s with an entire school of girls, and again in 1972 to report on striking miners in a village close to Pontypridd. Such was the warmth of the community that people would call out of their windows, 'Maeve, bach, you look cold and damp, come in to the fire and have a cup of tea.' She loved it so much that she spun her reporting job out far longer than was intended, going down the mine in the day and talking the night away with the miners in the Working Men's Club. She would return a third time in 1974 to follow the Welsh Nationalist Gwynfor Evans during his campaign to get back into Westminster.

Back at UCD, she sat her Higher Diploma of Education, believing that she had learned little of great use. She and her fellow students had been taught the psychology of teaching but nothing about *actual* teaching, which Maeve realised can only be learned when you do it, hands on.

For the next eight years she did just that – first in Cork, her 'year of misery', as she called it. 'We teachers used to huddle together in a tiny room so small that one person had to breathe in if the other breathed out – united in our loathing of the frightful headmistress!'[39]

She was so lonely that it seemed to her that she watched the same film – *Carthage in Flames* – week after week at the local cinema. She was so cold and so broke that she would carry pieces of coal back to burn at night and eventually, when it was all over, she boarded the 3.20 Friday train for Dublin with six sacks of the stuff – there was no other way to get rid of it!

Her time in Cork was not fun, but it did confirm that she liked teaching. On the train home she discovered something that would change her life. In the buffet car she met a handsome man who claimed also to have had a miserable time in Cork and suggested they drown their sorrows together.

'What do you like in your gin?' he asked her. Maeve replied, 'It!' at once, not having drunk alcohol before and not knowing what 'gin and it' was, but associating it with romantic situations in detective novels she'd read. It scarcely mattered: Italian vermouth was not a viable option on the train from Cork, and the barman suggested tonic instead.

It is fair to say that alcohol became an agreeable element in Maeve's life henceforth. 'So began a lifelong friendship which must have gladdened distilleries the world over,' as she herself put it.

There was no Jekyll and Hyde situation when Maeve had a drink. She admitted that occasionally she might stay on too long at a party, perhaps forget a few things and suffer the odd hangover, like everyone else, but she rarely lost control and, best of all, 'my liver held out!'

With a gin and tonic or a nip of whiskey her rapid-flow delivery of stories, anecdotes and observations on life was given a million-miles-an-hour enhancement. So it was that the Cork project, for all its shortcomings, did give her a new weapon in her arsenal, which would serve her well in the coming years. What Sartre had started, Gordon's completed!

Maeve's first teaching job in Dublin was to twelve- to eighteen-year-olds at Pembroke School in a Georgian mansion at No. 1 Pembroke Road, Dublin, close to UCD. History, Latin and religion were her subjects. Pembroke School was a girls-only, lay Catholic school which taught the middle-class daughters of liberal Catholics and was known as Miss Meredith's after its founder, who started the school in 1929 and had a reputation of being something of an eccentric. While academically strong, and superb at getting girls into top women's jobs, Miss Meredith's concentrated on letting pupils be what they wanted to be and do what they wanted to do. Miss Meredith herself still turned up with some ceremony mid-morning to call the roll. It was, altogether, a rather unusual establishment, both for its pupils and for its teachers. Maeve fitted in very well, for there was a great deal of the theatrical about her during this particularly liberal stage of her life in the early 1960s.

Maeve had embarked on her existential process with some verve and occasionally she would take flight to London, centring operations on Mary Holland's house in Palace Garden Terrace, behind Kensington Church Street, close to Kensington Palace. The house became a magnet for visiting Dubliners and there was quite a party scene.

Later, Mary would write for *The Observer* and for the *Irish Times* and forge a reputation for writing about Irish affairs, the Troubles in particular. Controversially, in Catholic Ireland, she also came to write about abortion, admitting that she herself had had one. But Maeve first entered her orbit at the start of Mary's career, which began after she won a competition and was taken on by *Vogue*.

'Mary hated working for *Vogue*,' says the sometime fashion journalist and writer Molly Parkin. 'We were neighbours in Palace Garden Terrace when I was married to [the art dealer] Michael Parkin and we had our first daughter, Sarah. I was painting professionally then. It was very arty up there at that time and we were all party people.'

London was now all about youth, all about fashion. The photographer David Bailey was working for *Vogue*. The clothes designer Mary Quant had set up in the King's Road in the mid-1950s in the vanguard of the style revolution, and was just then opening up in Knightsbridge, with Terence Conran designing the second of her shops. Conran himself was about to launch Habitat. The future was all about offering the masses a style to buy into. This was anathema to Maeve, whose whole thrust was for authenticity. Right up to her last novel, *A Week in Winter* (2012), she was exasperated by women being so weak as to allow themselves to be 'sucked into a world of labels and trends and the artificial demands of style'. Even so, Maeve clearly made an impression, as Molly Parkin remembers:

I had no idea that she was a teacher. I assumed she was an aspiring actress! Lots of people used to come over to Mary's house from the Abbey Theatre in Dublin. Maeve dressed stylishly in her own way, good shoes and gloves, handbags and little fur things round her neck. She looked good and was always beautifully perfumed. I remember her hair was lovely too. This was a time for hair, with Vidal Sassoon. Yes, Maeve enhanced a party and a room. She liked a drink, but we were all boozers.

So this was Maeve at the time she started teaching at Miss Meredith's. She dressed 'in her own way', individual, effective, looking after the edges, her hair, her hands, her feet and so on, letting her increasingly individual personality do the talking. And Molly took her for an actress. The girls at Miss Meredith's discovered the same persona, for her classes became something of a theatrical experience – even history, which was the first of the day.

Maeve's rule was that if a girl turned up late she would be locked out. One day, *she* was late and the girls locked *her* out and then watched, outraged, as she crossed the road to Searson's pub opposite and did not return until it was time for the next class. She never gave the girls the satisfaction of mentioning it.

For inspiration Maeve drew on the message of Cornelia Connelly: girls will not learn unless they are happy. And as with Mother St Dominic, presence, charisma, humour and attention to the individual were to the fore. Maeve followed Mother's example too (and her own experience) in making it her aim to raise the levels of self-confidence among her pupils, if not so wildly as her mother had done: 'Good teachers believe that their pupils can do anything,' she once said. 'When I was at school we had a teacher like that.' Such teachers – all women – turn up in her novels all the time.

In *Evening Class* (1996) that teacher is the Signora, Nora O'Donoghue. Maeve describes her as 'a wonderfully mad inspired teacher'.[40] Strong, eccentric, warm and wise, 'Signora burned with love. I think there's a message in that. Signora stands for the kind of people who do things from passion and fire and courage. We all love them.'[41]

Maeve's passion for teaching came, she said, from knowing that when she left the classroom after forty-five minutes her girls had something, however small, that they didn't have before. In *The Copper Beech*, a novel named after the great tree which spreads itself over the schoolhouse at Shancarrig where conscious life for the village children begins, Maddy Ross expresses her joy in seeing a child work out how to read a sentence for herself, or suddenly 'get' how a sum in maths works. Maeve once said that Maddy was one of the two characters in her fiction that she would most have liked to be (the other, Aisling O'Connor in *Light a Penny Candle*).

The girls at Miss Meredith's were all mad about Maeve, as they are mad about the gutsy Angela O'Hara in *Echoes*, and Miss Daly, the teacher in *A Week in Winter*. She became a role model to them, as Mother St Dominic had been for her, and would never be forgotten by them, as the tributes of many after she died showed.

Always she played the eccentric. Renagh Holohan, who would later hold positions at the *Irish Times* as London Editor and Features Editor, remembered that Maeve was so uncertain of Latin that she kept translations of the Virgil and Horace texts that the class would go through every day, under her desk, as cribs. There was no secret that she had them there, so that really it was all part of the theatre of Maeve's class, a ploy to keep the lessons lively. Some of her pupils may have been alert to the fact that exactly the same scene occurs at the beginning of Joyce's *Ulysses*, when Joyce's *alter ego*, Stephen Dedalus, is teaching at the school in Dalkey. He looks at the crib under the table 'and the boys are not quite in synchrony so they actually have to coach him what to do'.

Maeve's natural storytelling gifts brought the characters of history and Latin alive in memorable ways. Back in the 1960s Latin was essential for a number of degrees: law, medicine etc. Although it was one of her subjects at UCD, it was only a minor course and Maeve wasn't much interested in teaching it until one day a very bright child, who'd been studying Latin for about three years, let slip that she hadn't quite understood that people at one time actually *spoke* the language. On investigation it emerged that the whole class of thirty thought it was some kind of dead, out-of-date academic code which had been drawn on as a kind of source for modern European languages. From then on, Maeve made it her purpose to bring Latin to life for them, as Caroline Walsh, another alumna who worked for the *Irish Times*, variously as Features Editor and Literary Editor, remembered: 'Maeve made the people in Latin so real we expected them to come alive any minute. It was this vigour with which she approached it that I'm sure was the reason I got top-notch honours.'

The writer Felicity Hayes-McCoy, who would later script some of Maeve's stories for television, remembers being so taken with her description of the death of Julius Caesar that after one class she began recreating the scene with a group of friends, perhaps a little overdramatically. Suddenly she became aware that Maeve was looming over her and she found herself 'transfixed by a cold eye. My fellow assassins backed away leaving me frozen between the desks. Maeve gazed at me distantly for what felt like hours and then turned away with a weary sigh. That was it. Nothing more. But it was devastatingly effective.'[42]

Maeve could be an imposing presence. Indeed, for the first year the girls were more afraid of her than of the principal, particularly as she was not averse to giving the odd flick of a ruler as she passed by. Truth was that the new self-confident Maeve was not a woman to suffer fools gladly. But this, along with the theatre and eccentricity and storytelling magic, only served to bolster her reputation and gain her respect. What was especially attractive about her was that in private she didn't suffer the fool in herself any more gladly than she did the fool in anyone else.

In teaching, Maeve had found a platform to assert and express her increasingly individual persona. She became something of a legend wherever she taught, but especially at Miss Meredith's, many remembering especially the day she took the entire school to Wales, a trip she recorded in an article in the *Irish Times*.

The trip passed into the folklore of the school. Maeve said that it was the only thing she was *ever* remembered for – as an act of 'unbelievable folly' by the other teachers and as 'the best day out they ever had in their lives' by her pupils. That, surely, is a high point for any teacher to achieve.

Maeve related how forty girls under her sole care left Dún Laoghaire harbour for Holyhead one morning and by the evening, after a gorging of fish and chips in a Holyhead café, she realised she was six short. Fortunately five were found and returned before the ferry was due to sail, but the boat had to be held for the sixth while Maeve 'prised her away from the arms of some latter-day Hiram John'.

On the ferry, Maeve repaired to the bar, only to be disturbed by a deputation of girls who claimed that she was wanted on deck. Expecting to be faced by the police, she was in fact needed 'only to settle an argument about the Wicklow mountains, which had just come purplishly into view...'

Three days a week Maeve also taught conversational French to children in a Jewish primary school in Rathgar, the area of Dublin where James Joyce was born. Maeve had responded to an advertisement for a part-time French teacher and began work at Zion Schools soon afterwards. From the very first moment her interest was fired in all things Jewish – especially Israel.

It was to be another turning point.

At the start, things had not gone well. She made the mistake of telling the boys to take off their caps and refused to believe they were not defying her when they protested that wearing them was part of tradition, part of their religion. She investigated and apologised the next day, then switched tack, using Jewish customs – such as songs associated with the festival of Chanukkah[43] – as subjects for translation, which would at the same time take them and her further inside their culture. Soon the children were following her to the bus stop in their eagerness to learn, parents began inviting her into their homes and, seeing how completely enamoured of their traditions she became, they gave her a ticket to visit Israel.

Maeve decided to make it no ordinary holiday. With her companion Philippa O'Keefe, now a radiographer at a Dublin hospital, she made arrangements through the Zionist Federation to take a working holiday for two and a half months at Zikim, a kibbutz in southern Israel in the Negev Desert, about three miles west of the main road from Tel Aviv to the Gaza Strip.

The Federation Secretary looked the two young women up and down rather dubiously and said, 'You won't find an Ari Ben Canaan in every orange grove.' It was a reference to the hero of *Exodus*, the novel by Leon Uris about the founding of the state of Israel. The film had done plenty for the film star Paul Newman's reputation with the ladies.

Maeve said she realised that working on a kibbutz would be no picnic and agreed with the secretary that she and Philippa were totally ignorant and unfit, but they had made up their minds that that was what they wanted to do. They paid £48 for the fare and spent around £20 subsistence when there – a small price for what then transpired.

On arrival they were put to work in the kitchen peeling potatoes, in the chicken shed plucking chickens and in the garden weeding. Then, as the long hot summer wore on, Maeve was shifted from chicken duty to making yogurt from 6 a.m. until 2 p.m. Along the way she fell in love with the ideals of this desert kibbutz, writing home almost daily about the communal farms and the way of living and the separation of the children from their parents – how, as she put it, 'they had to learn to be grown-up and independent from their parents',[44] which wouldn't have been lost on William and Maureen, given that Maeve, at twenty-four, was still living at home.

She reckoned that, as a result of the separation, the children were more loving than ever when they did come into contact with their parents. However, at this stage she had had no personal contact with the kibbutz children. Only when she returned the following summer would she be allowed to supervise their swimming and only after she could prove that she could shout Hebrew phrases such as 'Come in at once' and 'Nobody out further than their waists'!

Such was the scene. There was nothing sentimental or idealistic about the people who ran the kibbutz. In many ways Maeve and Philippa were at the front line of a conflict between one cultural tradition and another, which was no less serious or potentially dangerous than what had been happening between Ireland and the UK, as it turned out.

The Jewish settlement in the Negev was at that time very sparse, and tensions between Arabs and Israelis were building towards the formation of the Palestine Liberation Organization (PLO), which came into being the following year. Maeve mentioned in letters home that there were air raids, and Zikim did later become a target. The people she and Philippa were working with in the kitchen – girls of their own age – had already spent two years in the army and knew that a war could start at any moment.

Maeve wrote that these girls were hard and cynical in some

ways and simple and innocent in others. They certainly weren't slow to question the Christian faith of two Catholic girls working in a kibbutz, and Maeve took their point: it would be a few years yet before the Vatican Council Fathers would vote to absolve the Jewish race for Christ's death.

However, the new Maeve didn't care what people thought, or that she and Philippa were the only gentiles there, or how she looked in shorts as she picked oranges from the trees. She was much more interested in talking to the Israeli girls and hearing their stories.

The kibbutz had been established in 1947 by a group of young Romanian Jews who belonged to a Zionist group called Hashomer Hatzair, which is the oldest Zionist youth movement still in existence. It grew out of two other groups, one a scouting movement (with roots in the ideas of Baden-Powell, who started the scout movement in Britain), the other more hard edged and political, its aim to integrate Marxism with psychoanalysis and shape Israeli children from birth to maturity through the commune regime, a process known as 'collectivist education'.

In effect, Zikim was run by a youth movement preparing for war to reinforce the state of Israel. The intensity of being in the front line was heightened by Maeve rising to the political idealism of the kibbutz – and then falling in love with one of its proponents.

This boy, like other members of Hashomer Hatzair, earnestly believed that the commune ideology would take over and the world would be perfect, with everyone equal. Communism and the commune ideals of collectivist education were at the root of the thinking of Kibbutz Zikim. To a young observer today, the fact that a member of the Jewish race should be communist (a political ideology in which private ownership is abolished in favour of communal production and subsistence, not profit) is difficult to comprehend. But in the 1950s and '60s communism had a utopian ring about it, and many Jews were communists, even in Britain.

Socialism and communism, only a little further towards the extreme end of the socialist spectrum, were viewed by many cultures as an evolutionary way forward. In Britain, communism had taken a hold in areas like Glasgow, where in 1918 Lenin appointed the first Bolshevik Consul for Scotland to Russia, and in Parliament, to which Communists were elected in the early 1920s, Cecil L'Estrange Malone, Shapurji Saklatvala and Walton Newbold among them. Indeed, the whole rise of left-wing politics in Britain, which gave vent to the feelings of the working classes for the first time, rode in on this revolutionary tide, and in the 1950s and '60s was widely viewed in America as a drift towards communist revolution. America was so concerned to prevent the spread of the ideology in Europe that it poured in billions of dollars, giving Britain the Macmillan years, when capitalism rooted down and the British 'never had it so good'. Meanwhile, from the late 1930s right through to the end of the 1960s, the police were ranged against far-left political protesters in cities all over the Western world.

There were people then who were political 'out of a kind of religious reason ... God-seekers, looking for the kingdom of God on earth,' as the writer and Nobel Prize winner Doris Lessing remembers. She was herself a communist with 'an inclination towards mysticism' (rather than religion).

At the kibbutz, political idealism and romance were in the air. Cool evenings under the stars were spent listening to music on a record player Maeve had borrowed from an old Hungarian. The songs and the clicking of the crickets mingled with the laughter of a group of army boys and girls who had been billeted on the kibbutz for a month. Maeve was knocked out by it all.

She was sure that her man loved her. She was so sure that she was wondering how she could explain to her parents that she was going to convert to the Jewish faith and that there would be a desert wedding. Everything combined to have an almost metaphysical effect upon her, which made such an extraordinary idea seem a real possibility.

Maeve had read Doris Lessing's *The Golden Notebook*, published a year earlier, and would now play 'The Game'. Think about the smallest objects in a room, then let the mind spread to absorb the house, the city, the country, the continent, while still holding the small original details in place until, as Lessing's character Anna Wulf thinks, 'the point was reached where I moved out into space, and watched the world, a sunlit ball in the sky, turning and rolling beneath me'.

What Anna wanted was 'a simultaneous knowledge of vastness and of smallness'. It was a game played by Lessing as a child in the vast open spaces of Africa. And now Maeve played it with her man under the stars over the Negev Desert and gained a new perspective on life.

In the context of infinity, not only did the goldfish bowl in which she lived in Dalkey seem less important somehow, but the need for a new, more meaningful philosophy of life became paramount and no doubt prepared her for what then happened.

Each week she and Philippa had a couple of days off and on this occasion Maeve decided to go to Jerusalem and see the Upper Room, where the Last Supper had taken place just before Christ's crucifixion. What she found was a cave. She couldn't say what exactly she had been expecting to find, but of course in her mind will have been the depiction of the Last Supper on the front of the High Altar of the Church of the Assumption at home in Dalkey, modelled on Leonardo da Vinci's.

What she found, she said, was a cave and a gun-toting Israeli soldier with a Brooklyn accent who, when she exclaimed that this couldn't possibly be the site of the Last Supper, said, barely looking up at her, 'What were you expecting, lady, a Renaissance table set for thirteen?'

Immediately white was black and black was white. Everything she had been taught with such certainty, everything she had taken on board with such trust and faith since she was a tiny child meant nothing. It all went – like that! – 'and never came back', she said.

Christian tradition has it that the Upper Room where the Last Supper was held is a second-storey room located directly above the Tomb of David and near the Dormition Abbey on Mount Zion, just outside the walls of the Old City of Jerusalem. It is not a cave; it has a low, vaulted ceiling, certainly, but it looks more like a crypt than a cave.

Of course, the room that stands today is not what it would have been at the time of Christ, and perhaps Maeve was told that the site had long ago been a cave. All that is known is that the room has been visited since at least the fourth century by pilgrims, who believe it to be the Upper Room. But there is no verification that it *was* the room where the Last Supper took place. Or indeed that there ever was a Last Supper (the words 'Last Supper' are not mentioned in the New Testament).

Was the experience reason to relinquish her faith as suddenly and impressively as St Paul found his? One has to say, rationally, no. But reason has little to do with faith and Maeve did lose hers at that moment: 'One minute I believed the lot, angels with wings and a special Irish God, and the next I didn't believe a word of it,' she said.[45]

When eventually Maeve told the story of her disillusionment with Catholicism, people in Ireland were stunned. Her declaration came as a shock to her parents' generation and some of her own. Her father beseeched her not to tell her mother. Even a television documentary about Maeve fifty years later managed still to stir people.

Denying Christ was a significant step, certainly, but it did not mean that she no longer had an inner life. As Maeve's brother William has said, her deepest reflection on the meaning of life should not be gauged by what she says about things on the surface.

Nevertheless, Maeve, at twenty-four, stood alone, an atheist for the next five years. All the things that she had been given to believe as a child had been shown to be untrue. Everyone had lied to her. There was no friendly Irish God waiting for her at the gates of Heaven, no family of saints looking out for her, no guardian angels. They'd all gone, just like *that*! And they never came back.

Then, to cap it all, there was betrayal too by the man she loved. Once again it had turned out that Maeve had poor judgement where men were concerned. Her Israeli did not love her after all. She was not the love of his life, only a summer fling. Maeve took this very badly.

She had gone away a Catholic and returned disillusioned by the Promised Land. The Israeli experiment did, however, have one immediately good consequence. When she arrived home there was a cheque waiting for her for £16, which represented a week and a half's salary as a teacher, though she hadn't earned it by teaching.

Her father had been so impressed by her letters home that he'd had them typed up and sent to the newspapers. The *Irish Independent* gave Maeve her first by-line under the title 'A Kibbutz Welcome'.

She had returned a published writer. Here was an opportunity which would ultimately confer lifelong meaning on her existence, and in the meantime it could be pursued alongside her teaching.

Then, of course, the next article she sent off wasn't accepted. Now that she was writing for publication she'd become self-conscious and overcooked it. Rejection followed rejection. Every day she would run down the steps to the garden gate in front of Eastmount to meet the postman, hoping for a letter of acceptance, but the postman – she said – developed curvature of the spine from the sheer weight of rejections.

Given that Maeve had not thought for a minute of having her letters published, it was clear that what had won the newspaper over was the *natural* style. She wrote them in her own voice. The letters were *real* Maeve, authentic Maeve, a chatty, intimate, enthusiastic *flow* of Maeve. There was nothing analytical involved – no objective intervention in what appeared on paper. It was *true*, and truth was what people were going to like about Maeve, because that is what she looked for in people.

But she still didn't know what newspapers wanted articles about. One day she met someone from the *Irish Times* and asked him straight. He said, 'What do you care most about, right now?' Maeve gave him the current bee in her bonnet – that teachers understand children better than their parents do, a point of view partly informed by her experience of collectivist education in Israel and partly by her own experience teaching in Dublin. He liked it, said it was contentious and might get the parents to write in. What a paper likes is a dialogue with its readers. So, she wrote the article and it was accepted.

Maeve had discovered the two principles behind her writing success. First, 'write about something you know and care about'; second, 'write like you speak'.

One clear focus of her interest was, following the Israeli experiment, travelling abroad, and she returned to the kibbutz for the next two summers (1964 and 1965). She had planned to go to Turkey and South America, but she could never forget *that summer*, 'that white hot sandy place', as she called it. Then she spread her wings. For two and a half months every year (during the school summer holiday) Maeve took off on her own. Cost? Not a problem.

She worked in children's camps, did cheap bus tours and slept on the decks of ships for free, having made a spectacular discovery: a timetable of world shipping called *The ABC Shipping Guide: An Alphabetical Guide to Passenger Services; Sailing Dates, Fares, Index to Shipping Lines and Ports.*

She got hold of a copy and spent months studying it. Every port was listed, with the shipping lines that made use of the port, when they arrived and when they left. Very probably she became a world authority on where passenger boats were going and when.

The guide also had an index which told her where to find out everything about the ships themselves. Maeve used it to plot journeys across the world. The journalist Michael O'Toole once described her as 'a great traveller, and the only person I know who can say things like "I remember one night in Bombay" without sounding affected'.

Many of the ships were not passenger boats at all. She would write letters to the shipping lines (addresses were available in the book) and ask whether she could be a guest on their boat going to ... wherever. She would either sleep on the deck of the boat for nothing or, if a berth was available, she would try and get work that would pay for it. She called the guide her 'favourite book'.

Travelling so much provided a good opportunity to write travel articles. From 1965 she started placing them quite regularly with the *Irish Times*, where her sometime pupil at Miss Meredith's, Renagh Holohan, now had a job and amused her colleagues in the office by insisting on calling the new contributor 'Miss Binchy'.

Maeve wrote more about the kibbutz, of course, and in 1965–6 about Tunisia, Sardinia, Crete, and the whole business of travelling alone, making a virtue of doing so and being in the unique position of being able to tell of its singular advantages, at a time when it was thought either racy or pathetic to go on holiday alone.

For Maeve, it was 'the obvious thing to do', it being more likely that people would befriend a lone traveller, that being alone you could explore where *you* wanted to explore (rather than indulge someone else's foibles), and of course it being more possible to engage in 'romantic encounters' without needing to worry about leaving a companion on their own. Her mother warned her that men could be intimidated by a well-travelled girl. Maeve laughed and so loved this anachronistic piece of mother-lore that thirty years later she put it in the mouth of Ria's mother in *Tara Road*.

Of course, Maureen wanted Maeve to settle down, to marry a solicitor or doctor and start a family. But where was the nine-to-five professional man who could tame a woman as resourceful, energetic and hot blooded as she? Nothing was further from Maeve's mind.

Realising that there was no Hell, she said, she no longer felt guilty drinking alcohol, and started to smoke, and also began to look on men 'with a nice beady eye and much more enthusiasm'.

Looking back on her life she was grateful that she didn't find fame and fortune when this period of her life began. 'If I'd been twenty-four when fame found me, I'd have probably snorted everything up my nose, bought a yacht and fallen off of it and drowned.'

Laying her Christian values aside, she now joined the generation that wanted no commitments, no ties, no promises and no lies – there would be no need to lie. Unfortunately, underneath, she was still as vulnerable as she had ever been.

Molly Parkin remembers Maeve coming round to her house one morning following a party on one of her visits to Mary Holland's house in London.

> Well, I remember her coming in the following day. It was long before mobile phones, of course, and she asked whether she could make a call. There'd been a very drunken evening and she'd ended up with the actor Jack MacGowran. There was nothing unusual about this in the 1960s. I was thrilled and excited for her. He was quite a brusque man, very short, not of a robust build, but he was one of those who came over from the Abbey Theatre in Dublin. Now she wanted to call him and she was very nervous. I remember she needed a couple of brandies before she could pick up the phone. He was a very good actor, at the Royal Court, Beckett, *Krapp's Last Tape*…

Jack MacGowran was Dublin born. He cut his teeth as a character actor at the Abbey Theatre and made his artistic reputation in Samuel Beckett's *Waiting for Godot* at the Royal

Court, in *Endgame* with the Royal Shakespeare Company, and on a record, a production he was working on when he met Maeve at the party – *MacGowran Speaking Beckett* was released to coincide with Beckett's sixtieth birthday in 1966. Nothing could have been a richer mix for Maeve, but the liaison did not work out.

'Well, it was terrible,' said Molly. 'Jack didn't want to know and Maeve was bitterly upset. I did my best to console her. She was a warm, wonderful person. I loved her. I'm not sure that men were very good for her.'

Hiram John, Jack MacGowran and her Israeli certainly weren't. Each of them had appealed to her for a serious reason that had little to do with the men themselves, more with what they represented to her – Hiram as an expression of the warm Welsh community culture; Jack as associated with the existentialist master, Beckett; and her Israeli for his political idealism.

Deep down there would always be the need for fulfilment at a level these fellows didn't provide; otherwise, what was it all for? Meanwhile, as each new summer approached she began to 'hunger again for wild sensations, for the escape' that summer brought.

In 1966–7, while still a teacher, she wrote articles about Singapore, Cyprus, La Rochelle, Portugal, Yugoslavia, Turkey, and about four days' incapacity when over-enthusiasm doing 'Le Madison' on a slippery dance floor on a boat called *Vietnam* practically paralysed her from the waist down, and meant not setting foot in the Philippines.

Then came Russia, India, Greece, the Canary Islands, Austria,

Tangier, Spain, Scotland, Lourdes, Bulgaria, Agadir, and she returned time and again to the Holy Land. Soon it was easier to list where she hadn't been.

Alongside the *Irish Times*, Maeve also submitted articles to *Punch* magazine; in October 1966 came 'Playtime in Palestine', which informed *Punch* readers that:

> the new 'in-person' to be in love with is the tourist guide in the Holy Land. He is usually called Ari, Hameed or perhaps Rafi, he is small, dark and invariably protective. He is Arab – but his ancestry is likely to include something that will please you. I spent a long time trying to convince Hameed that his father really couldn't have been called Mustapha O'Brien...

And so on. More and more people wanted Maeve to write for them because of her sense of humour, which now characterised her adventures – such as when she fell off a horse on the way to Petra.

> About a million tourists before and behind averted their eyes with shame for me. The adorable Rafi was unperturbed. Why was I worrying, he murmured soothingly, everyone knew that Arab steeds were wild and tempestuous, simply not to be trusted. The small, docile, broken-spirited mule listened in disbelief. It coughed reproachfully as I began to remount, it had never heard such lies.

People who knew Maeve recognised her immediately in stories

such as this. She had found her voice, which, as the months passed, more and more people got to know.

Then, tragedy. Maeve was in America when she received a phone call saying that her mother had been diagnosed with cancer. Apparently Maureen had been depressed for some months and had had tests, which showed that the cancer was far advanced and that she had little time to live. The approach in those days was really to deny that the patient was terminally ill and give them false hope. The last three months of Maureen's life – she died in December 1967 – were therefore lived as a lie, rather than as a loving preparation for death and in expression of just how wonderful a mother she had been. The fact that Maeve and her brother William actually made public their regret that this was so is a measure of just how desperately sad all the children were at Maureen's passing.

The pretence that the family kept up that she would get better was a terrible strain on everyone, including Maureen, who had been a nurse and was well aware of what was actually happening to her.

Maeve kept the pain of her mother's passing bottled up for two years and perhaps she never truly vented it until fifteen years later, when she wrote so beautifully of the last two weeks of Eileen O'Connor's life in *Light a Penny Candle*, the matriarch Eileen who towers above the lives of her children, just as Maureen did, until finally they too are shocked to learn that she has cancer. The prognosis is that she has two weeks to live. Like Maureen, she is a big woman who disappears physically before their eyes. Maeve paints the scene with loving detail, and there is time in her fictional world for proper goodbyes.

Eileen dies, but not before she settles a few important things to do with the girls' relationships and Aisling's future. Eileen knows things that Aisling can't think that she knows. But that's the point. Eileen knows, like Maureen always knew. As mothers do know.

Maureen and Eileen O'Connor were fashioned from the same archetype: the fictional Eileen is Maeve's great tribute to Maureen – feminine, passionate and deeply intuitive. In the novel there is even a sense of the continuity of the mother's spirit after death. When Aisling and Elizabeth return to Kilgarret to pay their respects to Eileen before she dies, they choose to sleep in the same beds in the room they shared as children when Eileen fulfilled the role of mother for both of them, and put Elizabeth's baby, named Eileen, in her carry-cot on the floor between them, as if they are the child's parents. It is a powerful, almost supernatural scene, confirmation of the continuity of the spirit of truth, which infuses the novel.

SIX

A WEEK IN SUMMER

In 1968, in the aftermath of Maureen's death, Maeve described herself as 'restless'. She was mourning her mother and with her sister Joan engaged to be married, Renie walking out with the man she would marry, and her brother married to Alice O'Connor, Maeve felt doomed to a life alone at Eastmount with her father.

William was still only in his fifties, active, working in Dublin, and Maeve couldn't see the situation changing for twenty or thirty years. 'She was staring down the barrel of spinsterhood,' as Donal Lynch put it succinctly.

She was also uncertain about remaining a teacher. Twelve months earlier she had written an article for the *Irish Times* entitled 'I Just Love Being a Teacher', but in 1968 Miss Meredith's had rejected the opportunity open to all schools in Eire to join the free or state school system, and this deeply upset Maeve on account of her views about social discrimination in education.

Another problem presented itself. She had been an atheist for five years. Travel and adventure had opened her eyes to the world, but hadn't replenished the spiritual vacuum left by her loss of faith. She was still and would always remain a God-seeker in Lessing's sense. 'Even when Catholics don't believe,' says Elizabeth White in *Light a Penny Candle*, 'they have something inside them that makes them think they do.' Maeve didn't believe in God, but deep down she remained sensitive to His absence.

She had returned to the kibbutz in 1964 and '65, not to chase her false lover, rather because of the new sense of purpose she had glimpsed there in '63.

She had been disappointed. She did not root down into the utopian commune culture of the kibbutz, because ultimately it was a political entity and real politicos were a different sort of animal to her. If anything, their aggressive stance threatened the very ideals of the commune they promoted.

Keeping her promise to William not to tell her mother that she had lost her faith had meant that she never spoke to Maureen about the hollow which, for all the adventure, freedom and wild sensation in her life, was eating at her inside.

When Doris Lessing became disenchanted with utopian communism she found what she was looking for in Sufism, believed by many to be 'the secret teaching within all religions',[46] while unaligned to the politics of any particular one of them.

Maeve acknowledged that 'many people of my age were affected by the dazzling novels of people such as Doris Lessing', but though she was sympathetic to Lessing's desire to look for meaning in the immaterial, Lessing would not provide the path that would appeal to Maeve.

That would be Maureen's legacy.

It happened on a trip that summer to Lisdoonvarna, a small town on the road from Ennistymon to Ballyvaghan in County Clare, far to the west of Ireland in one of its most beautiful, unspoiled areas.

It is possible that the trip had been planned in memory of Maureen, even perhaps originally to trace Maeve's maternal family tree, and was undertaken in the light of an ever increasing realisation of how important an influence her mother had been and how much Maeve was missing her.

As it happened, Lisdoonvarna was that year the host to the summer school of a festival known as Cumann Merriman, which had started up the year before and has been held at some town or other in the district of Thomond every year since.

Thomond includes parts of counties Tipperary (the county of Maureen's birth) and Limerick, and the whole of County Clare, a quite breathtaking area full of the remnants of Irish civilisation from three or four millennia ago – more than ninety megalithic tombs (dating to the fourth millennium BC), portal dolmens, a Celtic high cross in the village of Kilfenora and a number of ring forts.

The landscape is stunningly beautiful, especially the Atlantic seaboard and the Burren, from the Irish 'Boireann', meaning 'great rock'. It is one of the largest limestone terrains in Europe, a rich patchwork of criss-cross 'grikes' or cracks, full of Mediterranean and alpine plants in the summer and punctuated by secret underground streams and gorges. Around ninety-six square miles, the area is bounded by the Atlantic to the west,

Galway Bay to the north, and roughly demarcated by the villages of Ballyvaghan, Kinvara, Tubber, Corofin, Kilfenora and Lisdoonvarna, where there are still people who speak *an Ghailge* (Gaelic), the ancient language of Ireland.

Cumann Merriman plugged Maeve into the true spirit of Ireland. Here in County Clare the beauty, the language, the people, the archaeology strewn over the surface of the land, and the momentum of the festival itself, took Maeve by surprise.

At Lisdoonvarna Maeve discovered that tradition in Ireland goes right down into word and gesture, ritual and dance, mythology, song, poetry and music, art and architecture, custom and convention, even law. For there is a sixteenth-century School of Brehon Law here, the form of law originally built up from the customs, traditions and practices of the Irish people within the ancient pre-Christian kingdoms.

Cumann Merriman offered poetry readings, lectures, seminars, dance classes and 'conversations way into the night with poets, politicians, professors and polka dancers'. Most of all she loved how connected the regular festival-goers were, 'a great roaming band of people old and young', the friendliness of the *failtiú* (the welcome), and the unaffected fun of the craic – 'they urged us to pace ourselves … This, I think, had to do with not staying up until six o'clock in the morning singing, which was a danger.' In particular she loved how they all 'lapsed gently from English into Irish' and back again, slipping easily between their modern conscious selves and the collective unconscious of their ancient past, when Gaelic was the spoken word.

Here Maeve connected with the collective unconscious of her people, experiencing it in the resonances between them, expressed in a great sense of belonging, sensing this native warmth as the beauty that invests the hills and valleys of rural Ireland with a spirit all of its own.

She returned to the festival every year for forty years or more – as if for refreshment to a religious retreat (though that would have been a good deal more abstemious). But she remembered this first occasion especially. 'It was a great charge to my spirit to come here,' she said.

The visit confirmed who she was and gave her a kind of spiritual ballast to the new self-belief. In a literary sense it proved to be crucial too, for the festival, whose most recent patron was the Nobel Prize-winning poet Seamus Heaney, celebrates the eighteenth-century poet Brian Merriman, a legend in Ireland on account of his thousand-line poem 'Cúirt an Mheán Oíche' ('The Midnight Court').

'The Midnight Court' belongs to the ancient 'Aisling' poetic convention. 'Aisling' refers to what is in modern psychological terms the poet's 'anima', the spirit- or dream-girl who, like the Irish Muse-Goddess Bridget in myth, may appear to him as maiden, nymph or crone.

However she appears, Aisling is always female. She personifies the all-seeing intuitive feminine side of the poet's thinking, capable of cutting through the rational restraints of his day-to-day conscious thinking and engaging directly with the collective unconscious (the psychological drives that make his people tick). Aisling is, in short, the poet's inspiration or muse.

No wonder Maeve chose the name for her first heroine, Aisling O'Connor, who embodies the spirit of Ireland and who took Maeve into the hearts of millions.

'The Midnight Court' is comedic and Rabelaisian, embracing the reputation that the area has for matchmaking. For hundreds of years, in September, with the harvest safely in, bachelor farmers have flocked to Lisdoonvarna in search of wives – and still do. The current 'matchmaker' is a man with the appropriate name of Willie Daly. Although matchmaking sounds like merely a dating service, it has great symbolic significance, a first amorous step to fruitfulness and spiritual renewal for the year that will follow.

On account of its Rabelaisian style, Merriman's 'The Midnight Court' has been described as a parody of the Aisling tradition – misguidedly, for it is in every sense within the tradition. It celebrates the otherworldly feminine mystique of Ireland, and is set in a pre-Christian, matriarchal society ruled by the Aoibhea, Queen of the Fairies, who dispenses Ireland's ancient Brehon Law. So Merriman leads us to traditional pre-Christian, indeed to pre-Achaean (i.e. before 1900 BC), matriarchal Ireland, the remnants of which litter the local landscape in Thomond – the megalithic tombs, for example, which festival-goers can examine at their leisure every day.

Year after year Maeve drew from the deep well of inspiration at Cumann Merriman, and in the Aoibhea found a powerful matriarchal figure with whom to identify. The poem was of course written in Gaelic, though fortunately, as she observed, there is 'a rake of translations', the only problem being that 'everyone [at the Festival] recommended a different one'.

She saw her own literary career as starting here, and wrote a short story about her first experience of it, called 'A Week in Summer', which she gave to the festival in 2005, the bicentenary of Brian Merriman's death. The story is a delight and tells precisely how Cumann Merriman inspired her. A troubled couple, Kathleen Merman and her husband Brian, set off to trace Kathleen's forebears in Limerick, but are persuaded by a travel agent to choose Lisdoonvarna in neighbouring County Clare because, being a spa town, it will be better for Brian, a failed teacher who writes poetry in the attic and is a deep depressive.

As Maeve did, the Mermans arrive in the third week of August. On awakening after an afternoon nap in their hotel room they find themselves in the middle of the festival and are swept along in the warm current of good feeling. Everyone is very friendly and full of advice. They are made aware of every aspect of the place, including the Merriman poem, 'The Midnight Court', which becomes of particular interest to Brian.

Out of the window goes Kathleen's original plan to shuffle documents in search of her roots. And of course there is no need, for like Maeve she finds her roots in the warm compost of her mother's Ireland, singing and talking and reading and dancing her way back into the land of her birth, in Maeve's case a year after her mother's death, which is why when Kathleen finally coaxes Brian onto the dance floor, everyone in the hall is singing the words:

My mother died last springtime when Irish fields were green,
The neighbours said her funeral was the finest ever seen.

With the lightest of touches Maeve lifts Brian's spirits (as hers were lifted) and amidst the beauty of Fanore, 'a great place for the soul', a little village on the west coast of Clare beyond which you can look out over the Atlantic and see dolphins play, she accords him a revelation as mythical and inspiring as the one that she experienced on her first trip to Cumann Merriman in 1968.

At Fanore she delivers Brian's sweet insane notion that he and Kathleen are none other than the reincarnation of Brian Merriman and the poet's wife Kathleen Collins. They share their names almost – he is Brian Merman and Kathleen's maiden name is indeed Collins. He has followed the same career as the great poet, and he lists endless other similarities. It is mad, it is insane. Kathleen's heart sinks; she had thought that his depression was lifting. '"How EXACTLY a reincarnation?"' she asks 'with a deathbed smile', hoping she doesn't sound 'too like Nurse Ratchett in *One Flew Over the Cuckoo's Nest*'.

Maeve delivers Brian's joyous news in the context of her own hard-won freedom from the lobotomised society of Ken Kesey's classic beat generation book, and to Kathleen's joy her husband has returned to her spiritually refreshed, moving forward with his life, whatever Nurse Ratchett's medical diagnosis might have been.

The festival gives Brian Merman the strength to come out and share his poetry with other people. 'It had been the sign he

needed, something to prove to him that he wasn't worthless…'
It was the sign Maeve had needed, too. 'Suddenly everything in
their lives fitted into place and they felt confident and cheerful.'

From this moment it seemed that fate took a hand in Maeve's
life, but it was catalysed by a decision *she* took. When she got
home at the end of August 1968, she decided it was time to
change her job.

It had been five years since her first newspaper article was
published and although she couldn't have lived on the money
she was making, there was momentum in her writing. She
decided to give up her safe, permanent and pensionable job as a
teacher and become a freelance journalist, full time.

Her father was quite sanguine about it. He pointed out the
risks, but was probably aware that Maeve would go ahead whatever he said. He concluded that if Maureen were alive she would
have advised her to do it, and gave her his blessing.

The risk, in fact, was minimal. She could at any time go back
to teaching. Psychologically it was a good move because the
decision made a virtue of living at home with her father – money
would be short and the arrangement allowed her to live somewhere that cost nothing. In the event, her father even offered
to subsidise her a little in exchange for some light housework,
which Maeve described as 'notional'.

Then out of the blue she received a telephone call from the
Irish Times asking her to come in and see them. She feared there
must be some awful inaccuracy or legal problem with something
she'd written. Her father, a lawyer, advised her as he was wont
to do – 'Admit nothing. Whatever they say, admit nothing!' She

arrived at the office full of nerves but was told that there was going to be a vacancy for a Women's Editor. Was she interested?

Maeve claimed that the offer was a huge surprise. She was a 29-year-old teacher without a day's experience of working in a newspaper office. But after Merriman it seemed heaven sent. Call it fate – or perhaps a savvy move by News and Deputy Editor Donal Foley, the man who wanted her and later became immortalised in the rather different persona of Jack Foley, Benny's boyfriend in *Circle of Friends*. 'Savvy' because Maeve's belief that 'the secret of the universe is that we do have to take control of our own lives' was never more relevant than in the late 1960s. Women who all their lives had seen success as making a successful marriage – ceding control, in fact, and getting looked after by a man – were about to get a wake-up call.

When the *Irish Times* initially took the decision to introduce a women's page it was still predominantly a male preserve and introducing a page specifically for women readers set a precedent in Ireland. Within a few weeks its competitor, the *Irish Press*, followed suit and appointed Mary Kenny as Women's Editor; and the *Irish Independent* soon appointed its own women's editors too.

Mary Maher, an Irish-American journalist from Chicago and an early member of the Irish Women's Liberation Movement, founded in 1970, had begun working at the offices of the *Irish Times* in D'Olier Street in 1965, just before Maeve began to contribute articles about her travels. In 1967, Foley asked Maher to become the first Women's Editor of the paper. She started with a half-page five days a week called 'Women First', with Maeve a regular contributor.

But then Mary announced that she was to be married, 'and it was assumed I couldn't continue as editor', she said. The idea of leaving didn't come from her, then. There was no law to the effect that married women shouldn't work. In the 1940s and even in the 1950s, when women got married they might be expected to leave their jobs, because there were relatively few jobs to go round. But by the late 1960s this was very rare. Mary Maher has said that the paper was being 'very progressive' even allowing a freelance married woman to write for it. This may have been regarded as progressive in Ireland in 1968, but not in England. It is particularly surprising that a paper which was supposedly leading the way in women's rights by introducing a women's page was letting a senior female staffer go because she was getting married, and replacing her with someone with no experience of editing at all.

In any event, Donal Foley got the woman he wanted and in due course Mary began to write for Maeve's page. They literally swapped roles, which might have made for a difficult situation had not Maeve smoothed waters with her mischievous charm, telling Maher that she knew they'd be friends because they hated the same people.

Subsequently they became the closest of friends. Mary said that she saw from the start that Maeve had all the qualities needed to be a journalist, except typing, which she learned over a weekend using two fingers. Before that, as a freelance, she had had her articles typed by a woman in Dalkey.

For five years Maeve ran the *Irish Times* women's page and loved every minute of it. She wasn't interested in the cookery and knitting, and fashion and style were anathema to her, but she commissioned very good people to write about these things, while she wrote about women, their feelings and their changing world.

There never was a more exciting time to enter upon women's journalism than the late 1960s, when the world was waking up to the potential of women and there were new opportunities and pressures facing them. Imagine how the Catholic culture of Ireland, with marriage a sacred institution, family the principal unit since Celtic times, and contraception and abortion illegal, woke up to the news that love and marriage didn't necessarily have to go together, even that 'babies aren't always fulfilling. Children can be adorable but that doesn't stop most mothers wanting a life of their own outside their husband and children...' as British writer and feminist Shirley Conran exclaimed in the very year Maeve was offered the position of Women's Editor on the *Irish Times*. 'Three point five million women are working and 70 per cent would like to be out working. Half the mothers I met had been advised to get out and meet people as therapy for chronic depression. Eighty per cent of mothers would like to send their children to nursery school.'

Betty Friedan had set the feminist fuse alight in 1963 after attending a college reunion at Smith, a women's college in America. She'd handed out a questionnaire to 200 of her fellow alumnae. The results confirmed what she had already suspected – many women were unhappy and did not know why. After three women's magazines refused to publish Friedan's findings, because they contradicted conventional views, she spent five years researching and writing *The Feminine Mystique*.

Then, in 1970, came *The Female Eunuch*, Germaine Greer's bitter landmark examination of women's oppression, along with Kate Millett's *Sexual Politics*. Five years later Susan Brownmiller published *Against Our Will* and in 1977 came Marilyn French's *The Women's Room*, a novel about a woman who revolted against the constraints of domesticity. These were milestones in the development of feminism.

When the Women's Liberation movement was launched in Ireland there was no small degree of militancy, which kicked off with Gay Byrne's *Late Late Show*. Byrne's interview with the movement's leaders generated such heated argument that while it was being transmitted Garret FitzGerald (some years before he became Taoiseach) travelled to the studio to engage them. The meeting ended in a shouting match.

As Women's Editor, Maeve commissioned writers, civil rights campaigners and feminists such as Mary Cummins, Nell McCafferty and Elgy Gillespie. She had a strong sense of social revolution. But was she a feminist? 'I was not carrying a flag,' she said, 'but I am proud to have been there when something was happening.'[47]

In her articles she gave her readers the benefit of her own experience. For a start, she promoted feminism by example. In those days, young Irish girls didn't travel around the world, nor did many forge a career in journalism. Maeve had done both.

In many respects she typified 'the new woman': unmarried, career focused and engaging in maximising herself as a person. But her rise had been emotionally and psychologically moti-vated, not politically so. Her life over the previous decade had been a courageous existential strip-down to the point where she could stand alone and be secure in herself. Part of this had involved distancing herself from institutions that told her how to think, and she was now wary of waving a flag for *any* institution, feminism included. The only 'ism' she had ever countenanced of her own free will was existentialism, which passed the matter of how to live back to her, told her to be her own person and not to cede control of her thinking or to campaign for an institution, an ideology or a dogma ever again.

She now applied this to her advice to women. Because of the work she'd done on her own psyche, the angle she followed in her journalism wasn't something she even needed to think about. Each article served to reinforce the woman she had become. Editorially – and even in the design of the page – she was as instinctual as she now was in every other aspect of her life.

Being an existentialist made her wary of feminist extremists. The surprising thing about extreme feminism was its kinship to the repressive views of the nuns, which Maeve had taken pains to discard. Marilyn French, for example:

There is no question that men are predatory on women. Women are prey. They start to be prey when they are eight or ten or eleven years old. Women are frightened when they walk on a city street or any street at night. They are frightened of any man at all. He may not be a danger, but he may. We know we are prey and that is a horrible knowledge to live with about your own species.

Contrast that with the existentialist route to feminism. 'I think for too long women believed that somebody was going to come in and look after us. It's degrading for half the human race to have to behave like that,' said Maeve. 'So, in a sense, I think that women are much more interesting when they stop pretending to try to be nice for the sake of it … We must not allow ourselves to be lazy, we could do anything if we set out the time to do it.'[48]

On the issue of 'jobs for women' she might have invoked the 1916 Proclamation, in which 'equal rights and equal opportunities to all its citizens' had been included in the Constitution, long before Britain had achieved women's suffrage. For Maeve believed the opportunities for women were already there. She wrote that Irish women 'should, like Brutus, look not to their stars but to themselves that they are underlings'. This was absolutely in line with her philosophy, but sailed against feminism's dictum that women must hit out at the *status quo* and at men in particular.

Unlike others, Maeve shone the light not on male chauvinism but on the pity of women failing to seize the moment. What really hobbled women of the last generation, she said, was the way they were obsessed with 'what people were thinking', when in fact most of the time no one was thinking about them at all.

In this she was not only following the lessons of her own life but, as Mary Maher wrote, 'she was touching [on] exactly what women's fears were' and getting women to ask, 'Is it our own fault?' This was much more positive and useful than most other sentiments of the time.

By the mid-1970s pressure was mounting on the 'housewife'. The dreaded question at a dinner party was, 'What do you do?' The answer: 'Nothing. I'm a housewife.' You had to 'do' something and traditional housewifery was no longer a justifiable occupation.

The feminist Ann Oakley actually called for the housewife role to be abolished, even for the family to be abolished. More recently, with hindsight, she admitted that she had gone too far. 'There was quite a bit of suspicion of the family. I couldn't see that family was something I wanted to buy into. The trouble was we didn't think through it. How else do you bring up children?'

Maeve might have suggested 'in a kibbutz', but she didn't. She sensed a movement running away with itself, drunk on its own power, and she envisaged some potentially very unhappy women indeed. She was appalled that women should apologise for being 'only' a housewife. It sent her into a rage that anyone should be so controlling as to suggest that a woman should apologise for herself on *any* count. She did not intend to marginalise anyone who had decided to live their life in their own way.

There was no right or wrong about whether to work; it was down to the individual woman to maximise herself as a person, a wife, a mother, a career girl, whatever it may be; above all, to take control of her own life.

At the same time, she warned stay-at-home women to be aware of what was happening out there in a fast-changing world. For as women changed, so men's view of women was also changing. If you opt to be a housewife, fine, but be aware that your man will be more likely now to meet women at work and after work in the pub – women who have made a different decision about how they intend to live their lives. In this new environment, she warned, it was more likely that husbands would stray.

The increase in the number of women in careers meant that they did join the after-hours drinking crowd in every city in the world, a development that was bound to increase the opportunity for a married man to have an affair. And Maeve was in fact writing from personal experience. She, herself a new woman, admitted that after her mother's death, freed from the pressure to find a husband, she strayed in exactly this direction. 'I fell in love with unsuitable people that nobody would marry, even supposing they were free to marry, which they rarely were.'[49]

These articles in no way promoted Maeve herself as exemplary. She never mentioned her own story. What writing from her own experience depended on, however, was that *her* feelings were everyone's feelings – that all women actually did feel the same as she.

The first hint of a special connection with her readers came in their response to an article which had nothing to do with feminism, its subject chosen hastily after another writer had let her down. This time she wrote about her first stay at a hotel at the age of eighteen. In the morning she didn't know whether she should make the bed or not. If she didn't make the bed, when she came back to the hotel they'd think she was a slut. But if she did make it, and she wasn't meant to, they'd think she wasn't middle class enough to stay in a hotel, and think just as badly of her. In the end she pulled the bedclothes up a bit and folded them back.

She was amazed to get hundreds of letters in response to such an apparently trivial matter. But it wasn't so much the subject that got people writing in, it was the intimacy of the contract she'd entered into with her readers. With touching honesty she had appeared to lower her guard and had opened up her box of feelings about class, prejudice, and women always worrying about what people thought. She brought out the old Maeve, the pre-existential edition, and found a rapport with her readers that all writers long for.

Maeve was not a political feminist, any more than she was a utopian communist or a militant Irish Catholic. She wanted women to be themselves and have more fun. She wanted them to enjoy the same lovely, busy world of relationships that she now did, to stop worrying about what other people were thinking and to be aware of the great opportunities that were opening up.

In Ireland, this meant coming to grips with the secularisation of a God-fearing society. There were serious political issues emerging which called into question religious tradition as the basis of everyday life. Modernity was meeting Catholicism head on over such matters as sex before marriage, contraception, divorce and abortion. These were women's issues and she would have to deal with them publicly and not allow the Church to have the last word.

She sensed that she was not alone in her feelings about the Church. She wrote that organised religion was 'losing its grip' on the people. Travel and education were taking her paper's young readers to places where the Angelus didn't ring but where the values of local communities were as true as they were in old Ireland. She cited, too, the disappearance of censorship on books, films and theatre as a measure of change, as well as legal provisions for contraception and divorce.

But she also sensed that no revolution would succeed unless it was grafted onto what went before. The success of the feminist movement would lie not in its originality but in its ability to embrace and assimilate all that was true for women before it came along. She was not interested in promoting a new style of life that everyone could sign up for. She was interested in women's feelings.

From time to time a little bohemian anarchy did show itself, however. Mary Maher recalled a court case that hinged on the archaic notion that a married woman was still regarded as the 'chattel' of her husband, a key word in the Irish Women's Liberation manifesto – 'Chains or Change'.

Maeve was so annoyed about the case that throughout one issue she substituted 'Chattel First' for the running title of the women's page, 'Women First', wherever it occurred in the paper. She told no one she planned to do it, just slipped it in at the last minute.

Humour was of course fundamental to her journalism. 'She saw the funny side of everything,' said Maher. Time and again she made trenchant points about serious or sensitive issues by taking a light-hearted approach. On the sensitive issue of contraception, over which there were rallies, pickets, marches and demonstrations, with Women's Lib members walking out of Mass in protest over Archbishop McQuaid's letter on the subject and making public displays of illegally imported contraceptives at Connolly station in the centre of Dublin, Maeve took a characteristically witty line.

The pill was unavailable in Ireland unless prescribed for menstrual irregularity, so she ran a piece observing that the number of women in Ireland with menstrual irregularity was so staggering that perhaps the World Health Organization should look into it.

Of course contraception was a religious issue. It was actually important to Maeve not to force people out of their religious faith. She may have lost hers, but she let people make their own minds up. This was what she liked about the *Irish Times*, which was after all a traditionally Protestant paper: 'Nobody was forcing everybody out into the world,' as she put it. But those who didn't want to be confined by the Papal edicts and the laws of the Catholic state could find inclusion too. It was a mature but difficult line to tread, which she did with consummate ease.

Later, in another article, she has an argument with a woman she meets at a bus stop, who comments on the bad weather and observes that the gloom has spread to politics with the introduction in Ireland of doctor's prescriptions for contraceptives. Maeve misunderstands and thinks the woman is in favour of contraceptives being freely available. She goes on the attack against all those feeble politicians who are 'passing the buck to doctors'.

The woman falls silent. Maeve thinks she hasn't heard her, so she ups both volume and tempo, recommending that condoms and pills be stocked on chemists' shelves (a radical proposition in Ireland at the time), until finally the woman, appalled, asks in steely tones whether that is indeed her view, that she would like contraceptives in public places, there for all to see.

For a second Maeve considers that she may have misjudged the situation and backtracks – the condoms wouldn't need to be on show exactly, they'd be in packets… The woman remarks that Maeve seems very well informed. Maeve laughs and admits that she has seen a lot of condoms in her time, in fact she'd bought a number for friends just recently when she was in London.

The woman is now boiling with rage. Two red marks have appeared on her cheeks, her eyes are bulging out of their sockets. But mercifully the double-decker bus arrives and she waits to see whether Maeve will sit downstairs or look for a seat up top…

It is a masterful article, one of a series she wrote starting with the words 'Today I…' The journalist was becoming more than just that; the author was beginning to emerge. In the case of abortion, change has been the slowest of all. Mary Maher wrote a letter to the *Irish Times* as late as June 2012, only months before Savita Halappanavar died in a Galway hospital because she was not allowed an abortion, struggling with the feeling of horror at the shocking reality of what an unwanted pregnancy could mean.

Maher reminded readers that all of twenty years earlier, a fourteen-year-old rape victim had been forbidden by a High Court order to travel to England for an abortion. Thousands had marched through the streets and forced the Supreme Court to overturn the order. Finally a referendum decided in favour of allowing pregnant women information and abortion abroad.

Maeve did not attempt to treat abortion as lightly as she did contraception on the paper. Like Dickens before her, who had his own journalistic and fictional outlet in the magazine *Household Words*, Maeve saw that issues which polarise society as divisively as abortion does in Ireland are better handled in fiction, which has a way of dispelling prejudice and transforming at a level deeper than the argument of journalism.

What she was really good at was reaching out to her readers of the paper. On one occasion a ferry company was giving away a holiday as a prize and Maeve decided that the winner would be the person who wrote the best letter describing why they wanted to go with their best friend, not their husband. The response was enormous: women poured out their hearts about their female best friends, 'telling things about their lives', as Mary Maher recalled, 'that took your breath away'. In the office Maeve couldn't believe how truthful the correspondents had been, knowing that they might be published and named. It was a subject close to her heart, of course, and in the end she wrote three articles called 'Women Are Fools', fictionalising what the correspondents had told her. Once again, the response was amazing.

Another 'bridge' to writing fiction was being built in an ever more consistent movement towards writing in a 'case history' format. It began with an article about the Council of the Single Woman and her Dependants, an organisation started by Mary Webster in 1963 after she was forced to give up work at just thirty-one years of age to care for her parents. This was obviously a cause close to Maeve's heart but on the face of it, in journalistic terms, a dullish subject if sourced from statistics. So, she started writing little short stories of the people who had found themselves in this situation, bringing the carers one by one alive as real characters with beating hearts in their own stories, which carried all the points Maeve as a journalist wanted to make. It was a sympathetic emotional approach and people were very moved by it. In hindsight Maeve's readers will recognise it as the seedbed of the one she used later in fictional books like *The Lilac Bus* and *A Week in Winter*, which her long-term British editor would refer to as 'novels in episodes' – individual stories of characters who coalesce in the story in the end.

Meanwhile, so strong a following was she creating on the *Irish Times* that, just three years after beginning work as Women's Editor, she published her first non-fiction book, a book of her articles; the title – *My First Book* – a signal to her intentions for the future. Within a week it stood at No. 3 on the Irish bestseller list. Her wit and wisdom were exactly what readers of the paper wanted. So much so, in fact, that she attracted a stalker.

The *Irish Times* in those days had an 'open door' policy and readers would come in off the street, have a cup of coffee and tell them their stories. One day a woman came in claiming to be Maeve's muse. Maeve tried everything to avoid her and on one occasion had to dive under a desk while Mary Maher informed the woman that she wasn't in that day.

Joining the *Irish Times* brought a new circle of friends. Journalists, irrespective of which paper they worked for, like Mary Kenny on the *Press*, Janet McCutcheon and Mary Anderson on the *Independent* – 'rivals but friends' – belonged to a fun-loving sisterhood with Maeve which also included roving reporters from around the world. They were women who worked hard and played hard, worked out their ideas and schemes, and compared notes on life, living in the fast lane as they had chosen to do.

They'd drink together at the famous Pearl Bar in Dublin's Fleet Street. 'We became friends and some of us were feminists together,' said Maeve. 'We had a wonderful platform for airing our views and by God we didn't hide our views.'[50]

Marianne Heron remembers the first time she saw Maeve: 'She held half the editors in Dublin spellbound in a snug.' Maeve had been telling them about the time she'd woken up in the middle of the night and found a man in her room. She had engaged him in lively conversation and ended up getting him to fix her vacuum cleaner!

These were the days of long, boozy lunches, whether you were a journalist in Dublin or in London, and Maeve loved it. Fleet Street, which runs west off the bottom end of D'Olier Street, at one time formed the southern boundary of the Liffey, the great river that flows through Dublin. It was home to both the Palace Bar (still at No. 21) and the Pearl Bar (now, alas, no more). The Palace dates from 1880 and has all the dark wood and massive mirrors and tiled floors one would expect. Famed for making its own whiskey, it became the bar of choice of the legendary *Irish Times* Editor, Bertie Smyllie, who was at the helm from 1934 until he died twenty years later.

The story goes that he transferred his custom to the Pearl after he discovered that the Palace was stamping the back of his cash cheques with 'The Palace Bar' and he didn't like his bank manager knowing how much he spent there.

The famous five-cornered snug, which can be booked and shut off from the rest of the pub, survives and the atmosphere is still amazing today. Flann O'Brien, who died in Dublin aged fifty-four, in 1966, drank here and there are countless stories about his larks, most famously that he parked a car without an engine outside and pretended to be drunk in charge of it, was arrested and had to be released when it appeared that someone had taken its engine.

The 'cultured' Pearl Bar was evidently just as popular with the following generation. The craic has particular significance, of course, in Ireland – the urbanity, wit, laughter, conversation and spontaneous levity, generally laced with alcohol, can be had any night in any number of bars in Dublin.

This was a scene Maeve took to and contributed to and in some ways never really left. '"Moderation" is not a word I ever cleaved to in any way,' she once said. In the novels, parties are the great *test* of something essential about being Irish. You should be able to tell a good story and sing a good song and laugh and weep if you were partying with Maeve. In *Light a Penny Candle*, Elizabeth White's ineffectual father and Aisling O'Connor's impotent husband are hopeless when it comes to enjoying themselves. Aisling's husband Tony can't hold his liquor and looks down after every second sentence to his written notes when he's giving a speech – a sure sign that he has failed the test. When Elizabeth suggests to her father that perhaps he could make life more fun for her mother, she is mortified at how sad her intervention makes him and promises to God she'll never bring the subject up again. At her father's birthday party he does eventually pass the test, but it's like drawing blood out of a stone, because of course Mr White is English.

The English come in for a pasting on this score. Maeve once found an elderly Irishman to interview who lived in England and would go home to Tipperary every Christmas. He told her that he'd been going home for Christmas every year for thirty-eight years and each time he'd look forward to leaving so dreary a place and rediscovering the place where he experienced all the first happiness and warmth that he longs now to recapture, when all of a sudden, the very moment he'd be leaving, 'wouldn't they turn into cheerful, happy human beings and have a chat and a song…!'

For Maeve and the sisterhood, meeting at the Pearl would often start at lunchtime and go on until late in the evening, and sometimes there was no great distinction between the character, fun and humour of bar and office, as one of her most famous stories shows.

Two days a week, 'Women First' was all about food and fash-ion, and the rest of the time it was for women's issues. Theodora was the name of a journalist Maeve regularly commissioned to write foodie articles for the page. Theodora was every editor's dream: she required no editing at all. Moreover, Theodora's husband, George, was a film-maker and took pictures which would often appear in the paper illustrating her articles. On one occasion George hadn't sent a picture in to accompany an article by Theodora about making veal casserole. Maeve became unreasonably annoyed with George, who she doubted ever charged for his services to the paper, but soon realised that it was her own fault that she hadn't ensured that George would come up with a picture. She began to rush about looking for an alternative.

It was late. She was due to be home with her father for supper. He would be expecting her. She had to find an alternative fast. She went to her file of emergency pictures and found one that was the right shape for the space left on the page. It seemed to Maeve a good photo too, absolutely on theme, a colourful casserole with lots of knives and forks sticking out of it. She typed out a caption – something about a veal casserole being perfect for a winter evening – and went home to prepare a meal for her father. Afterwards, as they were settling down to watch the nine o'clock news on television, the second story made Maeve freeze.

There was her picture! It appeared after a shot of Dr Christiaan Barnard, the man who performed the world's first heart transplant operation, coming out of the Groote Schuur Hospital in Cape Town, South Africa. What she had seen as knives and forks were clamps and other utensils for the surgeon's second heart transplant operation. A picture of open-heart surgery illustrating an article about cooking veal casserole was being printed for the morning edition of the *Irish Times*.

She rang the Editor, Douglas Gageby, and told him that a photo had gone in that had been thought to be of a veal casserole and was in fact of a heart operation. She then ran down Knocknacree Road with Gageby's less than appreciative words still ringing in her ear, convinced that her job was in jeopardy.

The Binchys had no car and she had no idea when there'd be a train. She waved down a passing car, told her story to the man driving it and asked if he was going anywhere near D'Olier Street. 'I am now,' he replied.

The man even came up with her in the lift to the newspaper offices, where she found a crowd of serious-looking men standing around her desk. And all she could hear was, 'That bloody woman, that bloody woman.'

Maeve stood inside the door and announced her arrival. The printing of the paper had been held. People were rummaging around her desk and drawers for picture alternatives, finding things she'd rather they hadn't, like miniature bottles of gin.

Gageby was not happy and he gave her five minutes to find an alternative picture. The only one she could find, close to the dimensions of the other, was an advertisement sent in by Wedgwood. It was a picture of an egg cup with an egg in it. She sat down and wrote the caption – 'Why settle for an egg?'

Even before the veal casserole incident Maeve liked to pretend to be terrified of the boss, Douglas Gageby. It was all part of office theatre. She had every reason to be fearful at first, so naïve was she about the workings of a newspaper office. A year into the job and the paper received the first letter attacking Maeve for something she had written. It knocked her sideways. Not since she'd been arraigned before the school for smuggling out the boarders' love letters and was stripped of her Child of Mary medal had she been publicly shamed.

She thought it was the end of the world. For of course the paper would be publishing the letter from the disgruntled reader, and the very fact that the decision was taken to publish seemed to Maeve tantamount to her dismissal by the Editor. She decided the only thing to do was to offer her resignation. She tidied her desk and with her heart bursting with unhappiness went in to see Gageby.

It was a bad moment. Gageby was busy and didn't even break off from what he was doing while Maeve said her piece. He then paused only long enough to look up and say that the paper had a letter column for readers to write in with their views. If a reader thought Maeve was no good it was his right to say so. Maeve ventured, 'But do *you* think I am no good?' Gageby's 'No' was not as convincing as she would have liked. But it was enough to get her to go back to her desk and untidy it again.

She was in fact a favourite of both Gageby and Foley, her immediate boss, whose belief that a reporter could do a job irrespective of gender went down especially well. He didn't assign a woman to a woman's issue or a man to a man's issue on account of gender, but according to who, in his opinion, would do the job best.

※

The late 1960s was a period when all Maeve's friends were getting married or were occupied chasing their future husbands, and some of her closest friends, like Philippa, were leaving Ireland altogether.

Behind the craic and the laughs, Maeve admitted that she was a lonely young woman, envious of her friends getting married because marriage brought them a home of their own, while she was still living with her father, and they could have as much sex as they liked without anyone disapproving or panicking in case they got pregnant.

She longed for a mate, but nobody came Maeve's way with full-time commitment in mind. She said she consoled herself with her late mother's words that love was a matter of luck. You couldn't force the issue. It would happen when it happened, as it had for Maureen and William after they met by chance in Ballybunion. But Maeve knew in her heart that she was now too much of a handful for the sort of man that Maureen had had in mind for her when she said that.

Her loneliness found its way into a short story called 'I'm Not Really Mad, Doctor, Am I?', which introduces the reader to Valerie, who remembers one day coming home from work on the bus thinking that nobody had said 'I love you' to her like people had done to her friends. She dismisses it as only words until someone at a wedding tells her she should hurry up and get married, she's no spring chicken. Valerie starts stealing clothes to smarten up and eventually, realising something is wrong with her, makes an appointment to consult a psychiatrist.

It was Maeve's opinion that no psychiatrist ever knows which words precisely tip the cure, but the psychiatrist in this case does cure Valerie and he thinks that it could have been when he told her that she was a unique and special individual, that no one on earth had her history, her mind, her personality... This had been Maureen's line to Maeve when making her feel better about herself as a child. But now there was a danger of Maeve slipping back, with no one in Maureen's place to reassure her, not even her closest friends.

In 'Green Park' (in the *Victoria Line* collection), Maeve discusses how the sisterhood relationship – the type of blood bond with her closest girlfriends which had sustained Maeve since she was a girl – atrophies in adulthood. 'Blood brothers, you know, for life' – close friends who can say anything to each other and it won't be misconstrued; no one will tell, it'll remain a secret for life. The suggestion is that her old friends have grown out of it. She had not.

The story focuses on four women. Helen refuses to accept that the special bond isn't there any more. At school, Helen, not unlike Maeve with the boarders' love letters at Killiney, had fraternised with the senior girls, seeking their friendship by revealing secrets to them and trying to prove that she was mature as they were. In some ways Helen is still the innocent schoolgirl. She insists that the blood-kinship remains as strong as ever and says that she can still tell Margaret personal things about her life, her man and her money worries, and that Susie has just returned from Kuwait and told her how she has discovered that she is a lesbian. Susie hadn't been able to tell anyone else but Helen.

But when it comes to the test with Jane, who asks Helen and Margaret to join in a little deception with her, Helen is herself ultimately found wanting.

Maeve was aware how readily people could misconstrue her girl-friendships. Come the 1980s, in the novel *Tara Road*, Rosemary's sister Eileen goes to live with a woman from work called Stephanie and they become lovers. But that is not Maeve.

Her friendships with women are friendships – caring, trusting, almost frighteningly loyal, intimate certainly – but sex doesn't come into them at all.

Maeve wrote about women, she said, because she knew about them. She talked to women more than men 'and I know what they talk about more', she said. Women talk to one another about their feelings and emotions and relationships, and on that plane men were nowhere to be found.

Chewing over the spectrum of womanly love Maeve produced one of her best short stories of all – 'Holland Park' in *Central Line* (1978).

'Holland Park' is told in the first person by the author, and we immediately cast Maeve in the 'I' role. She and her friend Alice go to dinner with Malcolm and Melissa, a couple they met abroad on holiday who live in a beautiful house in Holland Park in west London. Alice is married; she isn't. There are all sorts of hidden messages in the description of the run-up to the party, particularly in her preparations. It is the first time that she and Alice have met Malcolm and Melissa on home territory.

What transpires is a wonderfully observed 'coming out', the sudden realisation that Malcolm and Melissa have all the time assumed that she and Alice are lesbians, which they are not – well, heavens, they wouldn't know what to do, would they?

But then she begins to examine her behaviour with Alice at the party objectively, and sees just why it could lead one to think that they were lesbians. And of course she does feel strongly about Alice. Woman to woman, there wasn't anything to touch the sort of relationship she had with Alice, totally trusting, intimate in all ways but not ... She didn't want Alice in that way. They'd laugh themselves silly! *'Kiss Alice?'*

As the evening progresses, the story begins to take on the hue of an Alan Ayckbourn play, but only a woman could write this. Alice becomes too drunk to drive home. Will Malcolm and Melissa offer them the double bed in the spare room? What will that mean, now that the friendship with Alice has been put in a different light? Her perception of their friendship has changed forever, but it hasn't for poor Alice, who is now paralytic and knows nothing of what she has been thinking.

Can anything ever be the same again? How will she respond to Alice in bed, thinking these things? Will her love for her, which has been bottled up for all these years, suddenly be released?

Friendships between girls were so utterly real and true to Maeve, and because they meant so much to her she was frighteningly vulnerable to them.

A fan once wrote about Maeve: 'It bothers me a little that in her books love almost always turns into betrayal.' Maeve said unequivocally, 'I know about love and disappointment – even betrayal – from my own life ... It's just so hard to believe that somebody with whom you've shared a great deal of intimacy would betray you.'[51]

Betrayal is everywhere in her fiction, and its opposites – truth, loyalty – are paramount. In *Circle of Friends* Nan carefully and coldly plans the betrayal of her friend Benny with her boyfriend Jack Foley. In *Quentins*, Don Richardson not only breaks Ella Brady's heart, he rips off her parents and others besides. Here is betrayal on a grand scale. Betrayal eats at this author, but it hurts most when it is the betrayal of a woman by a woman in the blood-tie friendship. This was the ultimate sin. The betrayal of Ria by Rosemary in *Tara Road* is the most painful of all. This is another novel full of betrayal: Danny betrays his wife Ria with Orla and Bernadette, but this – a man's betrayal of a woman – is insignificant next to the betrayal of Ria by her best friend Rosemary, who has a secret affair with Danny throughout the novel.

Nor does the betrayal stop there, for the question arises, if a girlfriend knows that your husband is cheating on you (as happens in the novel), should she tell you, and if she doesn't tell you, is she also guilty of betraying you? Maeve was still chewing on these questions in *A Week in Winter* shortly before she died.

What in Maeve's own life made her feel betrayal with this intensity? Did something happen in that period post-1963 when, liberated, she threw off the shackles, started drinking and smoking and had a series of doomed affairs? Was it the break-up of some close bond with one of her friends, which she treasured with the innocence of a child even when they became mature people, as the short story 'Green Park' suggests? Or was there perhaps a *Tara Road* Rosemary situation in those free-love years of the 1960s, where someone she knew cheated with her lover?

There was such innocent belief in Maeve, an idealism that had been sown in her by her loving family and the religious community. Mary Kenny once said of her, 'To the good, all things are good, and I used to say to Maeve that she didn't need formal religion – she was a saint already.'[52] Molly Parkin warmed to Maeve when they met in the early 1960s, but noted how badly she'd been hurt by what Maeve saw as the cruelty of Jack MacGowran. Molly was alarmed by the force of Maeve's response to what was, after all, a rejection after a spontaneous amorous episode well fuelled by alcohol, a common enough occurrence by the 1960s.

In spite of her new confident exterior Maeve was immensely vulnerable. Perhaps betrayal was always bound to crack her heart in two at some point.

As her close friends disappeared and her love life led nowhere, spinsterhood and caring for her father was the full reality, and there were down times for Maeve, real loneliness, though she claimed she didn't realise how lonely she was until later, when she could measure it against her happiness with her soulmate, the man who, as her friend the journalist Anne McHardy put it,[53] drove 'a series of bad-hat lovers out of her life, for ever'.

One St Patrick's Day Maeve found herself at a particular low point and booked into a hotel by the sea to be alone and sort things out. In the morning sunshine she walked along the sand and, finding a secluded spot, decided spontaneously to take a swim, throwing off her clothes and running naked into the sea. Minutes later a man and a woman appeared and sat down, right by her clothes. Appalled at first that they might be intending to rifle through her things, she then recognised them as an elderly couple she knew vaguely from Dublin and pondered what she should do.

Should she shout that she was stark naked and ask would they please avert their eyes as she alighted from the sea? Or should she walk out unabashed and be damned?

Concluding that her level of confidence did not meet the requirements of the latter option, she began yelling that she hadn't a bathing costume, that she had not expected to meet anyone, would they mind walking along the beach and she'd catch them up later?

The old couple stayed stoically where they were. Either out of ignorance, because they couldn't hear what Maeve said above the surf, or on account of their Irish sense of humour, they dug in.

Maeve realised what she had to do. Yelling and screaming she raced out of the water suddenly and flung herself belly down on her coat. Neither of them raised an eyebrow. He mumbled something about the March sea being chilly for a swim. She said Maeve really ought to have thought to bring a towel.

Maeve got dressed, walked with them back to the hotel and played poker with them for the rest of the afternoon.

At home with her father, at least life had a stable pattern. They would take the train into Dublin together each morning, he to his work in the Four Courts, she to the newspaper. In the evening they'd have supper together at home. Afterwards he'd go to his study and then join her and watch a bit of television – it was a peaceful life.

There had been times when she wanted to get him to go on holiday and felt bad that she hadn't pressed him to go with her. Maeve, after all, was travelling all over the place in pursuit of her career. She wrote a touching story about this, entitled

'Victoria'. She wonders what her father would say if she set up a trip for him and the reader soon gets a sense of her frustration. We know that he was far from helpless, a gentle intellectual, unpushy in his job and in his relations with others, but all is so quiet without the force of her mother's personality, and Maeve can only see him from her point of view.

In the story the father has his study and he manages to look after himself adequately when she is away. He never asks what his daughter is up to when she stays out overnight, but loves to discuss whatever adventures she may have had, if she wants to tell him. But it is life at a rate she cannot relate to, love of a sort that seems lost to this world already.

She suggests that they go together to Paris, which he's always talking about visiting. He says that it would be a good idea, some time, when he retires and has time to think it through and plan, but he won't commit. Was he now someone who said things that meant nothing? Is that what growing old is?

Truth seems constantly to be compromised in life. Why does the truth of so many loving things eventually have to slip away?

Then one time Maeve was away interviewing an American millionaire for the *Irish Times*. She spoke to her father on the telephone in the evening, made some joke about there being no one of marriage material for her there. And her father said something about wealth taking the life out of people.

Maeve's sister Renie was with him that evening. Later she went in to his study and saw him dozing with his book in his hand. The sisters used to joke that William would protest that he hadn't been dozing, 'just thinking with my eyes closed'.

Renie smiled and thought he was just thinking with his eyes closed, but then realised that he was not. William was dead. As peacefully as that, Maeve's father William Francis Binchy passed away.

Maeve had lost both her parents in three years, and now she would also lose the home in which she had been living since she was a child of twelve. The past was swept from under her in one moment and she was completely bereft.

She took a flat in Dublin and often of an evening she found that she'd forget that she had moved and would turn left out of the office, turning towards the station for the train to Dalkey, rather than right for the bus to her apartment.

She decided to work very hard to get it out of her system.

SEVEN

LONDON APPRENTICE

By the early 1970s, as well as working for the *Irish Times*, Maeve was broadcasting for RTÉ[54] in Dublin and working too for the BBC in London, sometimes down the phone line from Dublin and sometimes actually at the BBC studios, just north of Oxford Circus, in Portland Place.

One day she sent a letter to a theatre critic to attack him for something he'd written in a review. The critic had thought her letter very funny and told her she should get it broadcast. Why didn't she send it to *Woman's Hour*?[55]

Maeve did what the critic suggested and received a letter from *Woman's Hour* suggesting that if she was in London why didn't she come in and record a reading of the letter? So Maeve did just that. The producer of *Woman's Hour*, who later became a great friend, introduced her to a freelance broadcaster by the name of Gordon Snell. They got on very well and whenever Maeve found herself in London thereafter, they'd meet and have a drink, at first in the BBC Club, where Gordon would sometimes meet with his friends after work.

The Club was a short walk from the BBC's Portland Place studios. Maeve describes it perfectly as it was in the 1970s in 'Oxford Circus', another of her stories in the *Central Line* collection – a big room beyond the porter's desk, crowds of people, virtually no one to recognise from the telly, more like a constant party, really, than a gentleman's club with deep leather chairs. The heroine of Maeve's story doesn't like it at all and it wasn't a very womanly place, certainly. But it was a great meeting place for the many freelancers on whom the BBC depended, such as Maeve herself.

Gordon was tall and, although seven years older than Maeve, was boyishly handsome with quite a crop of hair, which he swept back over a high forehead and kept long at the back to the collar.

Measured against Maeve he was anything but the extrovert, but so were most people, and he couldn't be criticised for being shy. He was, after all, a broadcaster, and used to projecting his personality. The son of a chartered surveyor, Gordon was intelligent, congenial, open and sunny. He hailed from Watford in Hertfordshire, just to the north of London. Hertfordshire, though very suburban by then, was originally part of the Binchy heartland, before the family came to Ireland, indeed long before the Norman Conquest even.

Maeve and Gordon gelled immediately, partly because they shared the same kind of humour, but also because of their differences. He was really the perfect foil for Maeve. There were rarely silences in any company in which Maeve was involved, but here with Gordon the rapport was at once wholly natural and true.

She claimed not to have fancied him straight away, but liked being with him, thought him 'just great' and found him 'interesting', by which she meant she detected something singular in the way he related to people, which made her trust him. Trust was a key emotion in Maeve's repertoire.

And trust was not something she associated with men. She observed that Gordon had lots of long-term friends, many from when he was at school. He wasn't the kind of person who transferred from one circle to another according to what he was doing in his work.

Gordon was genuine. He was interested in people and cared about what they did. But it was his openness to Maeve herself that really swung it. She observed that his face lit up whenever he saw someone he knew and liked, and it lit up for her especially, which she found 'immensely cheering'.

After all the disappointment in her relations with men, he was exactly what Maeve needed. They were good friends for a year or two, then romance slowly blossomed. Ever spontaneous, Maeve once suggested hopping on the hovercraft to Boulogne for the day. In those days the 27-mile journey time from Dover to Boulogne was only thirty-five minutes, with six trips a day at peak times. Why not, said Gordon, so they did. Once there they walked up the hill in the town to the little square and spent the whole of the rest of the day in a restaurant, eating, drinking and talking and talking, until it was time for the hovercraft to return. By common consent it was that day in Boulogne which transformed their relationship into more than friendship.

Maeve confessed that she was 'beginning to fancy him dreadfully', but wanted at all costs not to put herself at risk in a relationship again. The good news was that Gordon wasn't married – she had promised herself never to fall for a married man again. But was it perhaps good between them, Maeve wondered, because they saw one another more or less only at weekends?

Maeve's main argument was always with herself. She spoke to herself like a teacher, just as she spoke to other people when they were at an uncertain point in their emotional lives. She told herself that the geographical distance between Ireland and England surely made it impossible for the relationship to become more serious. But then she and Gordon decided they would go on a holiday together to Sicily, and they had such a wonderful time that it seemed to Maeve ridiculous to be always saying goodbye to Gordon at airports. It was time to introduce him to her family.

Later she would write a very well-observed story for her *Victoria Line* collection called 'Highbury & Islington', in which Adam worries about what others might think of his partner when they first give her the once-over. Their two worlds are so different that for as long as he can he puts off the date when his fiancée, Heather, will meet his family, and even when the time arrives he finds a ridiculous excuse at the last minute to avoid the meeting. The reader realises that he will lose Heather's respect in the end, indeed he has already lost that of the readers. It was time Adam grew up.

After Gordon met Maeve's family for the first time he asked her at the airport what they'd thought of him. Maeve said they were absolutely delighted with him. 'Yes, but what did they say?' he asked. Maeve replied, as Aidan says to Orla in *A Week in Winter*, 'They said you'd be no trouble.'

'God, isn't that a recommendation,' Orla replies.

Gordon felt much the same. But Maeve reassured him it was the highest praise from her brother and sisters.

Of course, to begin with, the Irish–English issue was at the fulcrum of Maeve-and-Gordon relations and, as far as Maeve could see, the reason why they handled themselves so differently on social occasions. When Gordon first came to Ireland, if they found themselves at dinner with her friends, Maeve would criticise him for not saying more, not being more demonstrative. Gordon would protest that he liked to listen to what people said. She insisted that in Ireland that is simply not good enough, that the Irish are not listeners but talkers. Gordon objected that as far as he was concerned listening was good. But Maeve wouldn't hear of it. 'The etiquette books say you should have four good listeners and four good talkers at a dinner party,' she said once in interview with CBS News, 'but that would never work in Ireland, because where would you find the good listeners? And if you knew them, you wouldn't invite them to your house. You wouldn't let them in the door. What would they be so quiet about, what would they be listening for?'[56]

Maeve's criticism was hardly justified, for she herself was a great listener – she had to be. She made her name as a journalist by listening to, indeed eavesdropping on, other people, and later whole novels came out of chance words overheard. In any case, her dictum that Gordon should become a talker rather than a listener at parties is in contravention of her first principle: be who you are.

Maeve would not have been persuaded by any such argument. But Gordon soon began to fight his own corner a bit and when, a few years later, at a Christmas dinner in London's Fleet Street, Maeve, as always holding court until late, insisted that Gordon sing a song with her, joining the fray was no longer a problem for him, and according to their friend Patsey Murphy, Editor of the *Irish Times Magazine*, one of Maeve's favourite songs was 'Can't Help Lovin' Dat Man of Mine', which naturally she would sing on her own.

Later, Gordon could give as well as take and was not averse to a bit of badinage with the woman he came to love, though in the end it was hard to pip Maeve. Perhaps with tongue firmly in cheek, he once admitted that he never knew about the TV soap opera *Coronation Street* until he met Maeve. She replied, 'Life was limited in every way when you come to think about it. But you were keeping yourself in readiness.'[57]

It became a great double act. 'What struck me was the incredible relaxation of Maeve and Gordon in each other's company,' said Declan Kiberd. 'It radiated out and brought everyone into that zone of comfort and ease.'[58]

Maeve was aware of the differences between them, while at the same time knowing that he was the first man in her life who was true. Her friends realised she was in love with him long before she did, and the romance went on and on, with Maeve and Gordon travelling back and forth between England and

Ireland, Maeve increasingly concerned that it would never move onto a more certain footing.

How could it? The *Irish Times* was everything to her and she had built an enviable reputation through her features and the women's page. How could she just give that up and take the risk of a far less certain future with Gordon in London?

Leap in the Dark, with a nice touch of irony, was the name of a BBC TV series for which Gordon was anchor in 1973. Linda Blandford was his female counterpart. It was a kind of *Tomorrow's World* of the paranormal – the 1970s were full of mystics and magic, with people like Uri Geller bending spoons by looking at them and Erich von Däniken riding high in the bestseller charts with his extra-terrestrial-themed *Chariots of the Gods?*. *Leap in the Dark* went on to be a success and continued for four series (1973, 1975, 1977 and 1980). Gordon had performed very well in the initial stages with a less than ground-breaking script, trussed up in an olive-green safari jacket to give just the right air of 'gentleman adventurer with stories to make your hair curl', as one reviewer put it. But after they changed the format from documentary to docu-drama he wisely made a graceful retreat.

Maeve made her leap in the dark one day when she saw Douglas Gageby posting a job notice on the board at the *Irish Times* for 'a man on the ground in London' to write features for the paper. Maeve 'humphed' when she read the advertisement over his shoulder. Gageby looked at her over his glasses mildly disapprovingly and asked whether she was interested in the job – 'You've got a fella in England, haven't you?' Maeve replied that the discriminatory tone of the advertisement was her point. But Gageby could see that it wasn't: 'Well, do you want the job, or not?' Maeve did. It was the perfect solution.

She liked to say that that was how she came to pursue Gordon and 'nail his feet to the floor'. But at the time she still wasn't 100 per cent sure it would work out, and later said that it took a bit of courage. In the event, she got the job sewn up and telephoned Gordon, nonchalantly telling him that she'd 'got this job in London...' Asked later how he'd reacted, Gordon said, 'I was startled ... but pleased!'

'Love Gordon; hate London' would have been Maeve's telegram home a few months later, for working in London wasn't at all as she'd imagined it would be.

She had thought that it would be like Dublin, a world of journalism in which everybody knew everyone else. She expected that people would be shouting, 'Hello Maeve, are you coming for a drink in El Vino's?' every time she set foot on Fleet Street.

But with London more than twice the size of the whole of Ireland in population, it wasn't like that, and the London office for the *Irish Times* was but an outpost, shared with the *Cork Examiner*. When the writer Roisin McAuley became the *Examiner*'s London correspondent, there was only a partition between her desk and those of Maeve and the then London Editor, Conor O'Clery.

Maeve confessed she was 'a bit startled' at the relative scale of the whole thing. Suddenly, she didn't know anyone; even when she went on a press junket and was in among forty or fifty journalists it was likely that she wouldn't see a soul that she knew. Just occasionally she might bump into Mary Kenny or Mary Holland at some glittery celebrity party and run off to have a meal and some non-glittery conversation, which was 'like the nectar of the gods'. But it didn't happen often. It was all so utterly different to the daily round at home in Dublin.

London itself in the early 1970s was not a particularly great place in which to live. Striking miners had brought Britain almost to a standstill, with a three-day week operating from January 1974 until the following March, Prime Minister Ted Heath's makeshift idea to conserve electricity. Hospitals, supermarkets and other essential services (including newspaper printers) were exempt, but the whole place slowed down to a crawl.

At the same time the IRA had moved into the capital, and the next three decades were played out against their horrific activities, which made being Irish no easier.

On 8 March 1973, just as she arrived, the Provisional IRA conducted its first operation in England, planting four car bombs in London, killing one person and injuring 180. Ten members of the IRA unit were arrested at Heathrow airport trying to leave the country. On Christmas Eve, two packages exploded almost simultaneously in pubs in Swiss Cottage. On 17 June 1974, a bomb exploded at the Houses of Parliament. On 17 July bombs exploded in the Tower of London and at government buildings in Balham. On 7 November a bomb was thrown through the window of the Kings Arms pub in Woolwich. On 21 December bombs were defused in Harrods department store in Knightsbridge and outside London at the King's Arms pub in Warminster, Wiltshire. On 28 August 1975 a bomb exploded in Oxford Street. On 5 September another exploded in the lobby of the Hilton hotel. On 3 November a car bomb exploded in Connaught Square. From 6th to 12th December the IRA held two people hostage in the Balcombe Street Siege. And on 27 March 1976 a bomb exploded in a litter bin at the top of an escalator in a crowded exhibition hall at Earl's Court: 20,000 people were attending the *Daily Mail* Ideal Home Exhibition at the time; seventy were injured, four people lost limbs.

This is but one three-year window, a tiny sample of the endless actions by covert forces of the IRA against civilians who may or may not have been British and who couldn't fight back. The bombings continued through the 1970s, '80s and '90s, dealing out death and horrific injuries by the score.

In the *Irish Times* office, Maeve found herself drawn into political and social reporting. 'It extended me very much as a journalist,' she said. But first, on 14 November 1973, she announced her presence on Fleet Street with a scorcher of an article about Princess Anne's wedding to Captain Mark Phillips.

Maeve, who had been brought up to dislike pretension of any kind and had a sense of humour that liked to puncture it, delivered a series of satirical hits on the royal family which were very funny but ruffled some feathers.

She referred to the princess as looking 'as edgy as if it were the Badminton Horse Trials and she was waiting for the bell to gallop off', and the royal entourage as 'actors who were getting paid over the equity rate'. It caused a minor storm. Maeve was in Brussels when the article came out and returned to a mound of telegrams.

Recently, in a RTÉ documentary on Maeve's life, a fellow journalist made light of it, saying that it just wasn't 'reverential like the Brits are used to'. The line was that criticism had come from the English side and any from the Irish side always carried the codicil, 'We love you anyway.' This was not at all the case. Very few people in Britain even read the article, but many *Irish Times* readers across the sea were aghast. In letters to the Editor, Maeve's article was described as 'bitchy', the choice of her as worthy of the commission 'a serious indiscretion'. 'I am as Irish as the rest of us,' said one, but the article was 'something of which we all should be heartily ashamed'. That was from a resident of Killiney, Maeve's home patch: 'Lord preserve us from the "Binchys" of this world,' it ended. While Evelyn Scales satisfied herself with, 'pshwshwshwsh! – Yours, etc.'

The last article Maeve ever wrote in her life was for the professional magazine *The Journalist*, in which she confessed that the royal wedding piece was her worst journalistic experience ever, because she got such a torrent of hate mail. Maeve, a highly sensitive woman underneath it all, wasn't good at taking criticism, as she had shown in front of Douglas Gageby in 1969, and she confessed that the aftermath of the royal wedding had taken much more of a toll on her than she imagined it could.

Wisely, she turned her attention away from British royalty and back to the Irish.

One has a sharper awareness of one's identity when abroad anyway, but in London Maeve found herself alone among the English, living there as an émigré with an English lover, while the IRA was planting bombs in pubs, in litter bins and under people's cars, and causing mayhem on the street. It was not a good time to be Irish in London. When something went off the Irish were the first to be stopped on suspicion by the Metropolitan Police.

Donal Foley, who was himself at one time London Editor of the paper, was Maeve's great ally and support. He knew what it had been like to be an Irishman in London during the Second World War, long before the Troubles began.

Foley and his wife Pat Dowling had sought out the Irish enclaves in the metropolis, going to ceilidhs in Clapham Common and discovering that Irish émigré songs 'like "Galway Bay", "Moonlight on Mayo" or "An Carraig Doun" sung in the atmosphere of a quiet back room in a Camden Town pub by someone like Margaret Barry, could be just as haunting and authentic as Nicolas Toibin from Ring singing "Na Connerys"'.[59]

Foley was himself born in the Ring Gaeltacht in County Waterford, the beautiful peninsula west of Dungarvan, where Gaelic was the principal language. He lived and breathed Irish tradition, but Maeve wrote that one of his great strengths was that he never allowed himself to become a prisoner of it. He noted, for example, an affinity between the Irish and working-class people from London's East End, who urged them 'to sing "When Irish Eyes Are Smiling" in the middle of "Knees Up Mother Brown" and "The Old Kent Road"'.[60] But, at the same time, he told her that the recitation of the Irish during the London Blitz, when those self-same East Enders were being massacred by the score, was, 'May God's curse be on you England…' It was this terrifying antipathy that raged now in London, forty years on.

The new friends Maeve made in London loved her instantly, her generous Irish warmth, her accent, character and humour. She was a new woman, liberated, enlightened, apparently unburdened by religious or political affiliation and yet Irish through and through, traditional Irish in the Cumann Merriman sense – the festival to which she still returned for one week each summer for spiritual renewal.

Nevertheless, there were difficulties for the Irish in London during the Troubles. 'There are five and a half million people in Britain who can claim to be Irish,' she wrote in the Melbourne newspaper *The Age*. 'These days their claim is muted if heard at all. After almost every violent incident we hear on the radio or read in the papers that the police "want to interview someone with an Irish accent".'

She wrote little about the Troubles for the *Irish Times*, concentrating on the risks that ordinary folk were being put to and the damage being done to London businesses, particularly to restaurants. First, people were asking for tables away from windows, for fear of the glass killing them in the event of an explosion. Next they were asking for a table in the basement and before long it was more likely that they would stay at home. In the West End, theatres were soon closing because of the bombing and Maeve became nervous travelling on the London Underground, particularly when walking the long corridors. Parking a car had become impossible, because car bombs were now a real threat to ordinary people.

She gave no inkling in her articles about how she personally felt about the politics of the Troubles, however, saying later that she hadn't known enough about them and she only wrote about what she knew.

But later she did say that if she'd been writing a book at the time of the car bombing in Omagh, which killed twenty-nine, and injured around 220 people,

> the Troubles would be in, because nothing has touched people here like Omagh – honestly, nothing ever has. You might say what a heartless people not to be touched before, but I don't think it's true – it's just a different world, the North and the South [of Ireland]. But Omagh, it's the sheer madness…[61]

Her thinking on nationalist politics in the equally traditional country of Wales was, significantly, to keep the political and religious institutions out of the picture.

She had many heated arguments about this in 1974, when she followed the Welsh Nationalist candidate Gwynfor Evans for the *Irish Times* during his campaign to get back into Westminster. Her position was that Plaid Cymru, the Welsh Nationalist Party, was simply *unnecessary*, because Wales had retained its traditional culture, its language, music, songs and poetry already. Why did they need a political party to fight for it? Israel and Ireland are, like Wales, both traditional cultures and she had seen what happened when religious or political institutions took control of them. Sunrise 'came up unnoticed while they told me why', she said, and she loved every minute of it.

What inspired Maeve the writer were the values of these traditions, many of them endemic to cultures she had experienced all over the world, the implication being that all cultures belong to Tradition – with a capital 'T' – which is bigger than any one religion or political party can account for.

When James Joyce and his university friend Gogarty considered ways to 'Hellenise' Ireland in Dalkey in 1904 they were suggesting something similar – that in the centuries since the Romano-British missionary St Patrick had converted Ireland to Catholicism, the Church had lost sight of the 'theoria' of the Greeks – the Platonic ideas or forms out of which the Church had arisen, and that these ideals – beauty, love, truth – were intrinsic not only to ancient Irish culture but to Tradition itself, which is in no way restricted to a nation or to a religion, or indeed to a period in chronological time.

When Maeve spoke for Ireland, and when she wrote for Ireland, which she did with renewed vigour once she had found her feet as an Irish woman in London, Tradition is what she spoke for.

There is an interesting codicil to this. Maeve was not alone among the Binchys in championing native Irish culture at this time. So inspired was her uncle, Professor Daniel Binchy, by his undergraduate years, when he had been caught up in the martyrdom of those UCD boys back in 1920 – boys who were themselves fighting for the nation's identity – he began to write what became his life's work. The six-volume *Corpus Iuris Hibernici*, in its reinstatement of ancient Irish law [Brehon Law], speaks elegantly of the customs and values of Irish tradition and the identity of the Irish people within the pre-Christian kingdoms – Leinster, Ulster, Munster, Connacht and Meath.[62]

Daniel Binchy's work resulted in six volumes, 2,343 pages and 1.5 million words. *Corpus Iuris Hibernici* confirmed that Ireland, for all the horrors it had suffered, had a cultural identity which neither Britain nor the Catholic Church in Rome could, after all, redefine.

There was significant alignment between Daniel and his equally patriotic niece, in that the final volume of his master work came off the press in 1978, the very year that Maeve's first book of fiction – *Central Line* – was published.

Among the centres in London identified as Irish in Maeve's time were Camden Town, Kilburn, Shepherd's Bush and Hammersmith. She herself lived with Gordon in Hofland Road, West Kensington, just behind Olympia, on the borders of Hammersmith and Shepherd's Bush. The Royal Oak in Glenthorne Road was her local (now closed). She was much put out by the diminished opening hours on a Sunday at the Oak (and all pubs across Britain), as keen readers of the *Irish Times* may recall.

Ending her misadventure with royalty slightly wounded, Maeve mined a rich seam of articles about the Irish immigrant community in London. The history of Irish immigration goes back centuries, and is an unhappy one of exploitation, hunger (even starvation) and poverty, right into the time that Maeve was there in the 1970s.

February 1974 found her at the old Marmite factory in Kennington, which had closed its doors seven years earlier but was then reopening as the modern equivalent of a union workhouse (without the work). Here Maeve mingled with

300 down-and-outs seeking shelter – 'in by 11 p.m., out by 7'. Her mother would have been proud of her.

The aroma of Marmite had given way to the pong of dossers' feet, with Maeve in among it and the Irish to the fore. The 'case history' format – little cameos of people that make her points – was once again her chosen vehicle. *Irish Times* readers were introduced to, for example, John Anderson, the third of nine children who came to London from a farm in County Mayo in 1944, when things had looked poor in Ireland for a young man of twenty-four. For years, like so many Irish émigrés, he went home to his family at Christmas, but no longer. Returning costs too much in drink for his mates, because everyone assumes that having transferred to London he must be a secret millionaire.

A picture began to emerge of the Irish émigré which was less than stereotypical. In her stories she gave a glimpse of a multi-layered population which remained true to its roots and often worked a little harder to compete with the locals. A series called 'The Way We Live Now' again carried interviews with émigré Irish, though it was not all destitution. The first featured a doctor in Hampstead, with Joycean memories of the Jesuits at Stoneyhurst, the famous Roman Catholic school in the Ribble Valley in Lancashire. After years of travel through Burma, Malaya and Africa, Gerry Slattery had made his home in London and yielded his soul to Britishness, even if he still made the biennial trip to Twickenham to cheer for the Irish Fifteen. In contrast Paddy O'Connor, who left Wicklow for London penniless as a lad, experienced emigration at a different level, remembering 'raw Irish kids coming off the train at Euston and punch-ups between the pimps and the people from the Irish Centre to see who could get to them first'. By the time Maeve met him in 1974, Paddy was Deputy Chief Whip of the Greater London Council at County Hall. Taking over the Marmite factory for the homeless had been his idea, and he was about to take over the Charing Cross Hospital on the Strand as a second site, after the hospital's relocation to Fulham in 1973.

Her readers then meet a girl from Limerick, who came to London in 1967 and worked hard. In four years she'd saved £400 in a Post Office account. Enter a man who asks her to marry him. He's always wanted to live in Ireland so why not get a house there; her £400 would earn better interest in his building society account, which itself would look better for buying their own house together if it had £400 more in it. The girl begins making plans to go home to Ireland and hands her notice in at work. Suddenly her fiancé isn't to be found at his address.

Maeve was herself not only an émigré to London, but an émigré for love, and there is great precedent for that. Certainly the main drift across the water was of the legendary Irish 'spailpins' or trampsmen, of men to the factories of the old enemy, of 'McAlpine's fusiliers' to the building sites, as the famous Irish ballad of the early 1960s calls them (an allusion to Sir Robert McAlpine, a major employer of Irish workmen), and of the thousands who found work in the docks since the early nineteenth century. But it is a common misconception that only men emigrated from Ireland. There are countless examples in the twentieth century of Irish girls emigrating to England in search of love. The first thing an émigré girl would do was to go to the local Catholic church, of which there were many in Irish immigrant areas. The priest would find her a place to stay where she'd be safe, which would in turn give her the greater chance of securing employment. The Church had a hugely important role to play in safeguarding the immigrant community.

Then, from the mid-twentieth century, she could expect to find an Irish Centre in the great émigré cities, London, Manchester, Liverpool and Glasgow – a place of succour, but also somewhere to be Irish with your countrymen, a home from home. The years 1965 to 1990 were the golden age of the Irish community in Liverpool, thanks to the Irish Centre there. The feeling among the leaders there was that if an émigré didn't retain his own dancing, music, language, then he would have nothing to give to the community in which he lived, and the Irish as a body would sink without trace.

Now, the very same route – Irish Centre, Catholic priest – brought Maeve her first really successful story in England. At the Irish Centre in Camden Town Maeve met with a priest who told her a story of an Irish émigré, a builder's labourer in his parish, whose wife was preparing for Christmas when the news came from the hospital that her husband had died of pneumonia. She couldn't believe it, she kept thinking that it's a huge hospital and there must be some mistake. But there was no mistake and the family was suddenly without an earner. And if that wasn't bad enough, the man's brothers had turned up from Ireland to collect the body. The priest intervened and objected that he'd lived half his life in London. 'Won't he want to be buried where his wife and children can visit his grave?' 'No,' said the older brother. 'He'd want to be buried in the parish church at home, where his wife and seven children can visit the grave.'

The man had one wife and family in Ireland and another in London, neither one knowing about the other until the man died. The story first appeared in the *Irish Times* under the headline 'Death in Kilburn', and as a direct result became the basis of Maeve's most successful play, *Deeply Regretted By*, the classic Irish émigré tale that she wrote in 1976.

She felt that the most important thing about the bigamy story was that it was true, for bigamy among Irishmen in London, she discovered, was far from unusual. That it is a crime under Section 57 of the Offences Against the Person Act 1861 and carries a sentence of up to seven years in prison was not the point. She wanted our understanding. These men had been forced to emigrate to find work and fallen foul of the law because there was no work available at home. Her message to the Irish at home was, 'Don't forget us, just because you think there's plenty of jobs and money and we'll be fine; listen to that fleeting sense you have that we Irish in Britain do feel different and a little bit lost.'

But this was far from the only string to her bow. In the summer of 1974 she took a holiday in Cyprus and barely had she touched base in London on her return but she was ordered back on the plane to report on an Athens-backed coup on the island which had ignited a major international incident, the British offering sanctuary to the deposed President, Archbishop Makarios, and America sending seven ships to stand off Cyprus 'in readiness'.

Maeve always regarded Cyprus as the best thing that journalism ever landed her, as it meant that she got a story in the paper every day. Soon she was at the front, reporting from the Cypriot capital, Nicosia, describing the burnt-out remnants of Makarios's palace, the scene of strongest resistance, and being abandoned by her driver, who said he would rather 'vomit' than have anything to do with the rebels.

When serious bombing of the capital began, she, along with a hundred other reporters, retreated to the British base in Dhekelia in the south of the island, relating tales of horror about the mass evacuation from the north.

Desperate that her articles got through to Renagh Holohan, who was by now London Editor of the *Irish Times*, Maeve would sleep in the queue of journalists for the phone, the only means by which to relay her stories home, rather than risk losing her slot if she left.

Travelling abroad on her own in her twenties had nurtured useful skills for survival. Food and cigarettes were scarce and she bribed people to get supplies from the thousands of refugees. In the end she was among the last of the evacuees in an operation that transported over 6,000 people to Britain.

Characteristically, when she was categorised as a 'friendly national, Class 4A' she objected that '4A' didn't sound very friendly. They told her to 'shut up' and get on. Some British journalists flying out on the same plane had been classified 1A and didn't let her forget it all the way home.

Back home in England she launched her 'Inside London' column. In common with Joyce and Dickens, the two writers who influenced her most and whose work she loved, Maeve was becoming increasingly sympathetic to the everyday lives of ordinary people, to the minutiae of their day. This column was the first outlet for the particular skills she developed to pursue her interest, skills that would later be employed in her fiction. This is how it had worked for Dickens. *Sketches by Boz* carries in its very subtitle the writer's fascination for 'Every-day Life and Every-day People',[63] and the sketches led directly to his being commissioned to write fiction.

So it would be for Maeve. If reflection on Maureen's habit of talking to whoever she met on the bus or in the open-air market in Dublin's Moore Street planted the idea of 'the elements of the marvellous latent in ordinary living'[64] in Maeve's mind, Dickens and Joyce almost certainly gave her the idea of pursuing it in a literary vein.

Maeve's new column would be described as 'a veritable psychopathology of everyday life'.[65] It could have been conducted simply as a series of interviews. Instead, she took any opportunity she could find for eavesdropping on her subjects. She began listening in to people's conversations in restaurants, on buses, wherever she found herself. She even admitted to getting off a bus and pursuing two people down the street because their conversation hadn't finished.

The No. 73 bus was a favourite vehicle: from Victoria through Marble Arch, Oxford Circus, Tottenham Court Road, Euston, King's Cross and Islington, 'you hear everything eventually,' she once said. She even developed a vacant, 'not the full shilling' look, as if she wasn't quite there, so that people wouldn't think she had any particular interest in them. Gordon found it particularly dispiriting when suddenly she'd tune in to a conversation in a restaurant when he was mid-flow talking to her over a meal.

To give herself an edge, she decided to learn to lip-read. The idea came to her after catching a particularly bad cold, which made her a bit deaf, and when a programme came on television about lip-reading, she gave it a go, She would record the television news and play it back repeatedly with the volume turned down until she could read exactly what was said in the facial movements of the newscaster alone. She even attended classes in Kensington to hone her new skill, which on one occasion far in the future would give her unexpected and highly satisfying supremacy over a critical pair of her fans.

She was giving a talk to a large group of her readers. The format of the event included a lunch, followed by Maeve's talk and then a signing session afterwards. Maeve always got a bit tense before giving these talks and was so nervous before this one that she barely touched her lunch. Afterwards, feeling peckish, she asked the publicity PA to prepare her a plate of cheese and biscuits, which she was eating while the line of her readers was forming, each with a copy of her latest novel ready for her signature. Some way in the distance she noticed two women, one of whom was saying to the other, 'Would you look at her, eating a plate of cheese and biscuits after that huge meal, is it any wonder that she is the size she is?' Maeve had 'seen' them say this as clearly as if they had whispered it into her ear. And she was furious. She put the cheese aside and began the signing session, chatting to each of her readers in turn and writing a message in their books. Eventually, it was the turn of these two women. Maeve treated them as she had done every other. "'Lovely to see you and you look so well… And you mustn't worry about the cheese; I had it instead of the dinner, not as well." And their faces were scarlet and I loved it!'[66]

By the winter of 1975, delivering an eavesdropped conversation had become a Binchy format, an anticipated ingredient not only of her 'Inside London' column but of other articles too.

The very intrusiveness of her new private-lives technique was even sometimes used as the subject. In 'On a Pier Day' Maeve is back in Dublin. She has missed the train in Dún Laoghaire and is whiling away the time by walking the magnificent pier, a place no less imaginatively potent than the Cobb at Lyme Regis in Dorset, and equally popular for a stroll. It is a freezing day and Maeve notices a woman well wrapped up with a little dog which is looking less than happy with its situation, shivering uncomfortably in the cold. Maeve engages the woman in conversation, apparently concerned for the dog. The woman takes umbrage, protesting that her dog loves the bracing air and what's more it does him good, it shakes the surplus fat off him. Maeve retreats and embarks on a brisk walk herself, before espying a man looking out to sea, 'as if he were remembering a long life on the ocean or planning to end his life there'. She becomes convinced that he intends the latter and takes up a position close to him, intending quietly to divert him from his act of self-harm by talking about the cold weather and spring being around the corner, and when that fails, about the economy looking up. When he remains unmoved, she suggests that if he is planning to walk back to Dún Laoghaire she might walk back with him, and congratulates herself that so selfless an act of friendship would be bound to do the trick.

At last the man turns towards her, examines her thoughtfully for the first time, and replies to each of her points in turn, making it plain in measured tones that he disagrees with her prognosis in every case, that the weather is showing *no* signs of turning, the economy is getting *worse*, and no he does *not* intend to walk back to Dún Laoghaire. He wants simply to be left alone. It transpires he is engaged in working out the plot of a novel.

Moving on, Maeve comes upon two schoolgirls so scantily clad that surely they are close to developing hypothermia, if not in serious danger of being raped... She thinks for a moment of getting involved, but decides this time she'll let whatever will be happen.

Back in London she meets a woman at a party who has her bras and corsets made for her at a place in London's West End which also services the Queen. Maeve decides to go see for herself and maybe buy a bra, an item of no small import for a woman her size. She hopes they won't be snooty and put her down. 'It's bad enough to be put down when you're dressed. Naked, it's intolerable.' When she arrives the lady-in-waiting is a model of politeness and discretion, but what is required is a mould of Maeve's breasts – which is where the fun begins, as they scoop bits of her into a contraption 'like two huge steel horseshoes covered in fur'. What they create turns out to be 'the most cheering garment I ever bought ... firm to the point of being like reinforced steel. It will look fantastic if I'm knocked down by a bus.'

Gradually her articles became longer and more searching of the person being scrutinised; Maeve was not only on the hunt for a good story, but also for *character*. Indeed, from this point her stories tend to steer an uncertain course between journalistic fact and an imaginative work of fiction. 'She witnesses real life dramas in airports, overhears suicide plans in quick food queues. Is it all true or does she make it up?' wonders her friend the journalist Marianne Heron.[67]

Many of Maeve's articles were now really short stories in disguise, like the one about Elise, a French woman who attaches herself to her on holiday in Morocco.

Elise's genial, good-looking husband is paralysed from the waist down, but he is up for anything and is great fun, while Elise is precious, fastidious and snobbish. Everybody else seems to be enjoying themselves, but Maeve is stuck with Elise, who proceeds to grill Maeve about her wealth and social status, as if Elise were a cross between a tax inspector and a duchess looking for a maid companion. She then asks Maeve whether she thinks her husband is handsome. Maeve, thankful that the interrogation is at an end and keen to embrace this more positive turn in their conversation, agrees that he is fine looking indeed. Elise approves wholeheartedly. She values Maeve's judgement because it is always nice to hear what others think about one's choices in life. She then adds that of course she couldn't possibly tell Maeve about the sexual side of their marriage… And so it goes on. There is no escaping the woman. It is like Maeve is caught in a vice, and so shamelessly patronising is Elise about Maeve's social status that Maeve is eventually unable even to respond.

Time and again it is Maeve breaking the ice with strangers that gets a story off the ground. 'Oh, Why Can't the English?' made the most of her satirical émigré eye on the host nation. The episode occurs on a trip on the railway from London to Leeds, in the days when trains still had traditional six-seater compartments leading through their own door into a side corridor eventually into the next carriage. As the train gathers pace out of Euston, the door of the compartment is thrown open and the guard, a man in red braid, shouts in self-important railway-speak, 'Lusk Hall Varieties!' Maeve and the five businessmen, thrown together by chance into her compartment, look up wide eyed with non-comprehension, and with Maeve as catalyst, the unwritten rule of silence attached to train travel across England is broken. There develops a bizarre conversation as to what on earth 'Lusk Hall Varieties' might be, interest whipped up further by the sight of people hurrying along the corridor after the guard.

One by one, the members of the compartment – the nimble-minded crossword enthusiast, the management man, the fat budget man – each has his say, until finally, one of the group – 'the geologist' – cannot hold out any longer and goes to investigate, returning wiping tears of laughter from his eyes, to put the rest out of their misery. It was the way Red Braid had said it. 'Lusk Hall Varieties!' was in fact, 'Last call for High Teas.'

Now there can be no slinking back like tortoises into their all-too-English shells. The six continue to talk the whole way to

Leeds, making Maeve's tacit point, to be developed years later in such tales as *Nights of Rain and Stars* (2004),[68] that 'strangers are just friends you haven't met yet'.[69] When Red Braid reappears at the end and says, 'Trying survival please', they are all able to predict that the train was indeed *arriving at Leeds*.

Characterisation, social satire, comedy – it wasn't long before Gordon insisted that Maeve try her hand at fiction. He'd known she'd be good at it since she took to filling in what he called 'the word picture' of people she encountered. On one occasion, again on the harbourside at Dún Laoghaire, she'd seen three people, two men and a woman, walking towards her, dressed for sailing but looking very grim. At once she imagined that they were a married couple walking with a best friend, and that the woman (the wife) was unhappy because she secretly wished she'd married the best friend rather than her husband. The best friend was looking grim because he was wondering why he didn't marry the wife when he had the chance, instead of throwing his life away on his current girlfriend, a Barbie-doll blonde who always made herself scarce as soon as sailing was mentioned (which was why she wasn't there). The husband was looking grim only because he was absorbed with what problem the wind was going to cause them sailing that day. He knew that his wife would bite his head off if he started to explain the problem. She no longer provided him with sex in the bedroom. She lived for the moments when the three of them met at the yacht club, when she of course dressed up to look as good as she could in the presence of the Barbie doll...

Maeve did actually write the story for the Dún Laoghaire

Yacht Club, calling it 'An Enthusiastic Yacht Watcher', and it had come to her just like that.

The eavesdropping might give her an idea for a story. But once she had the story she couldn't help but imagine who the person was *in their entirety*. She couldn't help creating the whole character, the environment in which that person lived and her emotional life – her psychology and what she felt.

In fact, Gordon first mentioned writing fiction as something they could both do. He wanted to write children's books. For some time he'd had to put up with people saying, 'I saw/heard you on such-and-such a programme last night. Can't remember what it was about, but it was very good.' And Maeve said that that was exactly how she felt about journalism – you wrote your piece, expending great creative energy in the process, and it was history – unknown to anyone the very next day. 'Today's paper is tomorrow's fish-and-chip paper,' she said.

They both wanted something more lasting, something that could be accessed and be useful and entertaining long after it was written. Gordon had an idea for a fantasy story about a king who had great curiosity and a healthy scepticism for what he saw around him. In fact, he had a whole host of ideas of interest to young children.

Already Maeve had a useful contact in publishing called William Miller, an editor with a fine reputation who had, with three others, set up the trail-blazing Quartet Books in 1972. William, a former journalist and novelist himself, and a warm personality who liked to introduce himself as 'a Scot, a homosexual and a socialist', held court in bars or restaurants in whichever capital city he happened to be. It was a fair bet that eventually he and Maeve would meet, and when they did that they would get on. William invited Maeve to write a book of short stories and together they came up with the unique London Underground theme of *Central Line*. Soon Maeve also had an agent, very possibly suggested by William – Anna Cooper of the John Johnson Agency.

Women's feelings were always going to be the subject of the stories, because that is what Maeve knew about. But this 'metro' idea was brilliant because she found a story much easier to write once she had a setting with which she was familiar.

She started to travel the Central line, coming up occasionally at this station or that like a mole sniffing the air, then setting her imagination free to conjure up the atmosphere of the place and what people she might find living there.

Each story would have a point to make, putting into practice what she called 'one of the great lessons of feature journalism – the Power of the Parable' – to highlight something, some truth that had impressed itself on her in the course of her own challenging life over the past decade or so.

Less than a decade since her life had begun to fall into place, she was doing what she really wanted to do, writing fiction, and being with 'dear generous Gordon, who makes life great every single day'. Gordon believed that she could do anything she set her mind to, as her mother had believed. He helped make Maureen's confidence in her finally come true. For Maeve it was wonderful to have somebody by her side again who believed in her and who cheered her up when the going got tough, which it surely would. Through his love for her, Gordon, it seemed, had set her free.

Writing fiction changed her feelings even about living in London, for she saw now that it would never have been possible in Dublin. The social scene, the lunches in the Pearl Bar with her journalist friends, the fun, the harum-scarum things she got up to, were a distraction. In Dublin they'd sit in bars talking about their plans to write, but very few did it. In England it was different. Once she announced that she was writing a book, people were forever asking how it was going, which was good for her. In London she was in the right place to get the writing done.

Suddenly it no longer mattered that she didn't know anybody and didn't have things to do in the evening. Now, instead of feeling guilty about turning up at Gordon's workplace and being a hanger-on to his friends after she'd finished at the *Times*, she wrote short stories in the office between 6 and 8 p.m., after everyone else had gone home.

Combining writing fiction with daily journalism took some organisation. Roisin McAuley claimed that Maeve was the most organised person she had ever met, while Patsey Murphy described her levels of concentration in the office: 'No preciousness, no delay.'

In due course Gordon also got a contract, with A. & C. Black in Soho Square, a publisher of some distinction in children's books at the time. *The King of Quizzical Island*, as his book was called, would be illustrated by David McKee and published at the same time as Maeve's *Central Line*.

Once they were both contracted, the writing regime changed.

Roisin and Renagh Holohan remember that Maeve would work from about nine o'clock in the morning until two at the office, when she would break for lunch. She went to lunch 'always with company and lunch often continued late into the afternoon'.[70] She would then go home. Gordon might be out working for the BBC or he'd be writing at home. If the latter, they would write in the same room – twin typewriters next to one another. 'They worked together side by side, true mates,' said Patsey Murphy, 'their partnership in itself hugely inspiring.'[71]

They had a rule about showing each other their work. They had to tell the absolute truth. But then there would be what they called 'sulking time', ten minutes to decide whether the criticism would be taken on board or the original justified and kept.

Generally, they would break around seven. They'd be firm about this too, close up shop, have a shower, take a break, otherwise there'd be no end to the tinkering with what they had done. Maeve would put a cover on her typewriter to emphasise that that was all the attention the machine would be getting from her until the following day.

In the evening she and Gordon liked to entertain friends, many from the BBC or Fleet Street, and whenever anyone came over from Ireland they'd give a supper party in the house, just as Mary Holland had done. According to Roisin, Maeve was a demon card player and she recalled 'many wonderful evenings of wine, cards (mostly solo whist, I think) and an endless stream of visiting friends'.

If no one came round and they didn't go out to friends or the theatre (a favourite pastime), they'd have a quiet night with a meal and a bottle of wine in front of the television and watch one of the many films they recorded in the afternoons – old black-and-white ones, mostly shot at a time when the English accent sounded like the South African accent today, as Maeve put it, an amusing observation, and true.

Or they might talk about their next trip to Ireland or the colour of the garden – gardening being a skill, like chess, more satisfying talked about than expertly practised. Maeve claimed that anyone watching her and Gordon play chess wouldn't recognise it as the game they knew, but years later she so enjoyed it that she had a long-running postal series with her neighbour, whose moves would be despatched by hand through the cat flap onto the floor.

Then, no doubt influenced by her interest in old movies, Maeve decided she wanted to learn to tap dance and enrolled in a class in Covent Garden (as Orla does in *A Week in Winter*). She had a vision of herself dancing up a staircase like Ginger Rogers in *Swing Time*.

Maeve had always been a good dancer and she and Gordon attended the class twice a week with a group of friends. It was a serious commitment, involving practice at home to a record and the purchase of proper shoes. Not everyone kept it up, but Maeve and Gordon did.

✾

No doubt one of the reasons it was felt that publishers would be attracted to Maeve as a good long-term prospect was that her writing was already attracting interest from the Abbey Theatre in Dublin.

On 13 June 1975, Joe Dowling, Director of the Peacock Theatre, the small studio theatre below the foyer of the Abbey Theatre in Dublin, wrote on behalf of the National Theatre Society that he was looking for plays. 'I feel sure that with your splendid writing style and your consummate ear for dialogue, you could have a great contribution to make to the theatre.' He'd read her *Irish Times* pieces and was a great admirer of her work 'both as a reporter and as a witty and compassionate columnist'.

By the end of the month Maeve had replied to say that she was interested and suggested a play set in a classroom in an Irish convent school, with the action centred on three teachers whose lives are exposed by a devious schoolgirl. Dowling liked the idea, particularly as 'it would give a few parts for our young actresses, which would be a welcome change'.

Maeve delivered the script of *End of Term* at some point in the first half of November and heard nothing from Dowling until midway through the following January, 1976, when he wrote: 'I'm sure you are wondering what has happened to your play which you sent me in November.'

The script reviews had not been good. The problem seems to have been one of trying to pack too much into so short a play, too many characters and too much action. Of the three main plot elements – a blackmail attempt on a teacher by the devious schoolgirl, the reaction of the teacher and a love angle between them – it was felt that the first two alone would suffice. The reader's report described it as 'a rough and hurried first draft'.

In 1976 Maeve was only just beginning to progress from real-people journalism to fictional characterisation. *End of Term* was a huge learning curve. Particularly helpful was the award-winning playwright Hugh Leonard,[72] who lived in Dalkey.

Leonard was acting as Editor at the Abbey at this time and advised Maeve about writing dialogue for a modern play, pointing out the need for realism. Instead of having her characters make long speeches (as had been the way in Shakespeare's day), he suggested she look around at what actually happens. They were having lunch together at the time in a Dublin restaurant. Maeve looked around the room and saw at once that people don't wait respectfully to hear another person out, they interrupt and engage with them and there are a lot of unfinished sentences.

On 10 August 1976, Martin Fahey, Secretary of the Abbey Theatre, wrote to her with a contract. On signature of it she would receive £40.

Meanwhile producer Louis Lentin had read Maeve's story 'Death in Kilburn' in the *Irish Times* about the Irish bigamist, and commissioned a screenplay based on it, which she would call *Deeply Regretted By*.

Finally, on 12 December, *End of Term* – her first play – was produced for the Peacock stage of the Abbey Theatre.

Maeve was terrified before the opening night. A letter from Gordon shows just how much she needed reassurance. He advises her to regret nothing. Not being used to the gestation process of theatre or book publication, only to the instant turnaround of newspaper publishing, Maeve had hated the whole process – eighteen months from initial contact to the play opening to the public. There had been what seemed to her huge hassle. Was it worthwhile? Gordon urges her to wait and see how she feels afterwards, to be cool and not to make an instant decision to stick in future to her plans, which clearly now include novels as well as short stories. He advises her on the other hand not to appear too over-grateful that the Abbey has done the play at all. They are professionals in the business of putting on good theatre.

It is a wonderful letter, full of confidence and good advice. It puts Maeve in the driving seat. It is *her* work that all the fuss is about. He and she are too close to make a judgement about it, he advises, but he is sure that it will be a great success, and promises to come and get her when the Garda find her walking by the Liffey muttering, 'Nine out of ten – see me...'

He followed it up with a first-night telegram in the form of an end-of-term school report for a pupil called Maeve at St Thespis School. Every subject listed has a famous teacher appended who makes an appropriate comment. For example, for Drama the teacher is one W. Shakespeare, for Literature it is Jane Austen, and so on.

Very aptly, the last subject is simply 'Life', and the teacher is Jean-Paul Sartre, who comments, 'She knows the meaning of it.'

In the event, the reviews were mixed, but welcoming of a new talent. Notably, there was criticism of the plot. What they expected from Maeve was less plot and more relationships and feelings. Wrote Con Houlihan of the *Evening Press*, 'Alas Maeve

Binchy has not enough faith in her own talents and decides that her play must have a plot … Credibility so triumphantly achieved is thrown to the winds.' Dubliners, readers of the *Irish Times*, even those in the rival office of the *Irish Press*, already knew what Maeve was about and wanted her to have confidence in her particular talents. They would not have to wait long.

Things were moving forward well. Maeve had two plays under her belt and a collection of short stories, and was enjoying no small reputation on the *Irish Times*. Gordon now described himself as a writer and was working on a book about Amy Johnson, *Queen of the Air*. Both *The King of Quizzical Island* and Maeve's *Central Line* were due to appear in 1978 – along with the sixth volume of Daniel A. Binchy's *Corpus Iuris Hibernici*, of course.

With a year until publication and everything poised for lift-off, Gordon asked Maeve for her hand in marriage, a move that she later said consigned Myles McSwiney's suggestion that she join him on the L&H committee at UCD almost twenty years earlier to second place among invitations from men that had thrilled her! The only pity was that neither Gordon's parents nor Maeve's had survived to see the day.

So much had been said about fate and a love that is meant to be. William and Maureen had set the benchmark with their chance meeting in Ballybunion, but it all came round again with Maeve and Gordon, who had met by chance and made a match not between two families at war, like Shakespeare's star-crossed lovers, but between two nations at war, Ireland and England. Resolution was a topical theme at the time, for there had been a series of 'peace rallies' the previous summer and famously two Irish women, Mairéad Corrigan and Betty Williams, had formed the Community of Peace People, for which they were awarded the Nobel Peace Prize.

The wedding between Maeve and Gordon, set for 29 January 1977, was to be undertaken with minimum fuss in London, rather than in Ireland, where Belfast was in lockdown and Dublin the scene of the assassination of British Ambassador Christopher Ewart Biggs and his secretary Judith Cook the previous July. The reception would be held at an Irish hotel, like Olive's in 'Pimlico', a story Maeve was writing for the *Victoria Line* collection (which had now been signed up too, so high were the hopes for *Central Line*) – a hotel where at Christmas you got 'the Pope's Blessing in the morning and the Queen's speech in the afternoon – a combination of what was best about both cultures', as she wrote. Adrian Henri, principal among the Liverpool beat poets, who had a poetry band called the Liverpool Scene and wrote a lot about love, composed a poem especially for the occasion.

Afterwards, the plan was to make a fast getaway to Australia, followed by a very leisurely return, a period when Maeve would work their passage with commissions both from the *Irish Times* and from other newspapers along the way.

Gordon was forty-four, Maeve thirty-seven when they tied the knot at Hammersmith Register Office, travelling from ceremony to reception in a horse-drawn carriage. Thereafter they flew to Hillydale in the Dandenong mountains, near Melbourne, Australia, where they honeymooned at the house of Joe and Roni Greenberg.

Joe, until a short time before an art director for the London-based advertising company Waseys, had met Maeve through the photographer Liam White, who knew her well and was a firm friend. The Greenbergs had an unusual collection of African fertility masks, which seemed an appropriate enough setting for the start of the couple's life together as man and wife.

Almost immediately, Maeve arranged to write for the Australian newspaper *The Age*. She also wrote regular reports from Australia to the *Irish Times* and then drifted seamlessly into a memorable series called 'On the Beaches', enjoying some of the choice beaches of the world. Responding to one such article, a besotted reader wrote:

I disagree with your non-smoking correspondent, Mrs Courtney. I *like* the photograph of Miss Binchy lighting a cigarette. In fact I like all your photographs of her whatever she's doing. I particularly liked the one in today's issue of her lying on the beach with no clothes on, wasn't she? – Yours, etc.

EIGHT

NOVELIST

Maeve was thirty-eight when she discovered she couldn't have children. She and Gordon were bitterly disappointed, but as time went on they remained so occupied with writing their books that some friends of theirs believed at first that they were childless by choice, which wasn't so.

She approached the problem as she approached everything else that beset her in life: positively and pragmatically. The facts were that fertility treatment just wasn't good in the late 1970s and adoption wasn't possible after forty.

She rehearsed the whole panoply of problems attached to childless marriage in her novels. In *The Copper Beech*, the Kellys discover that it isn't easy to be a childless woman in a small town; Nora Kelly 'had been aware of the sideways glances for some time'. That God gave more and more children to the Brennans and the Dunnes when they couldn't feed or care for them while he passed Nora by was further evidence, she thought, that God wasn't operating in the world. But at the same time, Nora hears that childless couples do often grow very close to one another

– there being no distractions of family. The disappointment unites them into a shared lifestyle, something which Maeve and Gordon had already.

But in *Tara Road* when Hilary and Martin can't have children their marriage becomes sexless, while in *Quentins*, Brenda Brennan (co-owner of the restaurant Quentins, around which much of the action revolves) is childless and directs her maternal impulse into her work. Brenda mothers her clientele, who look to her for advice. Like Maeve in all her stories, Brenda brings her 'children' from disillusionment to self-belief and fulfilment in the end.

Traditionally the Irish mother, like Ria Lynch in *Tara Road*, 'passed on her standards and values to the next generation'. Maeve never had the chance to be a mother, but instead sat with her husband in the room where they worked and passed on her standards and values in her fictional parables to her family of readers.

There would soon be a publishing family too, one to which she was just as loyal. The sons and daughters of friends and family became Maeve's surrogate children. Maeve used to love them especially around the age of fourteen and fifteen, when she could play the role of ageing *enfant terrible* and do outrageous things with them, like taking them to movies for which they were underage.

But she could be schoolmarmish, too, insisting on a curfew and no smoking and spending half an hour every evening doing cocktails and scrapbooks – every evening they had to come up with a new idea for a non-alcoholic cocktail and make it in an electric cocktail maker which Maeve had, and then fill in a scrapbook of what they had done during the day. It was torture that she knew would give form to the whole experience – making them visit places and do things that they knew they would have to put into the scrapbook in the evening.

When these surrogate children grew up and married and had their own children, she asked them for photographs of her honorary grandchildren and made a picture collage. Mary Kenny remembered Maeve saying to her that she only ever wanted two things in life: 'to succeed in her work and be happily married. She achieved both of those aims abundantly.' But it seemed to her that Maeve might have missed having grandchildren more even than children. When she asked for a picture of Mary Kenny's, Maeve quoted Gore Vidal's famous saying, 'Never have children, only grandchildren.'

It is a fact, a coincidence perhaps, possibly more than that, that three female novelists who have been very successful in recent times (Maeve Binchy, Catherine Cookson and Barbara Taylor Bradford, their combined sales more than 250 million) were all childless. Cookson had a terrible time with it, fighting the temptation to snatch babies from prams and ending up in an asylum for a while, as she revealed in her autobiography. Taylor Bradford was deeply disappointed, but saw that she could never have written as many books or spent so much time writing had she had children hanging on her apron strings, the argument behind Cyril Connolly's point that 'there is no more sombre enemy of good art than the pram in the hall'.

For Cookson, her books *were* her children – she saw them

like that and she couldn't stop having them – she birthed more than 100 of them! It was a bit like that for Maeve and Gordon, not in terms of quantity, but they always worked at them together, in the same room, producing their fictional 'babies', conceiving them, nurturing them, even allowing each other to criticise the way they were nursing them, all the way through gestation to birth. And it must have been especially rewarding that one of them was all the time turning out books for other people's children.

Among the obituaries for Maeve, few omitted to mention that she was childless. An article in the *Daily Telegraph* seemed to suggest that female writers who didn't have children were missing a fundamental female experience of love which was bound ultimately to limit them as writers – a provocative point that was directed at Maeve but not backed up with reference to her work. There is only one instance where possibly the argument could be engaged, in *The Glass Lake* when Helen learns that her young daughter Kit burned the note that she left to explain why she has left the family home. Helen blames her in a way that seems to question her maternal qualities. But perhaps life is more complicated than many of us like to imagine.

Insightful of Maeve's surrogate maternal qualities is the reason she gave for showering blessings on her friends who shared their children with her: they didn't just revel in their children's successes with her, they shared their failures and problems too – the bad as well as the good. In that, she found an intimacy with the families that surpassed the expectations of everyone involved.

You can't truly love someone without the bad bits. What Maeve was describing was the unconditional love of motherhood, and is that not more powerfully conceived when it is so, as in her case, without hormonal assistance?

After their return from the extended honeymoon, *Central Line*, dedicated (like every one of Maeve's books) 'To Gordon with all my love', was published by Quartet, and *Deeply Regretted By*, the classic Irish émigré tale written by Maeve in 1976, was broadcast by RTÉ Television as part of its 'Thursday Playdate' series on 28 December. The play won a prize at the Prague Television Festival and two Jacob's Awards. In September 1979, rehearsals began for Maeve's third play, *Half-Promised Land*, which opened at the Abbey in October. The story was based on her experiences at Kibbutz Zikim in 1963.

Yet Maeve wasn't happy that drama was really her medium. Readers of her novels know that the very value of her fiction is that she explores her characters' emotional lives without any of the time constraints that drama placed on her – some of her books extend beyond 600 pages.

She once said, 'Plays don't come easy to me because I don't have a visual imagination.'[73] The different skills required were shown even more obviously when her work was scripted for film. When she saw the film script for *Circle of Friends* (1995) she said she had to lie down in a darkened room. It was only ninety-one pages, while the book was 551! She was sure that they must have emasculated the characters, who spoke mainly one-liners in the script. When she saw the film, however, she was thrilled to see that the actors expressed visually much of what she had written in the novel, and saw clearly just how different the media of book and film are.

The aptly entitled *Half-Promised Land* premiered at the Abbey Theatre on 11 October 1979. It tells of two Irish school-teachers who leave the convent school where they work to holiday in a kibbutz in the Negev Desert. The two women handle their newfound freedom in different ways. Sheila is a dedicated worker who finds herself forced to compromise her Catholic moral principles after a woman seeks her support to get an abortion. Meanwhile man-hungry Una forms a romantic attachment with an aggressive young Islamic soldier stationed at the kibbutz. Typically, Maeve uses humour to avoid head-on involvement with the reality of her relationship with her man back in 1963. Neither Una nor the soldier understands a word of the other's language – but there's little time for talk anyway...

Had Maeve traded the telling political and emotional burden of the relationship for laughs from the audience? Perhaps there had been compromise. Script editor Sean McCarthy discussed in detail what he thought was wrong with the first draft and locked her in a dressing room in the theatre until she got it right. Two hours later, theatre administrator Douglas Kennedy released her and discovered that she had long ago finished the task, was writing her column for the *Irish Times* and could use a double gin and tonic, which he went straight away to fetch. Maeve was never one to fight her ground with editors. She was already on to the next project.

Five weeks later the play 'opened to terrible reviews and sell-out business', according to Kennedy. 'Though Maeve was stoic about the largely negative critical response, she did admit to me some time later that it hurt.'[74]

Kennedy, today a novelist of renown, became friends with Maeve and benefited from her advice about failure, the taste of which every artist knows. He had left his job at the Abbey, had a less than successful experience with his first book and lost his column on the *Irish Times*. She took him to lunch and asked him, 'What next?' The only thing is to keep working, she said. Move on and whatever you do, don't let a hostile reviewer know that they've got to you.

Kennedy went on to give Maeve one of her great journalistic coups. The year after *Half-Promised Land* he managed to get the San Quentin Drama Workshop to perform Samuel Beckett's *Krapp's Last Tape* and *Endgame* at the Abbey with Beckett himself directing. But Beckett would rehearse only in London and on the condition he didn't have to do any press interviews.

Naturally when Kennedy went to London for rehearsals he sought out Maeve, who invited him to dinner and asked whether he could engineer a seat for her in rehearsal. He said it was unlikely, but to his amazement Beckett agreed, so long as she accepted that there would be no interview.

Samuel Beckett (1906–89) had been awarded the Nobel Prize in 1969 and was the most influential playwright alive. His interest in French existentialist literature, especially Camus, coincided with Maeve's. 'To anyone who can face the facts of human existence and not worry about some received dogma being thrown into question, Beckett is hugely enjoyable,' wrote John Calder.[75] As the author of *Waiting for Godot*, *Endgame* and *Krapp's Last*

Tape, he was singly one of the most interesting men in world theatre, had influenced Pinter, Fugard and Stoppard and would work with Ted Hughes. There was, also, as with James Joyce, a local frisson, because of Beckett being brought up in Foxrock, by Dalkey. Maeve may not have agreed with his bleak outlook on human existence, but to say that she was exhilarated at the prospect of meeting him was an understatement.

Come the day, Maeve sat in the auditorium watching the rehearsal, her 'pen darting across her reporter's pad'. Then, during a coffee break, Beckett, to her surprise, approached her, asked if she was the journalist from the *Irish Times*, and started chatting with her about Dublin. Kennedy calculates that they spoke for about seven minutes, 'a huge conversation' for Beckett to have with a journalist. During those precious minutes Maeve more or less destroyed the pencil in her hands in her efforts to stop herself writing anything down, which she knew would mark the end of the conversation. But when Beckett returned to the actors she sat down and scribbled manically for ten solid minutes, and when Kennedy saw the article in the *Irish Times*, the first interview with Beckett in an Irish newspaper for decades, Maeve, he said, had managed to regurgitate everything, verbatim, that he had heard Beckett say to her.

�֎

In the same year, when on a visit to Dalkey, Maeve spotted a little Georgian cottage for sale which fronted onto the road, and she and Gordon fell in love with it. An estate agency might call it 'unpretentious' or possibly 'bijou', but that says nothing about its singular architectural beauty, with its decorative ridge-work, swirling stone masonry over Georgian brickwork, and bold bay windows onto the street.

The cottage was already on Maeve's radar. When she and her father used to walk that way into town in the 1960s he would always say, 'Who in their sane senses would call their house Pollyvilla?' And Maeve would just as surely reply that the man who built it (and Annavilla next door) had two daughters, one called Polly, the other Anna, and that when the two cottages were built the builders' filling agent Polyfilla had yet to be invented.

Interestingly, the 1957 edition of *Thom's Street Directory of Ireland* states that the cottage, at that time owned by one John Fahey, was actually named Polly*ville*, which, so long as that is not a printer's error, means that somebody did rename it Pollyvilla within the era of Polyfilla. Perhaps Maeve would have returned it to the French original had she known!

The cottage consisted of a sitting room, dining room, kitchen and bathroom downstairs, and one bedroom upstairs. As a bolt-hole in Dublin, it was perfect. It would be a little while yet before she and Gordon moved there altogether.

By this time Anna Cooper, Maeve's agent, had left the John Johnson Agency to join Mother Teresa to become a nun and left behind her a list of editors who had expressed interest should Maeve ever look like writing a novel. When, subsequently, agency boss Andrew Hewson invited Christine Green, who was working for the literary publisher Faber & Faber, to take Anna's place, she met Maeve and discovered that while she was enjoying writing short stories, a novel was indeed very much on the cards, and Green rang the first name on that list.

Rosemary (Rosie) de Courcy worked for a company called Macdonald, which was engaged in publishing highly commercial hardbacks and paperbacks through its Futura imprint, all part of BPCC, the publishing and printing group run by the rogue entrepreneur Robert Maxwell, who would commit suicide in 1991 after plundering the *Daily Mirror* newspaper's pension fund.

Rosie had in 1977 published *The Thorn Birds*, one of the most successful novels of any era and the first by the Australian writer Colleen McCullough (who would become a friend of Maeve). Rosie recalls:

I put to Maeve an idea about a love story set in Northern Ireland. Quite rightly she dismissed this as not being up her street, but said that what she would like to write was a novel about best friends who underneath it all hated each other and ended up destroying one another. She always said that the fact that I immediately 'got' this paradoxical dynamic between girls convinced her that she wanted me to be her publisher.

That Maeve should suggest such a scenario may be thought a clue as to what had contributed to her own feelings of betrayal. But perhaps it is a common experience among girls, for it married with Rosie's own experience.

One of the reasons that Maeve and I bonded so immediately was that on the day we first met, I told her the story of my best childhood friend. Our mothers were best friends and this child was an intensely jealous bully. Everything I had, she wanted, including my life, my mother and – eventually – my first real boyfriend.

She and Maeve clicked instantly and became close friends.

She once told me that she caught sight of the pair of us reflected in a shop window and thought how strange it was that two such superficially different women, separated by more than a decade in age, should have become so close. I told her the truth – which was that I never saw any differences between us at all. We could have talked all day and all night and all the next day, without drawing breath. And we gave just that our very best shot – over copious glasses of wine. Mon Plaisir once asked us very politely if they could evict us just for an hour, while they set the tables for dinner. It was 6 p.m. and we had been there since lunchtime. We staggered off to a greasy spoon cafe and half-heartedly tried to sober up with coffee, before resuming at Mon Plaisir!

The two women had in common an attractive combination of success and vulnerability but they discussed this no more than they did Rosie's Irish side of the family. It seemed important to Maeve that Rosie was completely English. Perhaps no surprise; Maeve was thinking and writing about the Irish girl

Aisling's relationship with the English girl Elizabeth White when she and Rosie first became close. On the strength of Maeve's first synopsis Rosie agreed with Chris Green a £5,000 advance against royalties for UK hardcover and paperback rights for the novel, to be called *Light a Penny Candle*. The deal was not a particularly generous one at the time, but everything had fallen neatly into place and a contract was drawn.

Eventually, the part of the £5,000 advance due on signature of the contract, probably one third of it, arrived at Green's office. Green banked it and sent Maeve the amount less her commission. The sum of money that Maeve received at this point will have been in the region of £1,500. Not a lot, but she and Gordon had fallen a little behind with the mortgage payments on Pollyvilla and it was most welcome. Not only that, it was the first money earned by Maeve for her first novel.

When the cheque arrived, she and Gordon put it in pride of place on the mantelpiece at home in Hofland Street, danced round it, photographed it, kissed it, and celebrated the life out of it. The next day they came downstairs to discover the cheque was missing. They had lost the cheque for *Light a Penny Candle* on the day they received it!

They tore the house apart in search of it and eventually it was found. But the loss of it – temporary or permanent – wouldn't have mattered a jot: shortly afterwards they were asked to return it.

Anthony Cheetham, an old Etonian with an editorial background in mass-market paperbacks and entrepreneurial flair, was the force behind Macdonald and had founded the paperback imprint Futura for them, but had come to the conclusion that working for Maxwell was intolerable and made a move to set up his own publishing company with one or two other colleagues.

The new company was to be named Century. Rosie, who had risen from secretary to editor under Anthony's personal patronage and, indeed, become his wife, was naturally to be a part of this and they wanted Maeve to come with them.

'Anthony suggested that I should ask Maxwell if I could take two authors with me, but not to go for the obvious bestsellers,' said Rosie.

> Who should I ask for? I wondered. 'Ask for Eva Ibbotson (a brilliant children's writer who had turned her hand to historical fiction) and Maeve Binchy,' said Anthony. Maxwell had heard of neither author, so immediately gave me permission to approach their agents about transferring their contracts to the new venture.

In the light of this new state of affairs, Maeve was advised to cancel the contract with Macdonald, repay the advance and follow Anthony and Rosie to Century. *Light a Penny Candle* would lead the new list, which alone would be enough to get everyone jumping up and down about Rosie's great new signing. Most important, it would mean that Rosie would remain her editor. Maeve remained characteristically loyal to Anthony and Rosie throughout, moving with the duo after they ceded control of the company to the mighty US publisher Random House and started up again as Orion Publishing. She was always loyal and generous to those who helped her, staying with her new agent Chris Green after she left the John Johnson Agency and set up on her own, too, and moving twice with her American publisher and editor, Carole Baron.

So indispensable did Rosie become that 'Maeve and Chris decided that ever after the *Light a Penny Candle* contract, they would insist on having an "editor clause" in her contracts,' Rosie revealed. 'This stated that if I left the company, Maeve would have the right to cancel the contract and follow me.'

So began a relationship between Maeve, Rosie and Anthony that would continue for years, during which Century Publishing became the publishing sensation of Margaret Thatcher's making-it-happen Britain.

Green, meanwhile, turned her attention to her author, for whom she had very high hopes. She realised that Maeve needed a system of working that would enable her to write the novel and at the same time continue as a journalist for the *Irish Times*, which Maeve both needed and wanted to do.

Things had been coming to a head even before the contract for the first novel. Since *Central Line*'s publication in 1978, Maeve had had increasingly heavy duties both to promote the book and write new stories for *Victoria Line*, which was published in 1980. So divided were her priorities between the book world and journalism that in the run-up to Margaret Thatcher's election in May 1979, when she should have been turning in fascinating feature material about the possibility of the first female Prime Minister of Great Britain, she was instead sneaking off to do book tours and fobbing off the editor of the *Irish Times* with reassurances that Thatcher's would be a long campaign with plenty of time to cover it.

Maeve was adamant that she didn't want to stop writing for the *Times* and in any case £5,000 was not enough to secure her services full time on the novel. The plan was to carry on with her job and write the novel in short bursts. She would sit down every Friday afternoon when everyone else was in the pub and work on the manuscript until late afternoon on Sunday, or until 5,000 words were written.

Through the week she would get up at 5.12 a.m., having worked out that it took her eighteen minutes to get washed, dressed and make a cup of coffee, so she'd be at the typewriter at 5.30, work on the novel for three hours and then head off to the *Irish Times* office in Fleet Street.

Sacrosanct was the Monday morning deadline when she would put the 5,000 words in a taxi and send it to her agent. Gordon read each instalment and if Maeve descended into despair at any point he pulled her round.

Light a Penny Candle took a year to write but what immediately made it all worthwhile was the publishers' response. They were bowled over by it, which is not to say that it didn't cause some surprise. 'On the basis of the synopsis, I had been expecting a short, rather gloomy novel about best friends destroying each other,' Rosie told me. 'What I got was a great big heartwarming saga about best friends who stick up for each other through thick and thin – even suspected murder. That was when I knew I had something truly special on my hands.'

As soon as the contract was dry, Maeve said later, the synopsis which had earned her the contract had been torn up and she wrote the novel we all read.[76] Perhaps it wasn't in her nature to write so negative and destructive a story as had first been mooted. If it had had a real precedent then this may well have been the case. She told Donal O'Donoghue in 2010 that she had once tried to write a novel about revenge and found she couldn't. It was the only book she was never able to finish. This, after all, is the girl who at school never had anything bad to say about anybody. 'I couldn't get into the mind of the person who was plotting vengeance,' she said.

Maeve had much more important things to consider. Yes, like the short stories, her first novel would be about females, and yes, it would be about feelings and emotions, and it would tackle the social issues she'd been writing about in her journalism, many of which concerned Ireland as it changed from a God-fearing society into a secular one. But more than this, she wanted to see whether she could deliver the essence of who she had become, the stuff she'd been working on since that day on the bench on St Stephen's Green. It was no coincidence that the central character was called 'Aisling' (the name of the Merriman convention), Maeve's wild, free, all-seeing, intuitive self, fiercely passionate, capable of cutting through the rational restraints of everyday thinking, yet with a highly sensible attitude, clever, but not intellectual, a spirit whose speciality is feeling and emotion – laughing, really – and who is Irish to the core. This is Aisling O'Connor with the wild red hair in the novel, whose spirit we also detect in Aisling's mother Eileen and in Maeve's real mother Maureen, and in the side of Maeve which engaged freely with the otherworldly feminine mystique of Ireland itself.

Rosie predicted correctly that publication would make Maeve a millionaire. Everyone, including, most importantly, Century's marketing executive, Susan Lamb, was completely hooked on the story, although Maeve told her great friend Mary Kenny that there had been some misgivings that it was completely devoid of explicit sex.

Sex was an especially important ingredient in paperback fiction at this time. Anthony Cheetham's Futura had come to prominence partly on the back of a category of historical fiction pioneered by Avon, an American paperback publisher, where an editor called Nancy Coffey had been releasing passionate historical novels with explicit sex scenes. Known in the trade on both sides of the Atlantic as 'bodice-rippers', these were huge door-stopping books with a clear-cut editorial formula, which purportedly included a bedroom scene every nineteen pages. It led to writers such as Kathleen Woodiwiss (*The Flame & the Flower*, 1972) and Rosemary Rogers (*Sweet Savage Love*, 1974) among many others, becoming millionaires overnight.

These authors had a huge impact on the marketing of women's paperback fiction and, at Futura, Rosie had made her name as a white-hot mass-market editor after selling a series of home-grown bodice-rippers back across the Atlantic for hundreds of thousands of dollars.

Then along came Maeve with a novel with no explicit sex scenes at all! After publication she must have become sick of having to explain why. 'There's a huge interest in sex and writing about it very graphically,' Maeve told the *Daily Mail*. 'But I am not going to do it – not because I'm a Holy Joe, far from it. Not because I'm very moral, far from that. But because I'm afraid I'll get it wrong.' Nothing could have been more disarming. 'I've never been to an orgy,' she said, 'and I wouldn't know where legs should be and arms should be.'

Her personal sex life, much to her chagrin, she said, had not been as colourful as she would have liked.[77] But there is no doubt that Maeve was a hot-blooded, passionate woman who liked to use what she claimed was her lack of experience in lovemaking to amuse her friends. One time she and her drinking pals on Dublin's Fleet Street came up with the idea of writing a sex manual to make them some quick money, with each of them writing a chapter. Maeve was the only one to research hers; the others treated it as a boozy joke. But Maeve had the last laugh. She turned the situation into a brilliantly funny, sad and telling short story called 'Tottenham Court Road', which appeared in the *Central Line* collection.

Julia is a 29-year-old virgin who at last has a boyfriend, Michael, who wants to sleep with her. A very nervous Julia goes in search of a book to teach her what to do in bed and, having browsed the shelves in a porn shop in Tottenham Court Road, discovers that there is nothing specifically dedicated to 29-year-old virgins. People like her must be an embarrassment to society, she concludes.

Julia can't possibly tell her would-be lover that she is a virgin at twenty-nine and expect respect and tenderness. She must have a book which will make up for ten years' lack of experience in a few short hours. Michael is waiting, after all.

She needs to know whether he will expect her to undress him or whether she should strip off, lie down on the bed and wait for him. She needs detailed information about what to do with her pelvis, whether to go up and down or round and round. She would also like to know whether, because she has been a virgin so long, she might face some medical difficulty or associated consequences in getting it on at all.

Unable to find what she wants, Julia seeks the advice of the manager of the store. She says she's looking for a manual of instruction for a niece. The manager says they don't have anything quite like that and suggests that perhaps Julia would do better to have a talk with her niece. Julia answers that she can't advise her niece because she doesn't know anything about sex, adding (under her breath) 'I'm a nun.'

What the press had missed, of course, was that *Light a Penny Candle* was set in the 1950s. Maeve once said that she was thrilled by an editor's observation that in her books everybody is obsessed with sex but nobody ever actually has any, 'because I knew that I had got the 1950s right!' It was Oliver J. Flanagan, an Irish Fine Gael politician, who famously claimed that 'there was no sex in Ireland before television' – and the first TV station did not arrive until the early 1960s.

Century was already of the opinion that Maeve was unique and inimitable. Forget bodice-rippers, she was in a genre of her own. Maeve couldn't believe they were so excited about her work and kept examining the manuscript, wondering what it was that was so good.

But that only lasted a short while before she got on with the stories that became *The Lilac Bus* (1984), a clever idea – fictional case histories now – about a group of people whose lives are linked by a small schoolhouse in the little village of Shancarrig. They go up to work in Dublin during the week and then return to the country on a Friday. Their romances, secrets, betrayals and triumphs are the meat of each character's story. In 1990 it would become a ninety-minute television film.

Meanwhile, Anthony Cheetham, with no paperback imprint of his own at Century, planned to cover his investment in their new author by auctioning paperback rights in *Light a Penny Candle* to an outside publisher.

Maeve had asked whether she could attend the auction before it was explained to her that it wasn't like what went on at Sotheby's; it would be conducted by Anthony over the telephone after a multiple submission to selected paperback companies. On the day, she was so excited that she went out and looked for something to distract her and chanced on a shop offering ear piercing. She'd been afraid of having her ears pierced for years so thought that would be the ideal thing to stop her thinking about the auction.

Back home and with studs in her ears, the phone rang. It was Anthony, who asked whether she was sitting down. Maeve lied and said she was. Anthony knew she wasn't and commanded her to sit down. The deal had been done, he told her. Coronet, the paperback arm of Hodder & Stoughton, had bought UK and Commonwealth paperback rights in *Light a Penny Candle* for £52,000, the highest sum ever paid for a first novel commissioned by a British publisher.

Maeve asked ever so quietly, 'Excuse me, but do I get that, or do you?' Cheetham said that he was very much afraid that it was hers.

Light a Penny Candle was published by Century in 1982. It entered the Top 10 immediately and remained there for fifty-three weeks.

Gordon, meanwhile, had kept himself busy. Three of his books were published in the same year: *The Book of Theatre Quotes: Notes, Quotes & Anecdotes* came from Angus & Robertson, and two children's books from Cambridge University Press – *The Fastest Snail in the World* and *Tiddle and the Time Machine*, both illustrated by Alan Burton.

In celebration of his wife's bestseller status, he bought two garden chairs and a bottle of champagne and they sat in the garden together and drank it. That was as mad as they got.

No, Maeve told the press, she didn't think that the money would change her. (She had only just found herself. She wasn't about to reinvent who she was now.) As ever larger sums of money accrued she was generous to a number of charities, such as Arthritis Ireland, Alice Leahy's Trust (for the homeless), Amnesty International, the Hospice Foundation, Friends of the Elderly and Guide Dogs for the Blind, but first she was almost recklessly generous to her friends. A journalist colleague reported that when Maeve received the money for the paperback rights in *Light a Penny Candle*, she gave much of it to family, friends and colleagues, in his case enough to pay his mortgage for a month.

Publishers like authors who are also journalists because very often their journalist friends will review their books. But press reviews were never the mainstay of the marketing of Maeve. She was so successful so fast that perhaps a little envy crept in. Certainly she suffered a plethora of articles about how rich she had become and where she stood in the wealth stakes, rather than anything much being written about her work. 'Last year, she earned £1.4 million, more than Kate Moss and Naomi Campbell,' claimed one paper. She couldn't understand why it should be of interest to anyone that Maeve Binchy was one of the richest women in Britain.

In a review in the *Irish Times* in September 1994 Maeve tore into a biography of Catherine Cookson for its 'endless discussion of advances received and appearances in bestseller lists'.[78] This sort of thing was to her 'meaningless', even demeaning.

She was herself well read, in the French language as well as in English, and thought nothing of accepting an invitation to be interviewed in French on Bernard Pivot's highly cerebral arts programme, *Apostrophes*. Suddenly they had asked her, as only the French would, 'Madame, what is your philosophy of life?' She sensed impending confusion but answered spontaneously in French, 'I think that you've got to play the hand that you're dealt and stop wishing for another hand.' It was the first occasion she had coined a phrase which she would use time and again to describe how she had taken control of her life after her moment of truth at UCD. She looked up nervously to see how they took it and thankfully they were all nodding sagely in agreement. Afterwards, quite rightly, she applauded herself and said 'That's the kind of motif I bring to the books – that people take charge of their own lives.'

But precious, flapping literary London couldn't even be bothered to read her, and so she eschewed them, just as she did discussions about how much money she was worth.

Of course, there are snobs everywhere and Maeve never lost her sense of humour over it. One of her favourite moments, as an avid fan of the UK TV soap opera *Coronation Street* for many years, was an episode when Ken Barlow's mother-in-law, Blanche, presiding over a row between Ken and his partner Deirdre, suddenly says, 'Well, you can talk about literary life, I'm going to knock them down with my Maeve Binchy.' Blanche then bequeaths all her Maeve Binchy books to Ken, whose face contorts in horror when he hears the news.

Maeve watched flabbergasted. She thought she was having one of those crazy moments you hear about when people on the verge of going mad think the television is talking to them. And then she laughed 'til the tears ran down her face.

If being a real person in someone else's fiction appealed to Maeve's sense of the absurd, in 2005 she went one better by stepping into her own fictional world, making an appearance in a film of her novel *Tara Road*. Alert viewers will spot Maeve making a cameo appearance seated at the end of the bar after the scene when Ria takes a job at the cashier's counter at Colm's restaurant.

One significant reason behind Maeve's success was her

talent for promoting her books in front of an audience – she was a great speaker. So hard did she publicise her books for her publisher that Chris Green likened her to a swan, a bird that conceals a great deal of activity beneath the surface. And Maeve did put in a lot of work: three-week publicity tours in the UK and for months at a time around the world, the signing sessions, meeting the booksellers, meeting her public, creating her own family of readers in country after country, year after year.

The upside of these tours for Maeve was the opportunity actually to meet this new family. After months staring at a typewriter and wondering whether the book she was writing was of any interest, she thought it was great to meet her readers.

What sort of readers were they? She claimed to have had a letter from one, saying, 'In case you're looking for a readership profile, I bought your book for myself, for my weasel-like old rip of a mother-in-law and my serpent's tooth hell-cat of a daughter.'[79]

Members of her new family would stand in line, sometimes for hours, to tell her how much they liked her stories. Typically, in defiance of the parable of the vineyard,[80] she gave those who'd been standing in line longest the most attention, but that was because she did really care.

Barbara Taylor Bradford, whose first novel, *A Woman of Substance*, was published in 1980 and became a massive international hit around the same time as *Light a Penny Candle*, was also out on the book promotion circuit with Maeve. She relates how they appeared at one venue together.

She was on first and I was on second. Well, I may as well have gone home. She had the audience in stitches. She said nothing about her novel at all, until the audience were picking themselves up from the floor at the end, when she said, 'Oh, and my first novel – *Light a Penny Candle* – is out this week.' She was brilliant. It was a performance that I and the other authors knew we couldn't possibly compete with.

Touring could take up as many as three months in a year and she could be quite a challenge to interviewers. John Corr of the *Philadelphia Inquirer* once had an appointment to interview Maeve at ten in the morning. When he arrived at her hotel suite she indicated the bottle of Jameson's Irish whiskey on a nearby table with a nod of her head and said, 'I suppose it's a bit early to offer you a taste of the Irish.'

Chris Green had sold hardcover rights in *Light a Penny Candle* to Viking for $200,000 in time for US publication in 1982, the same year as the novel appeared in the UK. But the American public was actually quite late to take Maeve to its heart.

Her second novel, *Echoes*, came out there in 1985, but neither of these was a *New York Times* bestseller until they appeared in paperback under the Dell imprint. The paperback publisher then bought hardcover and paperback rights in the books that followed, right up until *Tara Road* (1998). But while the paperback editions continued to be bestsellers, it wasn't until *Circle of Friends*, first published eight years after *Light a Penny Candle*, that Dell's associated hardcover imprint Delacorte gave Maeve her first American hardback bestseller.[81]

It is part of publishing mythology that this was engineered by the best possible piece of publicity Maeve could have hoped for. Barbara Bush, First Lady of the United States from 1989 to 1993, let it be known that she was an avid fan of all Maeve's books and invited her to lunch at the White House.

On the day, Maeve's concern was not so much what to wear but whether she would know when to leave. When everyone was asked what they would like to drink, she politely requested a white wine rather than her usual gin and suffered increasing agony as one by one the other guests ordered non-alcoholic drinks, while a whole bottle of wine was fetched for her.

Carole Baron, Maeve's longstanding editor in America, denies that Barbara Bush's approbation of her author was the reason why the book did so well, however, dismissing it as

a column item. Maeve was already a hardcover bestseller [by the time of the luncheon]. It was a fun fact, but did not make the book sales. *Circle of Friends* was a hardcover best-seller because we intentionally changed her publication date from fall to winter (less competition) and went right for the St Patrick's Day promotions.

She recalls the occasion when the Mayor of Chicago gave Maeve a float of her own at the annual St Patrick's Day parade. And how she stood up and spoke to the multitude on the first night of the celebrations and slayed them all with her wit – the perfect way to conquer whole countries in the international publishing game.

On this occasion, Maeve took family and friends to Chicago with her, Mary Maher among them. Maher remembers how Maeve took an airline stewardess aside during the flight from New York to Chicago. The woman was about to be married, but wasn't at all sure that it was either the right time or the right man. Maeve listened attentively and thoroughly dissected both the woman and her problem. As ever, this girl-to-girl situation saw her at her best. She wanted every detail of the situation, and advised the stewardess in uncompromising terms according to her philosophy of life. With champagne in hand, the conversation took the entire flight. Having arrived in Chicago unsuccessful, Maeve was so upset that the stewardess was still going to go ahead with her marriage to a man she didn't love that that night she fell out of her hotel bed and broke her nose and toe.

Wherever she went, people came to her with their problems and she loved nothing better than to lift them out of their self-pity and turn them back on themselves, to galvanise them into making their own push to find and grow into and have confidence in themselves and make the right decisions, as she had managed to do in her own life.

Always, in the end, it was Maeve's interest in people, women especially, and rigorous adherence to her existential principles, which enabled her to meet her purpose and confer real meaning on her existence.

Remaining a journalist, even when she didn't need the money, meant that Maeve could exercise her developing matriarchal role through the *Irish Times* as well as through the novels, which she did right through the 1990s, the decade which marked the start of a new column called 'Unasked for Advice'. It became one of the most popular items in the newspaper.

But the novels would be the more subtle avenue for social purpose. Her journalism had led to her fiction. Now, the fiction took up the mantle of her social journalism in a different way. The trouble with giving people advice in a column, she used to say, is that they rarely listen. With a fictional story you can reach people in a way that you cannot by telling them straight. 'Sometimes, seeing seventeen-year-olds in agonies of self-consciousness, I'd love to tell them. But they wouldn't believe me. Perhaps, instead, I put the message into my books.'[82]

'The secret of the universe is that we do have to take control of our own lives' remained her mantra in the novels as it was in her journalism and in her life. In the novels the fictional hero-ines are ordinary women who over the course of the story begin to play the hand that they have been dealt and, realising that no one is going to ride in over the hill and change things for them, stand up for themselves and come to discover, enhance and believe in their own self-worth – hard work on yourself is required, dressing up and imagining it will not be enough. 'The ugly duckling does not become a beautiful swan. She becomes a confident duck able to take charge of her own life and prob-lems,' as Maeve put it so many times.

There's something akin to Helen Fielding's Bridget Jones, who appeared five years after Benny in *Circle of Friends*, her lack of self-esteem arising from obsessively following the advice of women's style magazines, the very medium that provides the stereotype that Benny and Maeve (because of their size) cannot hope to live up to.

Millions of readers identified with the heroines who were in part the alter egos of their author, like Benny, Clare O'Brien, Signora O'Donoghue and Angela O'Hara, and felt included in Maeve's world. 'She never marginalised us,' Cristina Odone wrote in the *New Statesman*.

> She fought the conspiracy to make us, the female readers, feel hopelessly inadequate ... We do not have to measure up to impossible feats of sexual acrobatics or aspire to unattainable levels of emotional toughness ... Her writing aims to *include* us in her world, rather than tell us what to do from her superior perch.

Maeve's world *is* inclusive. Her world gives people the confidence to become their own person. She abjured those who would sell you a style to buy into, which was what consumerism, from the 1960s on, had been all about. Consumerism, feminism, even Catholicism in its damning of Protestants to everlasting Hell – all the 'isms' were in the business of forming a membership that excludes or marginalises individuals as outsiders.

The goldfish bowl communities in which she sets the early novels provide the close but also often repressed environments where all this is played out. The early novels – up to *The Glass Lake* in 1994 – are set in small, traditional Catholic-Irish communities such as Kilgarret, Castlebay, Knockglen, Shancarrig and Lough Glass. They take us back to the 1950s and 1960s and record what women felt in those communities at that time. The value of these communities is very much in the balance.

In *Firefly Summer*, in sleepy little Mountfern, there is a great sense of belonging. In the end, when O'Neill's hotel, which has threatened traditional life there, is razed to the ground, a strange roar of approval goes up as the building collapses, as if emanating from some deep unconscious well of the town's people. But the American O'Neill himself, who had returned to the land of his ancestors, returns home wondering how on earth he ever thought that this was his place and these his people. There is a sense of the Mountfern community's roots feeding it from a rich bed of tradition, but also tying it down and limiting it, isolating it from the wider world.

In *The Glass Lake*, Kit McMahon lives in a similar community, Lough Glass, and understands its shortcomings. Her mother would love to have worked in the pharmacy, but working is only for women who are widows or unmarried or whose husband is somehow incapable of holding down a job. It wasn't proper for her father to have let his wife work. Now times are changing. Kit's mother expects that in the following decade (the 1960s) there'll be nothing a woman cannot do.

Maeve describes tradition – but nothing is static, and change is in the air. In *The Glass Lake* the phrase 'career woman' is in current usage in London in 1953. And in the same decade in *Light a Penny Candle*, Elizabeth tells her father that women are interested in getting work outside the home and men are no longer interested in settling down like they were. Her father makes it clear, however, that he would rather she lived what he calls 'a proper life' and 'be looked after'.

Tackling the 1950s and 1960s at a distance, in the time in which she was writing, the whole drift of Maeve's thinking was away from the political and authoritarian and towards the individual and the family, and the community values on which Christianity had been based originally. Maeve said that there was a horror of premarital pregnancy verging on hysteria, because using contraception and having an abortion had been made mortal sins. Since then the law has taken on the difficult role of bringing Ireland out of this kind of authoritarian, punitive theocracy into the modern world, and both sides of every argument have been made forcefully.

Maeve's younger brother William, educated at UCD like her, Professor of Law at Trinity College, a barrister practising at the Irish Bar from 1968 to 1970, served as a research counsellor to the Irish Law Reform Commission and as special legal advisor on family law reform to the Department of Justice, which put him in an important position on a number of campaigns about issues on which his sister was writing. He came out in favour of the constitutional ban on abortion in 1983 and against the introduction of divorce in Ireland in 1986, and again in 1995, unsuccessfully, when the Fifteenth Amendment of the Constitution of Ireland repealed the constitutional prohibition of divorce.

So, Maeve found herself in the unusual position not of arguing against her brother but of airing situations for her individual heroines which could sway public opinion against his. Abortion rears its head more than once in the novels and in 'Shepherd's Bush', a story in *Central Line*, England's role as Ireland's abortionist first gets an airing.

May is quiet, shy, naïve and pregnant, a girl from Ireland on her way to London for an abortion. There are no legal abortions in Dublin and May knows no one who has had an illegal one there. England is less than an hour away. We are with her all the way – declaring to Customs that her reason for the visit is 'business', arriving at Shepherd's Bush, seated in the pub where she will meet her friend Celia, where a lot of the accents are Irish, and in the doctor's surgery with Dr Harris, who of course knows May only as a name on his register, but who gently questions her as to her reasons for the abortion. The avuncular Dr Harris is not just ticking boxes here and he charges May not a penny for his services, which is the first thing in the day that really worries her. She is used to paying the doctor at home. Harris tells her to send him a postcard of her beautiful country, which he used to visit with his wife before the Troubles started. So finally to the surgeon, Mr White, not any old surgeon, but well known, where May learns that the cost will be around £180 or £200, in cash. The whole thing is done expertly and efficiently with clinical care, but May's room-mate in the private hospital turns out to be a girl who avails herself of the abortionist's services on a regular basis. Almost flippant about what she is undertaking, she introduces herself as Hell.

A deeper cut at this issue, still dividing Ireland today, is taken a few years later in *Light a Penny Candle*, where Elizabeth, having long ago returned to London, has an abortion after she becomes pregnant by her regular boyfriend Johnny, whom she loves. She hasn't told happy-go-lucky Johnny that she is pregnant because she knows he won't want to see her any more. Instead she asks Aisling, who has been brought up to see abortion as a fast route to Hell, to guide her.

Aisling can't see why she won't tell Johnny and argues that even if he won't marry Elizabeth when he discovers she's pregnant he'll admire her all the more for having the baby. If, on the other hand, Elizabeth is decided on having an abortion, then it is a brave thing to do and again Johnny should be informed so that he can respond one way or the other. But to say nothing and try to make out nothing has happened when next they meet is wrong. No good will come of it.

Elizabeth senses that Aisling's advice, however kind and caring, is plagued by the fact that she still lives under the shadow of the Church and believes everything about souls and limbo and Heaven and it being a mortal sin to have an abortion; that however modern she tries to be, Aisling cannot escape from the attitudes which were impressed upon her in Kilgarret since she was a child.

Going up the steps of the house where the abortionist, Mrs Norris, lives is for Aisling worse than going to confession after she's been messing around with Ned Barrett. Later she will deny that she knelt in prayer, crying and working her rosary beads while Mrs Norris did her stuff. But Elizabeth knows that she did kneel and pray, because when Mrs Norris told her, she said she used words from 'Hail Holy Queen' and Mrs Norris wasn't a Catholic and wouldn't have been able to make a prayer like that up, unless she heard Aisling say it:

Hail, holy Queen, Mother of mercy, hail, our life, our sweetness and our hope. To thee do we cry, poor banished children of Eve: to thee do we send up our sighs, mourning and weeping in this vale of tears. Turn then, most gracious Advocate, thine eyes of mercy toward us, and after this our exile, show unto us the blessed fruit of thy womb, Jesus, O merciful, O loving, O sweet Virgin Mary! Amen.

In *Light a Penny Candle* Maeve is mercilessly subtle in the way she embeds her disenchantment with Catholicism by allowing Aisling to 'educate' the naïve Protestant child Elizabeth in the catechism. Because Elizabeth is a Protestant she knows nothing. All must be explained to her. The way Maeve delivers Catholic beliefs is often charming, delightful, but as we smile she also makes us ask ourselves how rational adult minds could have believed some of these things to be true.

Maeve never encourages people not to believe in God – everyone is entitled to their own beliefs in her world – but matters of dogma, such as celibacy of the priesthood, are given a thorough going over, as in *Echoes*. Here her interest is in the hypocrisy that the rule engenders when the young priest Sean O'Hara takes a Japanese woman and makes a family with her. She shows the natural values of 'family' in conflict with what would seem to be the unnatural rules of the Church. Allied to this is the way the son's leaving the priesthood undermines the family morally, with the children hiding the truth, just as Maeve had been made to keep her mother in the dark about casting aside her faith.

Behind every issue she tackles in the novels lies her obsession with truth and its concomitants, hypocrisy and betrayal. Truth is what she looked for in fashioning herself after discarding the fantasies, half-truths and betrayals of her early life, which threatened the values that were endemic to her. In the end, Maeve's fictional world, while breaking away from the status quo, galvanises the individual with the very family and community values on which the Christianity she discarded was originally based. But her characters face truth rather than simply paying lip service to it.

Following the great success of *Light a Penny Candle*, Maeve had suffered agonies writing her second novel, *Echoes*, fearing that perhaps she only had the one novel in her. Rosie, her editor, remembers that at first the plan was for a novel again split between Ireland and England, with Oxford the main English focus, but it didn't work out and Maeve moved the action to Castlebay, lightly disguised setting for her fondly remembered summer holidays in Ballybunion. One character's physical characteristics are of particular interest, namely those of schoolteacher Angela O'Hara. The drama *The Jewel in the Crown*, based on Paul Scott's novel, was showing on television at the time she was writing the novel and along with millions of others Maeve was transfixed by the production. She was held particularly by Geraldine James in the role of Sarah Layton. She decided that if she would ever want to look like anyone other than herself it would have to be Geraldine James.

Maeve was so taken with the actress that she gave the good-looking O'Hara Geraldine's physical features – her red-brown hair, greenish eyes – and secretly longed for her to play the role in a film, the rights to which nobody had bought at this stage nor shown any interest in buying.

In 1985, the year of publication of *Echoes*, Maeve was thinking more about a projected film of *Light a Penny Candle*. A joint, four-part RTÉ and London Weekend TV production was mooted, but the producer, Bernard Kirchaesski, had terrible trouble finding a girl to play Aisling. 'Outside Ireland there is an image of an archetypal Irish beauty, influenced by Maureen O'Hara and Hollywood. It may be phoney, but we are looking for what the world thinks your Irish girl looks like, and we can't find her.'[83]

Phoney it is not and Kirchaesski's failure to grasp the one essential in the production that it was his responsibility to secure – the 'Aisling' persona – was lamentable. It is appropriate, however, that he likened the character to Maureen O'Hara. Maeve may even have had Maureen O'Hara in mind as a descriptive model when she created Aisling. The actress would have made the perfect Aisling had she been of an appropriate age. The famously red-headed film star was born into a Catholic-Irish family in Dublin in 1920 and trained at the Abbey Theatre from when she was a child, was noted for playing fiercely passionate heroines with a highly sensible attitude and, like Aisling, was abused by her husband. After her Hollywood success O'Hara returned to Ireland, to live mainly in Glengarriff, County Cork.

Perhaps this toying with Maureen O'Hara was the reason why Maeve chose the name O'Hara for the similarly pivotal character in her second novel – the schoolteacher Angela O'Hara in *Echoes*. But this time she modelled the fictional character on an actress who was of an age to play her. Imagine her surprise when, four years later, quite independently, Geraldine James was cast in the part of Angela O'Hara in Channel 4's television series of *Echoes*. Maeve had had no involvement in the casting. She couldn't believe it.

Actress and author subsequently became good friends. People rarely recognise themselves when fictional characters are based on them in novels, often because we don't see ourselves as other people see us. Geraldine was no exception. But in her case there was a surprise for her fictional creator too. Maeve had had her schoolteacher cycle down the hill in Castlebay with her hair flying in a straight line behind her and this is exactly what Geraldine had liked to do when she was a child. There was great synchronicity and the film turned out to be a magical experience for Maeve.

It was shot in the little seaside town of Dunmore East in County Waterford during a beautiful summer, and Maeve and Gordon used to find any excuse they could to go and watch. They got to know the people of the town, who were thrilled to have the film happening on their doorstep, many of them performing as extras in the film, so that if you go there today it is not difficult to find someone who was in it.

Maeve remembered one day in particular when she was watching the filming from the top of a cliff; there must have been 200 people involved. It suddenly hit her that all that was going on had emanated from one little idea she'd had, born of the balmy days of summer in Ballybunion, when she and her friends and family were so young. But what moved her was not nostalgic reminiscence, rather that the film had created work for so many. After that, whenever films were made of her books she waited in anticipation not for the denouement but for the credits, which she wanted to go on and on.

By the time of the filming of *Echoes*, Maeve had already published her third novel, *Firefly Summer* (1987). The following year came *Silver Wedding*. As with her journalism and short stories, so with the novels, the idea for *Silver Wedding* came while sitting on a bus. She overheard a girl saying to her friend that it was her parents' silver wedding and she must remember to get a card. Her friend said, 'Oh, that's nice, is there to be a party?' To which the first girl replied, 'No, it's a dreadful marriage – but the worse the marriage the bigger the card.'

The pathos of the exchange stunned Maeve; the sadness, delivered with a terrible matter-of-fact acceptance like that, on a bus, insisted on being allowed the chance to develop in her imagination and find resolution in one of her 'parables'.

Maeve was by now in the novel-writing groove, no longer worrying whether the next tale would be a bestseller. She was a novelist who was expected to deliver new works on a regular basis. When a small publisher has a success the size of Binchy's on their hands, turnover requires that she keeps producing. But there was no sense of being stuck on a treadmill.

Perhaps it was all this writing about her childhood, or perhaps, as she said, it was the invention of the fax machine, which had recently made communications between writer and publisher so good that it didn't matter where you were writing any more. Or perhaps she was now ready in herself to return. Whatever it was, she and Gordon decided that it was time to make Dalkey their principal home.

To the teenage Maeve thirty years earlier, Dalkey had been the dullest place on earth, the Kalahari Desert, and she and Philippa had wanted to escape. To the spinster in the 1960s, living there had seemed a life sentence. But now that she was in her forties and 'at one' with herself, dispensing her philosophy of life to an insatiable family of readers, the little town promised Maeve the deepest resonance of whom she had become.

Dalkey, as it turned out, had also changed. It was no longer the place it had been in the 1950s and 1960s – and neither was Ireland.

NINE

THE RETURN

The fortunes of Dalkey had changed dramatically through its history. In the fourteenth and fifteenth centuries, thanks to poor navigation of the river Liffey in Dublin, it was the main port for the capital, and was known as the 'Town of the Seven Castles'. Walled on three sides, to east, north and west, with a double ditch rampart to the south, its seven castles were quite small, more like fortified warehouses. Two only survive – Archbold's Castle, next to the Church of the Assumption, and Goat's Castle on the opposite side of the road, now the Town Hall and Heritage Centre.

In the sixteenth and seventeenth centuries the rise of Ringsend, a Dublin suburb on the south side of the Liffey, closer to the capital than Dalkey, and the successful navigation of the great river, took the life out of the town until, in 1815, hundreds of men were drafted in with their families to quarry stone high up on Dalkey Hill behind Knocknacree Road, for the construction of the great asylum harbour at Dún Laoghaire.

A metal track running between the quarry on the hill and

the harbour worked without power of any sort on a two-track pulley system, the weight of the stone-filled trucks coming down the steep hill pulling the empty trucks coming up it from the harbour. Today, the route of the old track is known as 'The Metals' and makes for a pleasant walk between the two towns.

Even with all this activity, however, Dalkey remained little more than 'a noisome fishing port of hovels, cabins and drinking taverns' until the mid-1800s, when the rising Dublin professional and business classes built themselves fine houses in the surrounding area.[84]

When Maeve returned to live in Dalkey in the 1980s, the sheer beauty of the place and its handy location meant that among the inhabitants of the big houses, built by the Victorian professional classes, were now some of the movers and shakers and beneficiaries of a newly prosperous Ireland. Dalkey was becoming trendy. Tina Turner, Chris de Burgh and members of U2 bought houses in the town, raising its profile considerably. Maeve and Gordon became neighbours of Gloria Hunniford, Bono and Neil Jordan. In Finnegan's, the local pub where Maeve and Gordon had their own table, one would encounter all sorts of people.

Fortunately the approach to celebrity was pleasantly casual in Dalkey and when Maeve returned as an international bestselling author there were still townsfolk who remembered her as a girl of ten, riding her old bicycle around the neighbourhood. Best of all, her brother William and two sisters, Joan and Renie, also found their way back to live within a few minutes of Maeve and Gordon at Pollyvilla.

For Maeve there was no moody nostalgia when she walked the streets of her childhood, rather the thrill of the future as she watched 'the girls coming up from Loreto in their uniforms, each one with hopes and dreams of what life will bring them'. And what a life now lay in store! She felt no regret for 'a vanished era and the ghosts of yesterday', only a sense of pride in the changes and the role she had played in some of them.[85]

Whether a child of the 1980s could, as an adult, afford to continue to live in Dalkey was less certain. Maeve's parents had bought Eastmount on Knocknacree Road, high above the town, for £3,000 in 1952. It went on the market in the spring of 2007 for €3.55 million, reducing later, with Ireland in the grip of recession, to €2.95 million.

As for her home with Gordon, which was now to become their principal address, they extended the first floor to make a studio where they could both continue to work side by side. Glass covered, and sun strewn in summer, it could be reached by means of a spiral staircase from the ground floor. A roof patio was laid outside where the ten minutes 'sulking time' could be spent dead-heading roses, and from which the big bunch of trees can be glimpsed behind which Eastmount stands.

Later, with part of the proceeds from the sale of her novel *Firefly Summer*, they bought the derelict house behind Pollyvilla for guest accommodation and to increase their privacy, naming it Firefly Cottage. Today, the whole dwelling is a bit like the Tardis. From the outside one would think it is a single-storey Georgian folly, but inside there was all the space they needed to live, work and entertain.

Maeve and Gordon continued their work on word processors – 'like twin pianos,' as she liked to put it – occupying opposite ends of a desk set along one wall of their glasshouse eyrie. Framed book covers and shelves of her books lined the walls, along with pictures of Maeve mixing it with powerful figures in the White House. Open lay a copy of *The Book of Kells*, the famous eighth-century illuminated manuscript of the Four Gospels, created by Celtic monks in the eighth century. This was not a contradiction for a Catholic who had lost her faith, it was something of a statement, because *The Book of Kells* is a relic of a time before the Irish Church was politicised, when Irish monasteries were the acknowledged centres of learning in Europe. It is often forgotten that St Patrick, besides bringing Christianity to Ireland, brought the written word. Maeve and Gordon would turn a page of this beautiful remnant of Tradition each day, just as is done with the original *Book of Kells* at Trinity College Dublin.

In preparation for writing a book Maeve would first detail her characters on large cardboard sheets. She regarded them as real creations, not to be discarded just because they had served her purpose in one story. Like Joyce, when required she had no hesitation in letting them wander into a second novel. For *Quentins*, for example, she welcomed Brenda Brennan and Ria and Danny Lynch from *Tara Road*, Cathy and Tom Feather, Maud and Simon Mitchell from *Scarlet Feather*, and Nora the Signora and Aidan Dunne from *Evening Class* in the new novel. Readers would comment on just how pleased they were to see them again.

Maeve was a consummate planner. Each novel, each project, had its own file, notebooks, timelines, headings, lists. First she would sit down and write out the story in maybe six or seven pages to confirm in her mind exactly where it was going. These would be sent to the publisher and, assuming they liked them, the project would go live.

In order to give the novel a clear sense of place she would often draw a map of the village where the action occurred. As soon as a character was introduced it would be given a house on the map, marked with the character's name. Hotels, pubs, shops would go on it too, as the whole village took shape.

Then there were time charts, which logged the duration of the writing and how many words Maeve needed to write each day; two to four pages (about 800 to 1,600 words) a day was the norm.

The working partnership with Gordon was extremely helpful. 'The discipline of another writer sitting beside you makes you work,' Maeve said. They'd work for four hours in the morning. Gordon would often put on a pair of silent headphones to cut out all sound. Maeve could answer the phone and think nothing of the interruption, but when she was writing she was gone to the world, total focus, total concentration.

At the end of each day they continued to read each other what they had written. But they were not at all competitive, even now that Maeve's career had taken off globally. Both being writers, they knew that some days go better than others. On a bad writing day, when things just didn't go well, they were a tremendous support to one another.

They claimed that they'd only ever had two arguments, one about the law of copyright and the Berne Convention, the other about Mexican cleaners working in Los Angeles airport. Not matters on which marriages have been known to founder, but the Mexican cleaners did provoke quite a stand-off, so much so that Maeve claimed that the divorce settlement – who was going to have what – was written out in a café at the airport itself. The next day they couldn't remember what they'd been fighting about.

Gordon developed a foolproof system to avoid a repetition. They'd separate 'Tone' from 'Content' of any argument and submit the content to 'A Working Party', made up of the two of them. They could have a working party on anything, and list the arguments for and against whatever was at issue. It never took long to reach an agreeable conclusion.

They had little systems for all sorts of things. For example, one left over from earlier days when money was tight was that they discussed financial matters only on Saturdays. Bills, cheques, whatever, all went into a drawer until then.

The only other occupants of the studio were two cats, Fred (a ginger) and Audrey (white with a black tail which it refused to acknowledge was its own). They would walk over everything and provide Maeve and Gordon with a good excuse not to work. Before Fred and Audrey were Tex and Sheelagh, immortalised in a painting by Norah Golden and in *The Tex and Sheelagh Omnibus* by Gordon, illustrated by Mary Murphy, which Poolbeg published in 1996.

Gordon's work powered ahead. Following his collaborations

with the illustrator Alan Burton, he teamed up with Maeve's sister, Joan Ryan, on two story collections, *The Haunted Hills* and *Sea Tales of Ireland*, before adding well over a dozen children's titles of his own over the next decade. Titles included adventure stories and mysteries, such as *The Cool MacCool*, *Tom's Amazing Machine* (which became a series), *Cruncher Sparrow High Flier* (also a series), *The Red Spectacles Gang*, *The Curse of Werewolf Castle*, and quirky projects such as *The Rhyming Irish Cookbook*, illustrated by Cathy Henderson, which no doubt raised a few laughs in the making.

After the planning, writing, for Maeve, was not so much a craft as a cutting off from conscious thought, a process almost of unthinking. Once everything was in place she would put all her notes and files away, let go and let the writing flow. Patsey Murphy wrote of 'a veil of mighty concentration' coming down and a clarity of purpose which meant that 'her fingers did not so much hit the keyboard as slap it like Jelly Roll Morton playing the piano'.

With enormous self-belief she put her subconscious to work – no analysis, just plug into tradition and go with the flow. When she was writing, her stories streamed through her uninhibited by conscious editing, as if delivered orally. In fact, Maeve saw herself as 'part of the great *seanchaí* oral tradition', proudly displaying her membership in a banner above the float she rode at the St Patrick's Day parade in Chicago in 2001. The banner read: 'Seanachai Storyteller Maeve Binchy'.[86]

Historically *seanchaithe* were servants to the chiefs of the four ancient clans and guardians of tradition, the O'Neills of Ulster, the O'Briens of Munster, the O'Conors of Connacht and the MacMurrough-Kavanaghs of Leinster. They appeared at wakes, christenings and quiltings (*cuilteireacht*), the last of which were attended only by women, but many were wanderers and might appear suddenly in the night and extemporise their stories around a winter fire. Where there were Irish speakers there were *seanchaithe* and singers and a folk-life which even hardship and grinding poverty could not eradicate.

A large corpus of *seanchaithe* tales was passed from one practitioner to another without being written down. There are associations with oral stories of Welsh mythology, such as the *Mabinogion*, a collection of eleven stories sustained orally for 2,000 or more years before Christ, and *The Book of Taliesin*, both passed down orally and not written down until the thirteenth century.

The difference is that while these Welsh stories were written down in the Middle Ages and preserved as almost sacred texts of Welsh tradition, all that is left of the *seanchaithe* tales – the original oral literature of 'that ancient and aristocratic world of Ireland,' as J. H. Delargy writes in his rarely found but fascinating extended essay, *The Gaelic Storyteller* (1945),[87] – 'are but pathetic fragments'. They were lost in the cleansing of Irish tradition by Cromwell and others, which Delargy refers to as those 'disastrous wars of the seventeenth century'.

Because of their role as oral custodians of tradition, *seanchaithe* are acknowledged to have inherited the function of the *filí* of pre-Christian Ireland, an elite class of poets or seers, the word 'filí' deriving from the proto-Celtic word meaning 'seer, one who sees', and so are linked, like the Aisling poetic convention, to the spirit of traditional Ireland, to the collective unconscious of the Irish people.

In *The Irish Writer and the World*, Declan Kiberd distinguishes between two levels of ancient storyteller. While a *seanchaí* would narrate local tales or lore, 'the *sgéalaí* enjoys higher status as the narrator of the *sean-sgéal* or international tale'. The *sgéalaí* was always a man whose tales were long and difficult to remember – amazing adventures, remote wonders, related in the third person – whereas the *seanchaí* could be a man or a woman and the tales recounted as if they themselves had experienced them. The tradition of the *seanchaí* is the one that Maeve more nearly follows, because her narratives are rooted in her personal quest.

As part of this oral tradition, Maeve 'speaks' to us in a characteristically lyrical, very Irish way. We love her Irish 'voice', and the rhythms and the music of it fit her task. Her books are popular worldwide because her stories are inspired by feelings which are experienced the world over, but most copies are sold wherever English is understood, because her voice seems to reflect the vibrant patterns of emotion that resonate between the characters. Irish-English is the perfect medium because emotional resonances are built into the musical syntax of the Irish tongue, individual 'notes' combining to sing of emotional qualities, while rhythmic structures and time values operate to reflect the emotional cadences of relationships. Altogether, the timbre of Maeve's authorial voice helps to inform and transform the reader at a level vastly more creative than simple information dissemination.

Marian Keyes, a great friend of Maeve who besides being a writer of renown knows plenty about the ancient Irish tongue, has argued that while the words Maeve used are English, 'they've been attached to the template of the older language we spoke'. And that is as it should be, for the *seanchaí* is associated with the Gaeltacht, the Irish-speaking areas of Ireland.

The distinction between an analytical writer and a spontaneous one is a valid point in the context of the *seanchaí*. 'You analyse things as a writer,' Maeve once said to fellow writer Felicity Hayes-McCoy, 'but I don't. I'm just delighted by them and write them down.' Hayes-McCoy wasn't sure that Maeve really thought that. But perhaps she did. There was little room for analytical thinking when she was writing. Then, she dared to lose herself in what she was doing. Lost to the conscious control tower of her thinking, the words just poured out. Writing this way, instinctively, was the ultimate in authenticity – a position she craved above all, the writer's self is lost to the task, along with all prejudice and affectation.

Traditionally, a *seanchaí* would point to this essential absence of self by ending their story with the phrase 'Sin é mo sgéal-sa! Má tá bréag ann bíodh! Ní mise a chum ná a cheap é.' 'That is my story! If there be a lie in it, be it so! It is not I who made or invented it.'

Maeve's editors were another vital part of the process. She had been brought up a journalist on the old adage, 'Don't get it right, get it finished.' Deadlines are sacrosanct on a newspaper and must be met at all costs. If the words don't come in, the paper doesn't go out – and you're in the firing line. The good news was that Maeve never had writer's block. A blank page never frightened a journalist as good as she. But it was up to the editor to get it right, which is no mean feat when faced with a manuscript of 250,000 words as opposed to a feature of a few hundred.

She was aware that people might think she was not a perfectionist, but 'I do not write poetry', she said, 'nor have I explored a new form of literature. I tell a story and I want to share it with my readers. I want my books to draw the readers into the tale that is being unfolded.'[88]

For her the priority was that here was a story that had to be told and she was for anything that would facilitate that process. She'd rarely dig in and have an argument about it. The initial problem her editors had to grapple with was that she was a rotten typist. Her agent, Chris Green, who edited and retyped the whole of *Light a Penny Candle* before sending it to Century, so convinced was she of its potential, recalls that whole sections of words would arrive in the form of anagrams, and there were occasions when even Maeve was unable to decipher what she had written. Green maintained her hands-on editorial involvement. In the Binchy archive there is a note from Maeve wishing Rosie, her editor, and Green 'courage and patience' as they set about editing *The Glass Lake* (1994).

Carole Baron, who subsequently looked after the editing on the American side, agrees: 'When Maeve sent in her manuscript her typing was abominable. You could barely read it. You said to yourself, "Oh my God, what am I going to do with this?" And then you started to punctuate it and paragraph it, and the magic

of her words would emerge.' She recalls that when word processors came in, her husband taught Maeve how to 'cut and paste',
which greatly speeded up her working life.

Speed was an attractive commodity, because it meant that
she could feed the publishing monster she was creating more
efficiently, but it was also potentially a destructive one. The
year 1990 saw publication of *Circle of Friends* (230,000 words),
a collection of short stories (*The Storyteller*) and the television
film of *The Lilac Bus*. In 1992 came her novel *The Copper Beech*
(113,000 words), and in 1993 the *Dublin People* collection of
stories. These were followed in 1994 by *The Glass Lake* (289,000
words) and in 1995 the film of *Circle of Friends*. There was also
her journalism in the *Irish Times* and elsewhere.

To write a 250,000-word novel involves an enormous amount
of energy and stamina. Maeve had to slow down, but was
showing no signs of doing so. She seemed to be operating in a
different time continuum to everyone else. Her conversation
was an enthusiastic, non-stop, generous flow of anecdotes,
information and observations, punctuated by quips, queries and
conspiratorial asides. It was a wonderful, delightful, endless flow,
like her books. But surely the sheer tempo of her working life
was bound to take its toll, particularly as in 1997 she was diagnosed with ischaemic heart disease (left ventricle dysfunction),
which would dog her until her death fifteen years later.

Maeve had been busy, busy, busy all her life since the moment
of truth at UCD in the late 1950s, and she couldn't see that life
should be any different. When, one Christmas, five friends
quite independently gave her copies of Paul Wilson's bestselling

self-help book *The Little Book of Calm*, she was for the first time alarmed. She said she couldn't understand it, she always thought she was *too* calm. 'How odd to be seen as some kind of tense, clenched fist.' It made amusing fodder for her hugely popular *Irish Times* column, 'Maeve's Week'. But it was a sign that she needed to change.

On the plus side her writing success had given her great self-belief and true confidence for the first time in her life. Gordon had helped bring her to it and now served and boosted her psychological equilibrium daily, as did her close friends and her publishers, as her acclaim spread throughout the world. With success came money. She cared nothing for it, but it too was a damn good tick in the box for her psyche.

This was self-esteem quite different to that induced by her mother's wonderful poetic phrases about her beauty taking the sight out of her eyes. With confidence, success and money came a reduced vulnerability, a toughness which was essential if she was to remain in control of her life.

Now, in her forties, she had achieved the fiscal turnover of a light engineering company and with the encouragement of her publishers and agent had begun to develop a strong sense of responsibility about her place in the enterprise, which was redefining her self and her place in the world.

She had an intuitive approach to decision making now and was unshakeable once she had chosen what to do. Within 'the enterprise', nobody was too close a friend to avoid censure, or worse. 'Once, during the writing of *Firefly Summer*, she got very cross with her agent Chris and me,' Rosie recalls. Maeve returned a section of the revised manuscript with a letter attached. 'I seem to remember that in it she told us she was beginning to think she no longer trusted us to give her the right editorial guidance.' Fortunately, there was a note from Gordon on top.

> It said something like: 'Under this note you will find a letter from Maeve which you may find upsetting. Pay no attention, girls. You are doing great, keep going.' After that we named him Director of Morale. He was absolutely marvellous. Without Gordon's soothing addendum, we would have slit our throats. But it was typical of Maeve that subsequently it became one of the episodes about which we laughed most.

The development was something to celebrate, the final maturation point in the existential process to which Maeve had submitted. People now knew that she had 'an invisible line, which, if you crossed, you became one of the unforgiven, sometimes forever,' as Rosie noted.

Maeve was becoming a very impressive lady indeed. Eventually she found herself capable of tackling head on the brightest and most talented of those she had never suffered gladly. She'd only bother with the brightest. And the wisest of them couldn't help but admire her style.

Colm Tóibín recalled sitting next to her at the make-up bench prior to a TV chat show. She had leaned across to him and said that she had been meaning to telephone him. During a recent interview in America, she'd been asked who she knew in Dublin and among others she had listed Colm, before realising that of course she didn't actually know him. Would he be sure never to let her down in America and say that he didn't know her, because 'I mean, that would be awful, wouldn't it? For me, it would anyway. And I know you wouldn't do it.'

She had then smiled knowingly and returned to discussing the impossible business of making her face up with the artist who was working on her. Tóibín hadn't known what to say. In fact, he had looked at himself in the mirror and said nothing, before realising that that had been precisely Maeve's purpose. An esteemed literary figure in Ireland, Tóibín is a member of Aosdána, a high-blown literary club, membership to which is by invitation only from current members and is limited to 250. Maeve had a loathing for any kind of exclusivity, anything that reeked of snobbery or pretention. Tóibín knew that he had been put down by a real professional, because she had made it seem that she was doing the exact opposite. Maeve had, he wrote, 'a sort of steely way of not ever being dull'.

'Steely' is the word that defined her now, as well as generous, fun and supportive, as she'd always been. 'Mischievous' describes how she sometimes went about her steely business. Her friends would not often refer to it, nor was it uppermost in her books or intimated in her public talks or her chats with readers in the signings. But without this steely and mischievous side she wouldn't have been able to achieve what she did.

A story that she told many times concerned a woman who once stopped her in a London street and asked whether she was Maeve Binchy, because she'd just read her latest book. Maeve replied that yes, she was indeed Maeve Binchy and hoped that she had enjoyed the book. To her great surprise the woman said that no, she hadn't in fact enjoyed it at all. When she put it down she felt that she could have written it just as well. To which Maeve replied, 'But you didn't, did you?'

It is easy to underestimate what it takes to write fiction with an authentic voice, because the very authenticity conceals all that it has taken to be authentic. The book remainder shops are littered with those who have tried but failed to write like Maeve, because they failed to see that it was the steely or ruthless honesty with which she set about herself from the late 1950s that gave her the vision, made her the authentic article and cleared the way for fate to become an effective element in her life.

On first impressions it was easy to miss Maeve's tougher side, so warm and generous a person was she. The American publisher Tom Dunne met her by chance in New York, around 1984. Tom was working at the time for St Martin's Press and the firm had been the under-bidder in the US auction for publishing rights in *Light a Penny Candle*. But it was his then boss, Tom McCormack, who had read the manuscript and been handling the negotiations, and Tom Dunne knew nothing at all about Maeve.

They met at a launch for Egon Ronay's famous restaurant guide at a hotel in New York, as Tom explains:

I published Egon Ronay in those days and he did a very grand launch of this particular edition of the book at the Pierre. He pulled in four great chefs and foodies from all over the world. It was amazing. As I recall you had sixteen dishes, quite small

– the four chefs presented four dishes each – wine flowed and it went on for hours. So, all these people are gathering at their tables and I look over mine and my eyes fall on the name 'Maeve Binchy', which means nothing to me, and I look up and this large lady in a very green dress comes walking over, says hello, plonks herself down and we get talking. When I say I work for St Martin's Press, she says, 'Oh, say hello to Tom McCormack for me. He was so generous even though he didn't get the book.' Now Tom, when reading an author's manuscript, couldn't help but edit it as he went along, and later over a drink Maeve handed me all these little notes he'd made on her manuscript. When he didn't win the auction he'd handed them to her and said, 'Here, you might find these of use.' Maeve said, 'No, I really shouldn't, they're yours.' But Tom, the great fiction editor, insisted, 'What am I going to do with them?' Maeve said to me, 'He was so kind, but I was really quite relieved that he didn't get the book, because I'd still be revising it!'

We then chatted some more and she said, 'Now, I do have one problem with a book St Martin's Press publishes.' I said, 'What's that?' She said, 'It's a disgraceful book.'

'What on earth is it?'

'Well, it's this supposedly humorous book called *Irish Erotic Art*.'

She didn't think it was funny. She said she thought it was insulting to the Irish people.

There is no such thing in Ireland as Irish erotic art and *Irish Erotic Art* is a blank book – there's not a word in it. That is the joke. It became a national bestseller in America. It wasn't that Maeve didn't find Irish jokes funny, she actually found them offensive. Tom didn't know the background but sensed the intensity of her feelings and that their enjoyable conversation could tip at any moment into disaster.

'I thought, right, here's a moment when you either do the right thing or the wrong thing and you're not quite sure until afterwards how what you say will be taken. I looked her straight in the eye and said, "I'll have you know I wrote that book!"'

There was little laughter, but it edged Maeve back into the comfort zone more effectively than if he'd said, 'Oh, get over yourself.'

In fact, they went on to become lifelong friends, his last name even to be attached to characters in her novels. With the tension gone, he revelled in Maeve's speculative analysis of their neighbours around their table, each cameo worthy of a place on the starting grid of one of her stories.

So we stayed right till the end, ate the four desserts and drank more wine and champagne. I suppose it was around four in the afternoon by then. And I look at her, and we really are now great pals, and all is forgotten about Irish erotic art, and I turn to her and say, 'Do you fancy splitting a bottle of champagne before we part?' She says, 'I'd love to!' Now she herself has told this story to any number of people, so I don't mind sharing it with you. Gordon wasn't with her on the trip. She had been meaning to go to the theatre but didn't make it. She went upstairs and called him. 'The first thing I said to him was,' she told me, 'Gordon, we have a new best friend.' And from that moment we *were* like best friends. I would visit her when I came to London. I used to hole up at a hotel – maybe three of us from St Martin's Press, meeting English publishers, reading manuscripts, sometimes there'd be long weekends when we didn't even leave the hotel. It was hard work but highly enjoyable. But I got into the habit of seeing Maeve and Gordon. If they were in London we'd go out to the Mirabelle or some grand place, or I'd hop over to Dublin and stay in Firefly Cottage.

In Dublin they would have these memorable dinners at the round table at Pollyvilla. They were such fun. I remember one occasion, I think it was the first time my friends Hope and Charlie came with me. Maeve invited them over to Dublin too, though they had to stay at the Shelbourne. Others at dinner included the *Irish Times* columnist Mary Maher, the district court judge Mary Kotsonouris, Maeve's cousin Dan Binchy, himself a writer, and his wife Joy, who are the loveliest and smartest people in the world in many ways, and we had a grand time. The wine, the food – dinner lasted at least five hours – Dan talking faster than Maeve. But the funny thing is I don't really remember people interrupting the one who was talking. Everybody at some time or other would chime in with something. Dan said, 'The Irish have learnt to be polite and wait. At a certain point someone has to stop and take a breath. It's like a slipstream, you get in.' They quite happily wait for you to take a breath and then the next one jumps in.

The next day we were trudging through the airport back to

London to work, and Hope, who's a very smart girl, Yale graduate, honours and so on, happens to be American, happens to be
Jewish – we were all a little hungover, I suppose – says: 'I want to
be Irish!' I said, 'Why?' 'Last night, the conversation, the people,
the stories, the laughter – they were even singing!' She said, 'This
place is amazing!'

That was Maeve. They showed a picture of the room in
Pollyvilla and the round table in the paper after Maeve died and
– because we had SUCH good times around that table – I cried.

In the early 1990s Maeve had much on her mind. Her UK
publishers, Century, had been caught up in the takeover game
that typified Britain in Margaret Thatcher's free market.
Century had been so successful that they had shrewdly targeted
and taken over a bigger company, Hutchinson. Now, in turn,
they had been bought by the mighty American publisher
Random House, who wanted to start up in the UK. Anthony
Cheetham was made chairman of the new UK Random House
board, while Gail Rebuck, who had been recruited to Century
in 1982 from Hamlyn, where she'd been a non-fiction editor and
gone on to show great management nous at Century, had also
received a place on the new Random House board.

In 1991 Anthony and Gail were invited to dinner by Random
House executives after their author Ben Okri had won the
Booker Prize for his novel *The Famished Road*. Anthony had
carried on celebrating at Soho's Groucho Club and not made the
dinner. The next morning he rolled up to breakfast at Claridge's
with his new bosses, only to find that he had been relieved of

his position in the new company and Gail Rebuck appointed in his place.

The same year, with some style, Anthony and wife Rosie formed a new company, Orion, and went on to acquire the time-honoured publisher Weidenfeld & Nicolson as the nucleus of a new, entrepreneurial publishing group. Thanks to the singular clause in her contract that stated that if Rosie left her publisher, Maeve would have the right to cancel the contract and follow her, Maeve was able to take her next book, *The Copper Beech*, away from Random House and give it to Orion. In 1993, Orion lodged an offer with Chris Green for a £500,000 advance for both UK hardcover and paperback rights in the next novel, *The Glass Lake* (at the time known as *Loughshee*). This was the first time that hardcover and paperback publication would be undertaken by one publisher in the UK and it was a big feather in Orion's cap.

Green wrote to Charles Nettleton at Maeve's UK paperback publisher, Coronet, to explain that she was in negotiation with Orion for both hardback and paperback rights, which effectively meant that he was being written out of the picture – a major loss for the company but a nice deal for Orion. At this stage Anthony Cheetham had started up two successful publishing companies, both spearheaded by Maeve.

More dealings followed which indicate just how hot a property Maeve had become and that there was room no longer for sentiment. After the marriage of Anthony and Rosie broke down and they separated, Hodder Headline, the company that now owned Coronet, which had lost out to Orion in respect of Maeve's UK paperback rights, offered Rosie employment as editor in the unspoken hope that Maeve would follow her. She didn't. Perhaps understandably, she had had enough of playing musical chairs.

'The parting of the ways editorially was sad for both of us,' Rosie remembers.

> Maeve felt that she was just too ill and tired to up sticks again and follow me to Headline, but she would have liked me to continue to edit her on a freelance basis. I felt that this would be problematic, having always been not only her editor but her publisher. At that point, therefore, Maeve decided that Carole Baron on the American side should take up the main editorial role and she would dispense with an English editor. I think hardly a day went by when we did not regret this parting of the ways, although we remained close friends to the end.

Resolution for Hodder Headline came when they joined forces with Maeve's publisher Orion in 2004.

In its UK edition alone, *The Copper Beech* sold in its first two years 72,614 in hardcover and 547,384 copies in paperback. Orion's targets over a similar time span for *The Glass Lake* were 100,000 in hardback and 800,000 in paperback. As the film of *Circle of Friends* was due to be released in 1995, the publishers would surely achieve these sales quickly.

One can begin to appreciate what an industry had been created around Maeve. But the UK wasn't all of it by any means.

In America, the first printing for the hardcover of *The Copper*

Beech (in November 1992 by Delacorte) was 160,000 copies. It was also a Book of the Month Club main selection and a Time–Life Book Digest Condensed Book selection; magazine rights were even sold to *Good Housekeeping*. Americans were now hungry for Maeve.

Then there were the editions published in thirty-six languages other than English.

Maeve's health, however, was under increasing stress and had been a disaster area for some time. She was overweight, exercise was anathema to her – other than tap dancing and tennis (she was 'a damned good tennis player') – and although she claimed not to have a sweet tooth, she admitted a penchant for quantities of butter, sauces, wine, curry and cheese.

After the drug-crazed 1960s, the 1970s in Britain saw a revolution in personal fitness, with jogging becoming a national British pastime. 'Joggers', Maeve wrote in the *Irish Times*, 'are mad', and revealed that her other pet hates were people breathing unnaturally after exerting themselves, men in tracksuits and, most of all, the 'aura of virtue' attached to getting fit. She was a hopeless case when it came to health. In addition to her diet of curry, wine and dairy foods, she confessed to smoking up to 100 cigarettes a day, including three before she got out of bed. In 1978 she visited the doctor with what she feared was pneumonia. She was 'fat, forty and had flu', he said. She never smoked another cigarette again.

The excess weight was less easily resolved. Maeve claimed to be a great walker as a child, for being the eldest of four there was always a pram that needed pushing. Her favourite walk took her beyond Eastmount over Dalkey Hill, along the Green Road in Killiney and down the Vico Road, but in later years she said she couldn't believe that there were people who liked walking, 'putting one leg in front of the other and looking round them and things. I regard walking as an absolute torture of getting from one place to the next place.'

She claimed that more unhappiness was caused in the world by people trying to change people than anything else. It was her lot in life to be big. Her personality and creativity depended on her being herself. She no more intended to snip at her weight problem by constant dieting or exercising than she intended to edit her glorious stream-of-consciousness outpourings, which defined her writing. Enough said. Get on with life.

But the other side of that was that at fifty even her large frame (six foot one) could not sustain her body weight. Osteoarthritis was crippling her; she couldn't walk or sleep for pain. For the battle-hardened writer, maintaining control over her life was increasingly a case of looking at a situation in a different way. On a promotional trip in Vancouver, she said:

I could say to you, 'Isn't it awfully sad for me, I have very bad arthritis in both hips and I am overweight, and I find it hard to move around, and I have to be helped up onto the stage, and I have to sit on a stool while I speak.' Or I could say, 'Isn't it wonderful I'm in Vancouver. I've been asked to speak, and there's a red stool waiting for me on the stage.'[89]

Four years of agony later, during which she could hardly stand

and would have to drag herself from the house to the car if she wanted to go out, she was diagnosed as in need of a hip replacement, but was too overweight to be operated on. The anaesthetic would have done for her heart. She was told to lose six stone in a year. She managed it in six months.

Desperate measures, a diet of Ryvita and the occasional slice of smoked salmon, so harmed her that she needed a blood transfusion as well as the hip replacement.

How she cut down on her beloved wine – an essential sacrifice in order to lose weight – is a story in itself. She developed a system whereby she would restrict herself to one evening of wine each month. The problem was that she looked forward to the evening so much, and her body's susceptibility to alcohol increased so dramatically, that each monthly outing became a spectacular hiatus which would take days of self-recrimination to get over.

Two glasses of wine at a restaurant to celebrate her wedding anniversary and she was holding forth listing the shortcomings of every man that she'd had a relationship with before meeting Gordon, sobbing great oceans of tears before the assembled throng, which included the kitchen staff who had come out to see what was going on.

That took her three days to get over.

The next time, one glass of red wine was enough to bring her close to passing out. Then followed the 'glass of champagne' on the flight to Chicago from New York when she spent the whole time trying to convince that stewardess not to marry the man she didn't love and ended up breaking her nose and a toe. She felt so ashamed that she cancelled the next evening of wine altogether.

But in the end she lost the weight – and in turn became terrified of the operation.

The harsh reality of it dawned on her when she was warned that her bones were so brittle that she might well have to spend the rest of her life in a wheelchair. To prepare for that she made all her friends learn to play bridge, something she had never wanted to do, thirty years after writing about Elizabeth White's elderly father looking upon bridge 'as some kind of survival raft' after his wife leaves him. So now it was for Maeve, except that she made sure to enjoy it. In reality, Mary Maher remembers, Maeve and her circle of friends developed their own version of the game which didn't adhere to the rule of silence which virtually defines bridge. They called it 'riverboat bridge', and it was a lot more fun.

Ahead of the hip operation Maeve was given an epidural and was conscious throughout. She felt nothing but couldn't understand why the hospital didn't call a stop to the building work going on outside – an incessant, dull cracking of hammer, she thought, on stone, unaware that it was in fact the surgeon's mallet going to work on her hip bone.

Thankfully, the operation was a great success. Maeve said that it changed her life. She spent seven weeks in hospital recuperating, reading thrillers, as she had loved to do as a child, and talking to the other patients, of course.

Studying the hip replacement manual with a group of them around the water dispenser one day, she noticed that it said that after eight weeks patients should be able to drive. 'That's great,' one of the group said drily. 'I always wanted to know how to drive but I never had the time to learn, it will be a huge advantage to me.'

What the massive loss of weight reveals about Maeve is an ability to turn willpower on and off like a tap. Unfortunately, once she'd had the operation, she turned the tap off and put four of the six stone back on again, saying that if she had to have the other hip replaced, so be it, she would simply lose the weight again.

Incredibly, it was during this period of great upheaval that she produced one of her best novels, *Evening Class*. She was in such pain that she had to call on Gordon more than usual, asking him to read back what she had written very carefully to check that it wasn't 'all mournful and dull and depressive'. *Evening Class* became one of her most popular and funniest books.

The mid-1990s was a pivotal time for her for other reasons. Ireland had changed and Maeve had played her part in effecting that change. Ireland was not only more prosperous, but more confident and tolerant. You could even get divorced now. The Fifteenth Amendment of the Constitution of Ireland repealed the constitutional prohibition of divorce in 1995.

Maeve wanted to write novels that reflected the *new* Ireland. *Evening Class* (1996) and *Tara Road* (1998) were the first to be designed to do just that. The idea for *Tara Road* came from over-hearing a woman say to her friend in a restaurant, 'I'm divorced. I always thought we had been happily married, but my husband said we hadn't been happy for years.' It so took Maeve aback that she set to wondering what she would do if such an awful thing happened to her.

Tara Road tells the story of Ria, who has been abandoned in a marriage that she had thought was happy. It put Maeve's sales in America into overdrive, thanks to a telephone call she received one evening out of the blue. The voice at the other end claimed to be the American chat show host Oprah Winfrey. 'Come on now, who is it really?' asked a stunned Maeve.

The Oprah Winfrey Show, the highest-rated talk show in American TV history, surely did not approach its interviewees this way. You would expect first to hear from a producer and probably via your agent. But here, on the telephone, was someone claiming to be the star of the show, the biggest star on American TV. In a firm voice came the words 'It is Oprah', and at that moment Maeve realised that yes, it was, and they began to chat.

Oprah told Maeve that she had selected *Tara Road* for her book club, which there and then, because Oprah's show went out all over the world, really guaranteed it enormous success. Maeve was 'delighted' and suggested that her publishers would be 'very pleased'. Her delight had nothing to do with sales or money. She didn't need them. What delighted her was that a condition of selection was that large quantities of the book would be going into American libraries, where people who couldn't afford to buy the book would be able to read it for nothing. That was the deal if you signed up with Oprah. 'She's brought reading very much into the public domain,' Maeve said, 'much more than people often realise.'

Six weeks later, Maeve went into a small studio with Oprah and four women who had read the book and had experienced similar problems to the characters in it. Maeve described Oprah as 'terribly natural and very nice and very easy to talk to', but there was quite a heated discussion among the women about whether Ria's friend Marilyn should have told her that her best friend Rosemary was having an affair with her husband – the great betrayal, with which Maeve continued to be so preoccupied. Oprah said she thought that in a situation such as this your friend should tell you; that truth always sets you free. Maeve did not disagree, but added that she often thought 'the truth can drive you mad'.

In these later novels Maeve sometimes uses allegory to introduce a symbolic dimension to the relationships she's writing about. In *Tara Road* the lives of her characters become an analogy for what is happening to Ireland in modern times. It is a small leap from Ria Lynch's awakening about her meaningless marriage, to modern Ireland's awakening. As for Ria, so for Ireland, all the old certainties have disappeared – and neither had seen it coming. Choosing the break-up of a family to make her point about the break-up of old Ireland was apt because family is at the core of what traditional Ireland was about.

In the later novel *Quentins*, she unites and organises her characters' stories to a similar end. The book draws on the lives of Brenda and Patrick Brennan's customers at their restaurant, Quentins, their clients' stories made available partly by Brenda's rare ability to lip-read those sitting at the tables. But there are hints early on that Quentins is more than a restaurant rendezvous for gossips. Quentin, the owner, has come by it through the generosity of Toby Hayward. His boyfriend, Katar, believes it has been given to him by God and Hayward's nickname, 'Tobe', raises expectations that Maeve is dealing with matters of existential significance for her characters, who represent Ireland itself.

Through Ella Brady we meet the charismatic Don Richardson. Ella's betrayal by Don is another example of a common theme in the novels, but it is served up in parallel with a plan to film the stories of the restaurant's clientele as a documentary of Ireland in change. Those brought up in a religious tradition and then disillusioned – 'One minute I believed the lot ... the next I didn't believe a word of it' – realise that a degree of hoodwinking, of confidence trickery has been going on. In *Quentins* Maeve is dealing not only with betrayal of one person by another, but of a nation by its political and religious institutions on a grand scale.

As she brings her heroines to self-belief and -sufficiency without reference to a romantic ideal, so she brings Ireland out of the sentimental into the truth culture which fashioned her own self-belief and -sufficiency, and passes the onus of its future onto individuals' shoulders, individuals such as those young Irish writers whose work Maeve encouraged at every turn.

When Danielle McLaughlin, a hugely talented young short-story writer from Donoughmore in County Cork, received the prize cheque of €1,000 for winning the annual Maeve Binchy Short Story competition at Cumann Merriman, she credited Maeve 'for her generosity and for her encouragement of emerging Irish writers. I am delighted and honoured to be yet another recipient of this legendary generosity and encouragement.'

There is a vibrant literary support structure in Ireland, publishing outlets for emerging fine writing like *The Stinging Fly*, *Boyne Berries*, *Crannóg*, and *Inktears*. Maeve did everything she could to encourage new writers, knowing how important they were to Ireland's future. And in 2008 she wrote *The Maeve Binchy Writer's Club*, inspired by a course that ran for twenty weeks at the National College of Ireland.[90]

After *Tara Road* came *Scarlet Feather* (2000), an idea she owed to two friends in catering on whom she based the characters of Cathy Scarlet and Tom Feather in the novel. Her friends kept telling her amazing stories about the people they catered for. Catering companies enter upon people's lives at times of high stress – at weddings, funerals, christenings, anniversaries, birthdays, retirements – when things of moment are happening and personal and family dramas unfold. So she thought a catering firm would be a good place to set a novel.

In *Quentins*, two years later, the catering idea is again part of the story, the lives of Brenda and Patrick Brennan's customers brought to the forefront once more.

What Maeve didn't say was that the two friends – inspiration for the catering theme of three novels, *Scarlet Feather*, *Quentins* and earlier in *Tara Road* – were none other than her best friend at school, Philippa O'Keefe, and Philippa's partner, Robert Hampton.

Maeve had supported Philippa's catering company, now called Lodge Catering after her house in South Hampstead, from its inception in 1985. Before long, she was catering for all the parties given by Century and whenever Maeve hosted functions or book launches from her London house, Philippa provided.

In 1999 awards for Maeve's achievements began to flow, with the British Book Award for Lifetime Achievement. Professor Kiberd, who brought to Maeve's reputation a certain literary gravitas, undertook a series of lunches with her and Gordon and remembers one occasion when Maeve dropped an earring on the floor. When she went under the table to retrieve it her arthritis took hold and, realising she was stuck fast and couldn't move, she looked up at Kiberd with one eye and said, 'Is there anything else useful I can be doing while I'm down here?'

Humour alternated with seriousness and tenderness, so that in the same year, she published a non-fiction book called *Aches and Pains*, a survival manual, a book of information and sometimes very funny along the way. She had been advised to stick to novels, and this would not be published by her regular publisher. But she was determined to write the book after a nurse had come to her in the middle of the night when she was lying awake in hospital clearly nervous about her impending hip operation. The nurse reassured Maeve and made her a cup of tea. Maeve told her how kind she was, and the nurse replied breezily, 'Oh, you'll forget me when you're better.' But Maeve didn't forget and this was by way of a thank you. Royalties went to the Arthritis Research Campaign.

There would, in time, be further changes made to Gordon and Maeve's home, to make it easier for her to get upstairs. A glass lift was fitted to the exterior of the building to enable easy access to the first-floor studio, for Maeve continued to work almost to the end.

During her final years she was in deep pain, with exercise of any sort out of the question because her back was full of arthritis. But she never complained. As Marian Keyes recalled in a tribute to Maeve, she continued to show her ability to laugh and look on the bright side to the end. 'In her most recent letter to me she admitted to the pain but ended by saying how lucky we were to have jobs we can do in our pyjamas!'

In the year 2000, the pain was the reason she announced her retirement. It meant the end of 'Maeve's Week' in the *Irish Times*. She had been working for the paper for thirty-two years, and readers had become used to receiving 'Maeve's Week' from wherever she happened to be.

It was also the end of the worldwide tours. In the previous year, she had spent 111 days promoting her books. But it was not the end of everything and she continued writing up to the end, though she would concentrate on novellas and on short stories rather than the lengthy novels she had produced in the past.

In the wake of the announcement of her 'retirement' everyone suddenly woke up to the fact that Maeve might be as fragile as the rest and what a figure might be lost. There was a flurry of awards – in 2000 a People of the Year Award and in 2001 the W. H. Smith Book Award for Fiction for *Scarlet Feather*, published the year before.

In 2002 there was another health crisis related to her heart disease, an episode that inspired her to write *Heart and Soul* (2008), the story of a doctor with a clinic in an under-served area. In 2004 came *Nights of Rain & Stars*, a tale of people on holiday in Greece linked by a shared tragedy. There was also radio drama – *Surprise*, a four-part play, and the award-winning *Infancy and*

Tia Maria, starring Oscar-winner Kathy Bates. Maeve was also a driving force behind the RTÉ Radio 1 *Human Rights* drama seasons, while in 2009 her story 'The Games Room' was adapted for RTÉ Radio 1 by Anne-Marie Casey.

In 2005 she was one of a clutch of writers responsible for 'She Was Wearing', a series of interconnecting monologues specially commissioned in response to Amnesty International's Stop Violence Against Women campaign. In the same year a portrait of her by Maeve McCarthy was hung at the National Gallery of Ireland.

Then, in 2006, she began writing novellas for the series of books called *Quick Reads*, an opportunity for readers to snatch a taste of a whole host of different living authors, a scheme chaired by Gail Rebuck, who had been with Maeve at Century in 1982. And so it went on: *Whitehorn Woods* (2006), a film called *How About You* (2007) and a television film, *Anner House* (2007), both based on short stories.

This was not the sort of schedule normally associated with retirement, but the body of work was so rich and varied that it must have been one of her happiest periods, at last to be able to slow down a little and enjoy what she was doing (as much as the pain would allow).

In 2007, she was presented with the Irish PEN Award by Professor Kiberd, and the University College Dublin Foundation Day Medal by her alma mater. *Minding Frankie* also came that year, a novel about Noel Lynch, an alcoholic who enlists his neighbours' help to raise his infant daughter, Frankie, following the death of her mother, Stella. The Lynch family have lived in Dublin's St Jarlath Crescent for years, but Noel's friends find him and Frankie a flat seven minutes away in Chestnut Court, in a community Maeve wrote about but didn't include in *Minding Frankie*.

'Every once in a while,' said her agent, Christine Green, 'Maeve would write about one of these people. She would then put it in a drawer. "For the future," she would say.'

Now, her publishers have announced that these sketches are to appear in 'a collection of linked short stories' in a book called *Chestnut Street*, which will be released in 2014. Readers will be interested to see how faithful to Maeve's very distinctive style the posthumous work turns out to be.

❦

Maeve died on Monday 30 July 2012. She had been in and out of the Blackrock Clinic, a private hospital the other side of Dún Laoghaire, for a while, but there was no thought among her friends that it was time. The writer Roisin McAuley had lunched with Maeve and Gordon at their home only four weeks earlier. Maeve had mentioned that she was to return to the hospital the following week, but there was as much laughter and warmth as there always had been and she had no reason to think they would not see each other again. The expectation on all sides had been that life would go on, and events seemed to confirm that. Dolores Mackenna woke to the announcement of Maeve's demise on the Tuesday morning and went downstairs to find a letter enclosing a recipe from Maeve for a book she was

compiling to raise funds for the Irish Motor Neurone
Association. It was all so sudden a surprise.

The news spread like wildfire around the world. Her first
publisher, Rosie de Courcy, had caught the news on television
just before setting off into the wilds of Africa.

A few nights later I had a most vivid dream in which she had
written me two letters: the first – in her unmistakable handwrit-
ing – had scrawled on the envelope: 'Don't worry if journalists
want to interview you in Chipping Norton [her home town]' –
typical mad dream stuff. But the second one was eerie. It began:
'Dearest Rosie, The game's up. My back's broke...' I woke up,
thinking, how strange. Hips, knees, heart – yes. But back?

When she returned she discovered that although the final blow
came from a heart attack, the end had begun four weeks earlier
with a severe spinal infection – acute discitis, an infection in the
disc space between the vertebrae in her spinal column.

In response to the news, tributes flooded in from dozens
of countries, from publishers and politicians (including from
President Michael D. Higgins and from Taoiseach Enda Kenny),
from friends and colleagues, from people she had helped, from
veterans of book signings and émigrés from Ireland, for whom
reading her had been like coming home.

Readers worldwide who had never met her responded without
knowing quite why, but with a sense that the passing of this exhil-
arating, joyful spirit who made people feel happier for reading
her was something to be lamented. One, from Birmingham,

remembered writing to Maeve three years earlier to ask her for a signed copy of a book for her mother's eightieth birthday. A few days later she received a phone call from Maeve herself!

Then there was the woman who had lost an earring and seen a photo in a magazine of Maeve wearing a pair just like them. She had written to ask where she'd got hers. Maeve had dropped her a postcard saying that Gordon had bought her the earrings from a gallery in Foxrock and wished her good luck in finding another.

Another wrote simply, 'There will be a rare old time in Heaven tonight.'

The great feeling of uplift transferred from the stories. 'That's her legacy,' someone concluded. A feeling not engineered through escapism, but by her vision of life as it turns on passion and anxiety, and by galvanising her characters and her readers to take the lead part in their own life-dramas, as she had done in hers. Her books have 'an emotional reality that most authors can't capture,' said another reader. 'Next to the bible,' confessed a third, perhaps seeing the novels as parables, 'the writings that I have learned the most about life from was her wonderful books.'

Maeve's relationship with her readers was an intimate one. 'We felt like we knew her somehow,' one person wrote. In the ferment of her stories she laid out so much of herself at a deeper level than the memoirist can. 'I could "feel" her heart in each book,' wrote a reader from Ohio.

Tributes poured in to Maeve's website and publications such as the *Irish Times*, with Jennifer Johnston writing of Maeve as the essential Irishwoman, generous, warm hearted, funny, great to see and drink with. On the Lodge Catering site there were tributes from staff members who remembered 'Maeve always holding court and talking for Ireland and never to be outdone in a yarn' at all those legendary parties in her London house with which two Irish girls from the Holy Child Killiney, Philippa and Maeve, had wowed the British media and book trade. Sometime staff member Helder Maia Moco even found time to tweet from Brazil and send Philippa 'a big hug', knowing how hopeless she would be feeling.

As the day of the funeral approached, journalists roamed through Dalkey with the thought that here could be one of Maeve's fictional communities – and in some respects they were not disappointed.

Before Maeve started writing novels, the playwright Hugh Leonard (1926–2009) had put the modern town on the literary map, using actual Dalkey characters in his books and plays, people with whom the townspeople were familiar – Maeve herself commented that audiences as far apart as the Abbey Theatre Dublin, London's West End and Broadway knew Dalkey friends of hers, the Comerfords and Dr Enright, thanks to Leonard.

And she was not averse to doing something similar. Finnegan's, the Dalkey bar where Gordon and Maeve kept a reserved table in an alcove and came several times a week for lunch, was the venue for a public reading by Maeve a month before she died. She had written a short story for the Dalkey Book Festival which was set in the town and mentioned various local businesses.

Until his death in 2009, Hugh Leonard had been a great

supporter of the two local drama societies, the Dalkey Players and St Patrick's, and had organised author walks and presented the story of the area at the Dalkey Heritage Centre. It all helped to strengthen the sense of community, a spirit which, with Maeve's funeral imminent, journalists from afar were now looking for from the locals.

Matt Malone of the Senso Studios hair salon told the press how Maeve would entertain them all with her stories and a hair appointment would turn into a signing session with customers racing down to the Book Exchange to buy the latest of her books and get her signature on it before she left. An assistant at the library told a journalist she had nothing appropriate to put in the window, what with all Maeve's books out on loan since the announcement of her death. And Hilary McCabe at McCabe's Select Stores café and grocery, who had known Maeve since she was four, confirmed that she'd been the talk of the town all day.

No one quite knew how to handle the funeral. Was it to be a very public occasion with Dalkey reaching out to the world or a more personal one, out of respect for her family's feelings? Maeve herself had wanted a funeral for friends and family only.

In the event, a Requiem Mass was celebrated on Friday 3 August at the Church of the Assumption in Castle Street, in the old Dalkey lands where half a century earlier Maeve had waited on tenterhooks for her Matriculation results and her adult life had begun.

Inevitably there wasn't room for everyone who turned up. Hundreds more than the church could hold watched proceedings on an RTÉ webcast in the Heritage Centre at Goat's Castle on the opposite side of the street.

Representatives from the highest political office attended along with high-profile members of the arts, the media and the literary world, as well as representatives of charities that Maeve supported.

The flowers at the funeral were *Rosa* 'Gordon Snell'. Maeve had commissioned the bloom – a yellow floribunda – as a special birthday present to Gordon in 1999, when it was shown for the first time at the annual Royal Horticultural Society's Chelsea Flower Show in London.

The Mass was celebrated by four priests, including past and present administrators at Dalkey (Fr John McDonagh and Fr Paddy Devitt), visiting priest Fr William Stuart, and Fr Michael Collins of Haddington Road parish in Dublin.

Maeve's cousin, the actress Kate Binchy, and her brother William gave readings, as did Maeve's neighbour, the *Father Ted* actor Frank Kelly. Music was provided partly by uilleann piper Liam O'Flynn, whose 'Brendan Theme' Maeve had selected as her favourite track on the BBC radio programme *Desert Island Discs*.

After the Mass, Rita Connolly sang 'The Deer's Cry (St Patrick's Breastplate)' and the coffin was taken from the church to the strains of 'Mo Ghile Mear', the time-honoured lament of the female spirit of Ireland, again sung by Rita Connolly. There then followed a private cremation.

TEN

A WEEK IN WINTER

Four months later came *A Week in Winter*, the last book Maeve had written and her final opportunity to reach her millions of readers. It was not a wasted one. In it she describes Freda, who 'sees true', as if Maeve wrote the story knowing she was leaving, standing on the threshold of Freda's 'other world'.

Carole Baron had to edit the novel with no Maeve to consult. She worked with a copy editor and they'd say things like, 'That doesn't sound like the kind of word Maeve would use' or 'This sounds like a Maeve word' to each other. Carole said she felt Maeve at her shoulder the whole time.[91]

In the dying of the light Maeve sought resolution in symmetry, echoing the opening page of her first novel in the final words of her last. *Light a Penny Candle* opens with Elizabeth White's mother Violet reading a library book, an escapist romance starring a masterful man and a bird-brain heroine who does nothing for herself – the type of book, Maeve was announcing back in 1982, that she was not about to write. Now, *A Week in Winter* ends with Freda, who understands how a library can be the seat and lifeblood of a community, and what books can do other than to provide mere escapist entertainment.

Gordon had closed his literary output with similar symmetry the previous year, a second adventure of the King of Quizzical Island, the character of his first book, published at the same time as Maeve's first fiction in 1978.[92]

One of Maeve's school friends, who hadn't been able to attend her funeral, wondered that it had been a Catholic ceremony, given that she was agnostic. 'Maybe,' she said, 'coming to face death, maybe there was a turnaround.' The thought was bound to cross the minds of people aware of Maeve's loss of faith in 1963.

The 'turnaround' scenario doesn't sound like her. In Father William Stuart's homily he said: 'Maeve came from the tradition of the Magi. She was a searcher, a seeker of the divine, but it eluded her.' Perhaps what she understood to be divine did not elude her. Sometimes one must lose a life to find a new one. She discarded Catholicism certainly, but a new inner life had begun to form in 1968, with her visit to Cumann Merriman in County Clare.

And therein lies the real message of *A Week in Winter*. Forty-four years after first dipping her finger in the cauldron of inspiration of Cumann Merriman, celebrated in the short story 'A Week in Summer', she rounded off her literary career, and her life, knowing that she was dying, with a book entitled *A Week in Winter*. The novel is set in Merriman's birthplace at Ennistymon, less than eight miles south of Lisdoonvarna.

The 'West of Ireland paradise' of Ennistymon is the fictional

Stoneybridge of the novel. It is named Stoneybridge after Ennistymon's seven-arch stone bridge, which stands astride the Cullenagh.

Stone House in the novel, 'a picture of a house', is converted into a hotel by its fictional proprietor Chicky Starr, who has come home with her burden of secrets and regrets, and it is here that Maeve throws together an ill-assorted group of strangers. Stone House is in fact the house in Ennistymon which the poet Francis McNamara (1884–1946) converted into the Falls Hotel in the 1930s, and where, for three successive years from 2002, Cumann Merriman held its summer school.[93]

Merriman was born illegitimately at Ennistymon in 1749. Shortly after his birth his mother married a local stonemason who was working on the walls of the local Deerpark estate. Stone is what Ennistymon is all about. 'Built by the best stonemasons in Ireland, there is a congruence of shape and form about this place which comes from a long tradition of knowing how to express vernacular art in stone,' writes Margaret MacCurtain in the best short account of the town.[94]

The symmetry of returning to Cumann Merriman in *A Week in Winter* to complete the circle that had begun there in 1968 was no mere tidy tying up of ends, it said something about her inner life.

When she returned to Dalkey in the 1980s, Maeve did so not sentimentally to rediscover the town of her youth, nor prosperously to connect with modern celebrity Dalkey, but spiritually to reconnect with the collective unconscious of her people, which was her inspiration.

Connections with Ireland's ancient past were to be found, like so much else, on her doorstep. Dalkey came into existence as Killbegnet, which means 'Begnet's Church', which takes us back to the ruins of the seventh-century church in Castle Street. But at the eastern end of Sorrento Road, beyond Sorrento Point (the far promontory of the modern town), there lies a bewitching 25-acre island in a huddle with three smaller fragments,[95] and a sense of Ireland far, far back in the mists of time.

It is no surprise to learn that Dalkey Island was inhabited at least as early as 4000 BC, long before St Patrick was brought to Dún Laoghaire from his home in England as a sixteen-year-old slave, long before Laoghaire himself was crowned High King of Ireland on the Hill of Tara – to a time even before Tara itself was a symbol of national kingship in Ireland.[96]

When Dalkey Island came into its own in the fourth millennium before the birth of Christ, Tara was a ceremonial site of a different kind. Its vast passage tomb, known as Duma na nGiall, takes us back to the era of the megalithic tombs of Thomond, which the festival-goers of Cumann Merriman know so well.

This was a time when Ireland, one of the oldest nations in Europe, was known as 'Ierne', after early colonisation by Greek and other eastern European peoples had left a certain *matriarchal* impress upon the Irish mind.

The Celtic Mother Goddess, Danu (descended from the goddess Danae of Argos), was brought to Ireland's shores in neolithic times (4000–2400 BC) and still finds reference in two hills in County Kerry – Da Chich Anann ('the Breast of Anu') to this day.

Danae, or Danu, is the matriarchal goddess celebrated in Brian Merriman's poem as the Aoibhea, Queen of the Fairies, the matriarchal figure Maeve found to identify with, a formidable, mysterious feminine principle recognised by the poet's intuitive side (Merriman's 'Aisling' dream-girl) as the voice of the collective unconscious of the Irish people.[97]

The more one discovers about Maeve, the more this powerful matriarchal impress fits. Queen Maeve, the matriarch whose acolytes, friends and family paraded alongside her throne on the St Patrick Day parade; Maeve the counsellor and advisor, who at the end could still think, as she did when she was twenty, that she could run everybody else's life; intuitive Maeve, whose unassailable authority could strike to the very core of one's being; and Maeve the *seanchaí*, whose values arose from somewhere deep in her country's past and were enshrined in modern parables, her purpose to offer resolution to divisions everywhere.

She herself recognised the moment when this unconscious 'goddess' personality suddenly and unexpectedly put in an appearance. She called it 'an unbalanced kind of time', often at 5.30 in the morning when she was up before the world writing a book. At that time, 'You have absolutely no judgement about your own work.' There is no objectivity, no analysis, you just cut off and the work flows.

Sometimes it seems perfectly pleasant, a good story that might hold the attention, and sometimes it seems like the ramblings of a mad person. Sitting there, a sad pool of light in a sleeping world, it's easy to ask yourself cosmic questions. Not only what is it all about, but what is it all for? The answers are hard to find.[98]

A thing of no idle interest is that in a lifetime process of realising her true matriarchal self, it seems that Maeve was fulfilling a destiny pre-ordained at the very moment of naming her.

This goddess found expression in various personae, none more famously than as Medb, the Queen of Connacht in the Ulster Cycle of Irish mythology. The matriarchal people of County Sligo built a massive passage tomb for her known in Gaelic as Meascán Méabha, the tomb of Medb, a large cairn about 180 feet wide and 30 feet high of some 40,000 tons of stone, making it the largest in Ireland outside the Brú na Bóinne. And on the hillside below Tara, just north of Dublin, there is a protected national monument, a large ceremonial enclosure or 'henge' 800 feet in diameter dedicated to Medb. But the sign to it reads, 'Rath Maeve'. For 'Medb', in English, translates as 'Queen Maeve'.

So, when Maureen named her beloved child Maeve she was, as an out-and-out Irishwoman steeped in these things, putting her baby plumb central in the great matriarchal mythology that lies at the heart of what being Irish means.

There is more. Very often when a great sea change in the beliefs of a people occurs, as it did when St Patrick brought Christianity to Ireland, custom, ritual and characters of the old religion are grafted onto the new, facilitating the leap of faith and making the transition less dramatic. The memory of the goddess worshipped as Danu was preserved for Christians in fifth-century Ireland in the figure of St Anne, who in the

Christian story is the mother (i.e. the forerunner) of the Virgin Mary.[99]

It is so apt, then, that Maureen christened her daughter both Anne and Maeve, the two names that point to an identification with the matriarchal tradition in Ireland as far back as we can tell.

It is also appropriate that *our* Maeve lived in Knocknacree Road on Dalkey Hill thousands of years after Medb. For the large hill on which Queen Maeve lies buried in Sligo is called Knocknarea, and like Maeve's hill overlooks a beautiful bay.

Finally, both Maeve's brother and her literary agent quite independently described her as a swan gliding apparently effortlessly across a pool, while underneath everything is going like the clappers. And Queen Maeve was commonly identified with the swan, even sometimes taking a swan's form in myth.

Over the millennia the Sligo people have remained highly protective of the tomb of Medb, resisting its excavation. It is just about the oldest thing of Irish Tradition we have.

APPENDIX A

The issuing of the 'Proclamation of the Republic' by Patrick Pearse in 1916 marked the beginning of modern Irish history.

IRISHMEN AND IRISHWOMEN: In the name of God and of the dead generations from which she receives her old tradition of nationhood, Ireland, through us, summons her children to her flag and strikes for her freedom.

Having organised and trained her manhood through her secret revolutionary organisation, the Irish Republican Brotherhood, and through her open military organisations, the Irish Volunteers and the Irish Citizen Army, having patiently perfected her discipline, having resolutely waited for the right moment to reveal itself, she now seizes that moment, and, supported by her exiled children in America and by gallant allies in Europe, but relying in the first on her own strength, she strikes in full confidence of victory.

We declare the right of the people of Ireland to the ownership of Ireland, and to the unfettered control of Irish destinies, to be sovereign and indefeasible. The long usurpation of that right by a foreign people and government has not extinguished the right, nor can it ever be extinguished except by the destruction of the Irish people. In every generation the Irish people have asserted their right to national freedom and sovereignty: six times during the past three hundred years they have asserted it in arms. Standing on that fundamental right and again asserting it in arms in the face of the world, we hereby proclaim the Irish Republic as a Sovereign Independent State, and we pledge our lives and the lives of our comrades-in-arms to the cause of its freedom, of its welfare, and its exaltation among the nations.

The Irish Republic is entitled to, and hereby claims, the allegiance of every Irishman and Irishwoman. The Republic guarantees religious and civil liberty, equal rights and equal opportunities to all its citizens, and declares its resolve to pursue the happiness and prosperity of the whole nation and of all its parts, cherishing all the children of the nation equally, and oblivious of the differences carefully fostered by an alien government, which have divided a minority from the majority in the past.

Until our arms have brought the opportune moment for the establishment of a permanent National Government, representative of the whole people of Ireland and elected by the suffrages of all her men and women, the Provisional Government, hereby constituted, will administer the civil and military affairs of the Republic in trust for the people.

We place the cause of the Irish Republic under the protection of the Most High God, Whose blessing we invoke upon our arms, and we pray that no one who serves that cause will dishonour it by cowardice, inhumanity, or rapine. In this supreme hour the Irish nation must, by its valour and discipline and by the readiness of its children to sacrifice themselves for the common good, prove itself worthy of the august destiny to which it is called.

APPENDIX B

'The Ballad of Kevin Barry'

In Mountjoy jail one Monday morning
High upon the gallows tree,
Kevin Barry gave his young life
For the cause of liberty.
Just a lad of eighteen summers,
Still there's no one can deny,
As he walked to death that morning,
He proudly held his head on high.

[Chorus]
Shoot me like an Irish soldier.
Do not hang me like a dog,
For I fought to free old Ireland
On that still September morn.
All around the little bakery
Where we fought them hand to hand,
Shoot me like an Irish soldier,
For I fought to free Ireland.

Just before he faced the hangman,
In his dreary prison cell,
British soldiers tortured Barry,
Just because he would not tell
The names of his brave comrades,
And other things they wished to know.
'Turn informer or we'll kill you.'
Kevin Barry answered 'No'.

Proudly standing to attention
While he bade his last farewell
To his broken-hearted mother
Whose grief no one can tell.
For the cause he proudly cherished
This sad parting had to be
Then to death walked softly smiling
That old Ireland might be free.

Another martyr for old Ireland,
Another murder for the crown,
Whose brutal laws may kill the Irish,
But can't keep their spirit down.
Lads like Barry are no cowards.
From the foe they will not fly.
Lads like Barry will free Ireland,
For her sake they'll live and die.

APPENDIX C

Brehon law arose through the roots of society as it were by osmosis, quite unlike the rule of the Jesuit Society of Jesus, which was imposed – top down – from Rome. It differs in significant ways to canon law, the law of the Catholic Church. For example, Brehon law allows polygyny (more than one lover) and divorce. It is also more enlightened in its treatment of women. By the eighth century, although Irish society was male dominated, it allowed women greater freedom, independence and rights to property than any other European society. Divorce was provided for on a number of grounds and property was divided fairly according to the contribution each spouse made. A husband was legally permitted to hit his wife to 'correct' her, but if the blow left a mark she was entitled to compensation and could, if she wished, divorce him.

There are also many differences between Brehon law and British law, which the British government had for centuries been imposing upon the Irish people. Capital punishment, for example, was not permitted.

TIMELINE

1858 William Patrick Binchy, Maeve's grandfather, is born.

1909 William Francis Binchy, Maeve's father, is born at Charleville, County Cork.

1910 Maureen Blackmore, Maeve's mother, is born in Cregg by Carrick-on-Suir, County Tipperary.

1911 Michael Binchy (17), James Binchy (14), Joseph Binchy (11), Owen S. Binchy (14) and Daniel A. Binchy (11) attend Clongowes Wood Jesuit College for boys in Balraheen, County Kildare, with John Charles McQuaid.

1916 On Easter Monday, the Irish Volunteers, the Irish Citizen Army of James Connolly and 200 members of another revolutionary body, Cumann na mBan, seize certain locations in Dublin, and at a key moment Patrick Pearse reads the famous Proclamation on behalf of the Military Council of the Irish Republican Brotherhood, outside the Post Office in Sackville Street. The leaders are executed by the British.

1918 Daniel A. Binchy takes up a place at University College Dublin and becomes active in the student union.

1920 Kevin Barry, a nineteen-year-old undergraduate at University College Dublin reading Medicine, is executed by hanging at Mountjoy Prison for his part in an action which resulted in the deaths of three British soldiers.

1921 Frank Flood, a nineteen-year-old scholarship boy at University College Dublin reading Engineering, is arrested while attacking the Dublin Metropolitan Police at Drumcondra, charged with high treason and executed by hanging at Mountjoy Prison.

1924 Daniel A. Binchy is appointed Professor of Legal History and Jurisprudence at University College Dublin.

1925 William Francis Binchy, Maeve's father, goes up to University College Dublin to read English Language and Literature.

1928 William Francis Binchy graduates from University College Dublin with First Class Honours.

1938 William Francis Binchy, by now a barrister, marries Maureen Blackmore on 29 March at the Catholic church of Dún Laoghaire.

1939 Anne Maeve Binchy (Maeve) is born on 28 May at 26 Upper Pembroke Street, Dublin 2. The family goes to live at Beechgrove, Lower Glenageary Road, close to Dalkey.

1940 Daniel W. J. Binchy, Maeve's first cousin, is born.

1942 Joan M. Binchy, Maeve's sister, is born.

1944 Irene (Renie) A. Binchy, Maeve's sister, is born.

1945 Maeve attends St Anne's Private School nursery at 36 Clarinda Park East.

1947 William F. T. Binchy, Maeve's brother, is born.

1947 The Holy Child, a Jesuit convent, opens at Killiney, at the invitation of Archbishop John Charles McQuaid.

1949 Last tram to leave Dalkey.

1949 First English translation of *Nausea* by Jean-Paul Sartre.

1950 Maeve attends the Holy Child Convent in Killiney. This is the model of the convent school attended by Aisling O'Connor and Elizabeth White in Maeve's first novel, *Light a Penny Candle*.

1952 Maeve's family move to a large house called Eastmount, on the Knocknacree Road in Dalkey.

1953 First English publication of *The Second Sex* by Simone de Beauvoir.

1953 Maeve's first date, an invitation to the cinema at Dún Laoghaire, to see *Roman Holiday*, starring Gregory Peck and Audrey Hepburn. Hepburn won an Academy Award. Maeve's date was a disaster.

1956 Maeve takes her Leaving Certificate at seventeen, and leaves the Holy Child Killiney for university.

1956 Maeve goes up to University College Dublin to read Law, but swiftly changes course to read English, French and History, with Latin her fourth subject, sitting First Arts in these subjects in 1957, then focusing just on French and History for her honours degree, taken in 1959.

1956 First English edition published of *Being and Nothingness* by Jean-Paul Sartre.

1959 Maeve sits her finals at University College Dublin.

1959 Maeve accepts a summer-term teaching position at St Leonards-on-Sea on the south coast of England.

1960 Maeve studies for a DipEd at University College.

1960 Maeve teaches at a school in Cork. On the train home the following year she has her first taste of alcohol. She is twenty-two.

1961 Maeve begins teaching Latin and history to girls from twelve to eighteen at a lay Catholic girls' school in Dublin, Miss Meredith's on Pembroke Road, close by the canal in Dublin 4. Three days a week she teaches conversational French to children at Zion Schools in Dublin's Jewish quarter.

1963 The parents of children Maeve is teaching at the Jewish school give her a trip to Israel as a present. She has no money, so she goes and works in Kibbutz Zikim in Ashkelon, Israel with her best friend, Philippa O'Keefe. Maeve also spends the following two summers (1964 and 1965) at the kibbutz.

1963 Maeve loses her Christian faith while in Israel. Returns home to find that she is a published writer. Her father had sold her letters to the *Irish Independent*.

1965 Travels to Tunisia, Sardinia, Crete…

1966 Begins freelancing as a journalist. Feminism articles, backs the convent schools.

1966 Travels widely over the next two years – Singapore, Cyprus, La Rochelle, Portugal, Yugoslavia, Turkey, the Philippines, Russia, India, Greece, Canaries, Austria, Tangier, Spain, Scotland, Lourdes, Bulgaria, Agadir and Palestine.

1967 Maureen, Maeve's mother, dies aged fifty-seven of cancer at St Luke's Hospital, Rathgar, Dublin.

1967 Maeve's first visit to Cumann Merriman, which aims to promote interest in all aspects of Irish culture. The Merriman Summer School is held during the last week of August in the district of Thomond, Co. Clare. Past patrons include the poet, writer and Nobel Prize winner Seamus Heaney.

1967 Maeve writes article for the *Irish Times* entitled 'I just love being a teacher'.

1968 Maeve gives up teaching and is hired as Women's Editor of the *Irish Times*.

1968 Maeve becomes a frequent contributor to RTÉ Radio.

1968 Maeve's sister Renie qualifies as a doctor.

1968 Maeve's brother William Binchy becomes a barrister-at-law.

1970 Publication of *The Female Eunuch* by Germaine Greer.

1970 The Irish Women's Liberation movement is founded.

1970 Publication of *My First Book* by Maeve Binchy, a collection of her *Irish Times* articles.

1971 Maeve's father dies at sixty-two. Maeve, absolutely bereft, sells the family house and moves to a flat in Dublin. Meets freelance BBC broadcaster Gordon Snell in London when she is there to do some work on *Woman's Hour*.

1973 Maeve leaves Dublin for a job with the *Irish Times* in its London office, and to pursue her relationship with Gordon Snell.

1973 On 8 March, the Provisional Irish Republican Army (IRA) conducts its first operation in England, planting four car bombs in London.

1973 On 14 November Maeve covers Princess Anne's marriage to Captain Mark Phillips and causes a stir.

1974 Maeve covers the war in Cyprus after she and Gordon had holidayed there.

1974 Maeve follows the Welsh Nationalist Gwynfor Evans during his campaign to get back into Westminster.

1975 Maeve begins her 'Inside London' column.

1975 Maeve receives a letter from Joc Dowling from the Abbey Theatre, Peacock Stage, asking whether she'd ever thought of writing plays.

1976 27 March, a bomb placed by the Provisional IRA explodes in a litter bin at the top of an escalator in a crowded exhibition hall, Earl's Court. 20,000 people were attending the *Daily Mail* Ideal Home Exhibition at the time. Seventy were injured, four people lost limbs.

1976 9 December, Maeve's first play, *End of Term*, is produced by the Abbey Theatre. It is about three teachers in an Irish convent school as their lives are exposed by a devious schoolgirl.

1977 Maeve and Gordon Snell marry on 29 January at Hammersmith Register Office. They honeymoon in Australia.

1978 Maeve first collection of fictional short stories – *Central Line* – is published on 19 June.

1978 The sixth volume of Maeve's uncle Daniel A. Binchy's life's work, *Corpus Iuris Hibernici*, is published.

1978 *Deeply Regretted By*, a screenplay written by Maeve in 1976, is broadcast on 28 December as part of RTÉ Television's 'Thursday Play Date' series, with Louis Lentin producing. It wins a prize at the Prague Television Festival and two Jacob's awards for Maeve Binchy and Donall Farmer. It is an account of a tragedy affecting a woman in London who discovers, on the death of her husband, that their married life was a lie. It first appeared as 'Death in Kilburn' in the *Irish Times*.

1979 Maeve's play *Half-Promised Land* is produced by the Abbey Theatre, Peacock Stage, on 11 October. The play tells of two Irish schoolteachers, Sheila and Una, working on a kibbutz in Israel.

1980 Maeve's second collection of fictional short stories – *Victoria Line* – is published.

1980 Maeve and Gordon spot Pollyvilla up for sale in Dalkey. They buy it.

1980 *Ireland of the Welcomes* play transmitted on 'Thursday Playdate', 16 October. Concerns the dream of an Irish emigrant to return and settle with his family in his native town.

1981 Century Publishing pay Maeve £5,000 advance for her first novel, *Light a Penny Candle*, and sell UK paperback rights for £52,000, the highest sum ever paid for a first novel commissioned by a British publisher. Maeve's agent Christine Green sells US hardcover rights to Viking for $200,000.

1981 Maeve's short-story collection *Dublin 4* is published.

1982 *Light a Penny Candle*, which follows the friendship of two young women through two decades, is published and remains in the UK Top 10 for fifty-three weeks.

1982 Binchy's Bakery in Charleville closes.

1983 Maeve's short-story collection *London Transports* is published.

1984 Maeve's linked story collection *The Lilac Bus* is published.

1983 William Binchy campaigns for the constitutional ban on abortion as an amendment to the Irish Constitution, successfully.

1985 *Echoes*, Maeve's second novel, is published. It tells of the struggle of an impoverished young woman to escape a narrow-minded resort town.

1985 Founding of Philippa O'Keefe's catering company, Lodge Catering, which becomes the model for Scarlet Feather in future novels.

1986 William Binchy campaigns against the introduction of divorce in Ireland (successfully in 1986, and unsuccessfully in 1995).

1987 Maeve's novel *Firefly Summer* is published. It concerns an Irish-American who is forced to reconsider his misconceptions about Ireland when he goes there to live.

1988 Maeve's novel *Silver Wedding* is published, the story of a couple celebrating their twenty-fifth wedding anniversary and the events that led them there.

1988 The four-part television miniseries based on *Echoes* is broadcast on Channel 4.

1989 Daniel A. Binchy, Maeve's uncle, dies.

1990 Maeve's novel *Circle of Friends* is published. It is about two friends who attend university in Dublin.

1990 Maeve's short-story collection *The Storyteller* is published.

1990 The ninety-minute TV film of *The Lilac Bus* is transmitted.

1992 Maeve's novel *The Copper Beech* is published by Orion Publishing. The great tree spreads itself over the schoolhouse where conscious life for Shancarrig's children begins.

1993 Maeve's short-story collection *Dublin People* is published.

1993 Photograph of Maeve by Richard Whitehead becomes part of the National Portrait Gallery Collection in London.

1993 Orion offer £500,000 advance for UK rights in Maeve's new novel, *The Glass Lake*.

1994 *The Glass Lake* is published, about a woman who disappears, believed to have committed suicide, but she has left her family to start a new life.

1995 The film of *Circle of Friends* is premiered.

1995 Screenplays by Jim Culleton based on short stories by Maeve are produced under the title *Troubled Hearts* by Belltable Arts Centre, Limerick, Dublin.

1995 The Fifteenth Amendment of the Constitution of Ireland repeals the constitutional prohibition of divorce, approved by referendum on 24 November 1995 and signed into law on 17 June 1996.

1996 Maeve's short-story collection *Cross Lines* is published.

1996 Maeve's short-story collection *This Year It Will Be Different: And Other Stories* is published.

1996 Maeve's novel *Evening Class* is published, in which a group of people gather for an evening class at a high school. The class represents the chance to make a dream come true for each one of them.

1997 Maeve's radio play *The Visit* broadcast by RTE Radio.

1997 The collection *Finbar's Hotel*, to which Maeve is a contributor, is published.

1998 Maeve's novel *Tara Road* is published, in which two women – one Irish, one American – try to improve their lives by trading houses.

1998 Maeve's short-story collection *The Return Journey* is published.

1999 Maeve's non-fiction book *Aches & Pains* is published.

1999 Maeve appears on *The Oprah Winfrey Show* in New York.

1999 Maeve receives the British Book Award for Lifetime Achievement.

1999 The collection *Ladies' Night at Finbar's Hotel*, to which Maeve is a contributor, is published.

2000 Maeve's novel *Scarlet Feather* is published. Two friends who were caterers in real life – Cathy Scarlet and Tom Feather in the novel – tell amazing stories about the people they cater for.

2000 Maeve announces her retirement.

2000 Maeve receives a People of the Year Award.

2001 Maeve's novel *Scarlet Feather* wins the W. H. Smith Book Award for Fiction.

2001 Maeve's *Wired to the Moon* is produced at the Andrews Lane Theatre, Dublin. The play follows six characters who all allow problems in their lives to spiral out of control. The six stories are interwoven, as the characters try to come to terms with their dilemmas and confront the insecurities that cause them.

2002 Maeve's novel *Quentins*, about the customers in a Dublin restaurant, is published.

2002 Maeve's novella *The Builders* is published.

2002 Maeve is editor with Cathy Kelly and Marian Keyes of *Irish Girls About Town*.

2002 Maeve suffers a health crisis related to a heart condition. It inspires her to write the novel *Heart and Soul*.

2004 Maeve campaigns against the restriction of the automatic, constitutional right to citizenship of all of those born on the island of Ireland (unsuccessfully).

2004 Maeve's novel *Nights of Rain & Stars*, a tale of vacationers in Greece who are linked by a shared tragedy, is published.

2005 The film of Maeve's novel *Tara Road* is premiered.

2005 Maeve's *Surprise*, a four-part radio drama, is broadcast. Maeve is a driving force behind the RTÉ Radio 1 *Human Rights* drama seasons.

2005 Maeve is one of the writers for *She Was Wearing*, a play produced at Smock Alley Theatre & Studio in Dublin. It's a series of short, interconnecting monologues specially commissioned in response to Amnesty International's Stop Violence Against Women campaign.

2005 Maeve Binchy has her portrait, by Maeve McCarthy, hung at the National Gallery in London.

2006 Maeve's non-fiction book *A Time to Dance* is published.

2006 Maeve's novella *Star Sullivan* is published.

2006 Maeve's novel *Whitehorn Woods* is published.

2007 A film, *How About You*, is based on Maeve's short story by the same name from the short-story collection titled *This Year It Will Be Different: And Other Stories*, but sometimes published as *The Hard Core*. The film stars Vanessa Redgrave, Joss Ackland, Brenda Fricker and Imelda Staunton.

2007 Maeve's story 'Anner House' becomes a ninety-minute TV film written by Anne-Marie Casey.

2007 Maeve receives the Irish PEN Award, joining such luminaries as John B. Keane, Brian Friel, Edna O'Brien, William Trevor, John McGahern and Seamus Heaney.

2007 Maeve is awarded the University College Dublin Foundation Day Medal by her alma mater.

2008 Maeve's sister Renie dies on 12 January.

2008 Maeve's novel *Heart & Soul*, about a doctor who establishes a clinic in an under-served area while trying to juggle her own affairs, is published.

2008 Maeve's non-fiction book *The Maeve Binchy Writer's Club* is published.

2009 Maeve appears on *The Meaning of Life* TV chat show with Gay Byrne.

2010 Maeve's novel *Minding Frankie* is published. It centres on a single father who enlists the aid of his neighbours to help raise his infant daughter.

2010 Maeve receives a lifetime achievement award from the Irish Book Awards.

2011 Maeve and Gordon make appear in RTÉ's TV soap opera *Fair City*.

2012 Maeve's novella *Full House* is published.

2012 Maeve dies from a heart attack at the Blackrock Clinic, County Dublin, on 30 July.

2012 Her last novel, *A Week in Winter*, is published in November.

2014 *Chestnut Street*, a book of linked short stories, is published posthumously.

NOTES

1   Maeve Binchy in interview with Donal O'Donoghue, *RTÉ Guide* (2010).

2   Maeve Binchy in *A Portrait of the Artist as a Young Girl*, edited by John Quinn (Methuen, 1986).

3   Every biography and newspaper gives 1940 as the year in which she was born, and her age was given as seventy-two when she died in July 2012. But her birth certificate states plainly and unequivocally that she was born on 29 May 1939.

4   Maeve Binchy, *A Week in Winter* (Orion, 2012).

5   Donal Lynch, *Sunday Independent*, 2012.

6   Clifton School, which today is a private residence called Summerfield Lodge. Joyce taught there for a term.

7   The Martello tower at Sandycove has contained a museum dedicated to Joyce since Bloomsday 1962, though, as I write, cutbacks have reduced staffing to volunteer status.

8   The Binchy Archive, James Joyce Library, University College Dublin.

9   Interview with Jessica Simmons, *The Guardian*, November 2010.

10   Not to be confused with the novelist Daniel W. J. Binchy, who is Maeve's first cousin. Daniel Anthony, Maeve's uncle, was born in 1900

(though sometimes it is recorded as 1889) and became a scholar of Irish linguistics and early Irish law.

11   John Quinn (ed.), *A Portrait of the Artist as a Young Girl* (Methuen, 1986).

12   Ibid.

13   Maeve Binchy, *Aches and Pains* (Orion, 1999).

14   Interview of Maeve Binchy with Mary Buscher, *Irish America*, 2001.

15   John Quinn (ed.), *A Portrait of the Artist as a Young Girl* (Methuen, 1986).

16   *Maeve Binchy: At Home in the World* (2010). Documentary directed by Sinéad O'Brien; produced by Noel Pearson. A Ferndale Films production for RTÉ.

17   Interview of Maeve Binchy with Mary Buscher, *Irish America*, 2001.

18   Maeve Binchy in *A Portrait of the Artist as a Young Girl*, edited by John Quinn (Methuen, 1986).

19   Interview with Professor Declan Kiberd on the occasion at the Royal St George Yacht Club in Dún Laoghaire in January 2007 when Professor Kiberd, at that time Professor of Anglo-Irish Literature at UCD, took to the podium to praise a national treasure. Maeve Binchy was being conferred with the Irish PEN/A. T. Cross Literary Award, joining a distinguished roll-call of Irish writers who had received it before her, including John McGahern and Seamus Heaney. Declan Kiberd is now Professor of Irish Studies at Notre Dame University, USA.

20   Frank Budgen, *James Joyce and the Making of Ulysses* (Oxford University Press, 1972).

21   Jack Matthews, *Newsday*, March 1995.

22   Founder member of Fianna Fáil, the Republican Party, and Taoiseach (Prime Minister) from 1959–66.

23   From 1959–65 the leader of Fine Gael, a centre-right party in the Republic, and a great orator.

24 The Irish Citizen Army of James Connolly and 200 members of another revolutionary body, Cumann na mBan.

25 See Appendix A.

26 The Literary and Historical Society was founded as a student debating society (known as the L&H) in 1855–6 by John Henry Newman (1801–90), rector of the Catholic University of Ireland, founded in 1854, to be chartered as University College Dublin in 1908. The society ceased to function in December 1880 and emerged again in November 1882 as the Union Literary Society (until 1883). Many members of the society went on to play important roles in public, professional, ecclesiastical, business and judicial life in Ireland.

27 See Appendix B.

28 The six counties of Northern Ireland are Londonderry, Antrim, Tyrone, Fermanagh, Armagh and Down.

29 'Art straight from Carole's kitchen table', *West End Extra*, New Journal Enterprises.

30 Interview with Professor Declan Kiberd on the occasion in January 2007 when Maeve Binchy was conferred with the Irish PEN/A.T. Cross Literary Award.

31 *The Light of Experience* (BBC, 1977).

32 Andrew G. Marshall, *The Independent*, September 1998.

33 See allusion to Jean-Paul Sartre as Maeve's life guide in a letter from Gordon Snell (Chapter Seven: London Apprentice).

34 Andrew G. Marshall, *The Independent*, September 1998.

35 Jack Kerouac quoted by the late Al Aronowitz in *The Blacklisted Journalist*.

36 Andrew G. Marshall, *The Independent*, September 1998.

37 She would tackle it in her journalism and also in *Echoes*, where David Power can become a doctor like his father easily enough, but it is very

hard for Clare O'Brien, whose father runs a sweetshop, to be anything at all.

38   Now part of St Leonards-Mayfield, an independent Catholic school.

39   Katharine Webber, *Publishers Weekly*, October 1992.

40   Margaret Bernstein, *Everywoman*, May 1999.

41   Ibid.

42   Felicity Hayes-McCoy, *The Guardian*, July 2012.

43   Chanukkah, the Jewish festival of rededication, also known as the festival of lights, is an eight-day festival beginning on the 25th day of the Jewish month of Kislev (29/30 days within November–December in the Gregorian calendar).

44   Lewis Burke Frumkes, *The Writer*, February 2000.

45   Acorn Media Publishing Inc., 2001.

46   Robert Graves, introduction to *The Sufis* by Idries Shah (Doubleday, 1964).

47   *Undercover Portraits: Maeve Binchy* (2000), produced and directed by Michael Garvey. An Orpheus production for RTÉ.

48   Acorn Media Publishing Inc., 2001.

49   *Good Housekeeping*, September 1996.

50   *Undercover Portraits: Maeve Binchy* (2000), produced and directed by Michael Garvey. An Orpheus production for RTÉ.

51   Amanda Cable, *The People*, October 1999.

52   Mary Kenny, *Daily Telegraph*, July 2012.

53   Anne McHardy, *The Guardian*, July 2012.

54   Ireland's national radio and television broadcaster.

55 A famous women's magazine programme first broadcast by the BBC in 1946 and still going today.

56 CBS *This Morning*. Burelle's Information Services, 1995.

57 *Maeve Binchy: At Home in the World* (2010). Documentary directed by Sinéad O'Brien; produced by Noel Pearson. A Ferndale Films production for RTÉ.

58 A Boxing Day 2012 tribute to Maeve Binchy on RTÉ Radio 1, the programme presented by Evelyn O'Rourke. Declan Kiberd, sometime Professor of Anglo-Irish Literature at University College Dublin, is now Professor of Irish Studies at Notre Dame University, USA.

59 Margaret Barry (1917–89) was a traditional Irish singer and banjo player.

60 Donal Foley, *Three Villages: An Autobiography*, with an introduction by Maeve Binchy and Mary Maher (Ballylough Books, 1977 and 2003).

61 Interview by Dina Rabinovitch for *The Guardian*, September 1998. The Omagh bombing occurred the previous month.

62 See Appendix C.

63 Charles Dickens, *Sketches by 'Boz', Illustrative of Every-day Life and Every-day People* (1836–7).

64 Declan Kiberd, *Ulysses and Us: The Art of Everyday Living* (Faber, 2009).

65 Professor Anthony Clare in *Dear Maeve* by Maeve Binchy (Poolbeg, 1995).

66 A Boxing Day 2012 tribute to Maeve Binchy on RTÉ Radio 1.

67 *Irish Independent*, 1979.

68 Four strangers meet in a Greek taverna high above the village of Aghia Anna.

69 Maeve Binchy, *A Week in Winter* (Orion, 2012).

70 www.roisinmcauley.com/uncategorized/976/maeve-binchy/

71 Patsey Murphy, *Irish Times*, August 2012.

72   Besides writing TV adaptations, novels, essays, autobiographies and some forty stage plays, three of which were produced on Broadway (*The Au Pair Man* (1973), *Da* (1978), and *A Life* (1980)), Hugh Leonard was commissioned by the national broadcasting body RTÉ to write the TV play *Insurrection* to coincide with the fiftieth anniversary of the 1916 Easter Rising.

73   *Undercover Portraits: Maeve Binchy* (2000), produced and directed by Michael Garvey. An Orpheus production for RTÉ.

74   Douglas Kennedy, *Irish Times*, August 2012.

75   John Calder, *The Garden of Eros* (Calder, 2013).

76   *Undercover Portraits: Maeve Binchy* (2000), produced and directed by Michael Garvey. An Orpheus Production for RTÉ.

77   Mary Kenny, *Daily Telegraph*, July 2012.

78   Cliff Goodwin, *To Be a Lady: A Biography of Catherine Cookson* (Century, 1994).

79   'Life in the Day of...' feature in the *Sunday Times*.

80   In the parable of the vineyard, the labourers who worked least hours received the same reward as the labourers who worked most hours.

81   In America, after leaving Delacorte and Dell, Maeve Binchy was published by Dutton in hardcover and New American Library in paperback for *Scarlet Feather*, *Quentins*, and *Night of Rain and Stars*, all *New York Times* bestsellers in hardcover and paperback. She then moved, with her editor, Carole Baron, to Knopf and its paperback company Anchor for publication of *Whitethorn Woods*. They are her publishers to this day. Maeve's last book, *A Week in Winter*, reached No. 1 in America in its first week on sale.

82   Andrew G. Marshall, *The Independent*, 1998.

83   *Irish Times*, 18 April 1985.

84   Conan Kennedy, *Grandfather's House: Monte Alverno, Dalkey, Co. Dublin* (Morrigan New Century, 2008).

85 *Dalkey: An Anthology*, Volume 2, compiled by Frank Mullen; edited by Padraig Yeates (2009).

86 Anthony Kirby, *Christian Science Monitor*, 1999.

87 One, in decrepit condition, is available in the James Joyce Library at University College Dublin.

88 *Daily Telegraph*, 1998.

89 Hester Riches, *Vancouver Sun*, 1994.

90 *The Maeve Binchy Writer's Club* includes twenty letters from Maeve, offering encouragement to aspiring writers, and contributions by Marian Keyes, Alison Walsh, Norah Casey, Paula Campbell, Ivy Bannister, Gerald Dawe, Jim Culleton, Ferdia McAnna and Julie Parsons.

91 RTÉ Radio 1 tribute to Maeve Binchy, presented by Evelyn O'Rourke, December 2012.

92 *The King of Quizzical Island Digs Through the World* (Walker, 2011).

93 The literary associations of the hotel were enhanced when one of McNamara's daughters married the poet Dylan Thomas. There is a bar named after him today.

94 Thomas Davis lecture by Dr Margaret MacCurtain in *Irish Country Towns* (Mercier, 1994).

95 Lamb Island, Clare Island and Maiden Rock.

96 The Hill of Tara is a World Heritage site just north of Dublin, regarded as one of the most important prehistoric sites in Europe.

97 Robert Graves, *The White Goddess: A Historical Grammar of Poetic Myth* (Faber, 1961).

98 'Life in the Day of...' feature in the *Sunday Times*.

99 Robert Graves, *The White Goddess: A Historical Grammar of Poetic Myth* (Faber, 1961).

ACKNOWLEDGEMENTS

Special thanks go to my publisher, Jeremy Robson, for giving me the opportunity to write this book, to Hollie Teague and the whole team at Biteback Publishing and The Robson Press for engaging with it with such enthusiasm, and to Maeve Binchy's literary executor for wishing me well with it. Principally, I would like to thank my wife, Dee, for her textual research, support and advice, and the following for the generous help they gave me in the early stages: Evelyn Flanagan (Special Collections Librarian) and Eugene Roche, Special Collections, James Joyce Library, University College Dublin; Kate Manning, Archives, University College Dublin; Professor Declan Kiberd, Keough Professor of Irish Studies and Professor of English, the University of Notre Dame, Indiana, USA, previously Chair of Anglo-Irish Literature and Drama at University College Dublin; Ms Gerardine Hackett, Principal, Holy Child Killiney; Robin Adams, Librarian, and Iris Bedford, Admissions, Berkeley Library, Trinity College Dublin; Darragh Begley, Reference Team, National Library of Ireland, Dublin; Geraldine

MacCarthy, Holy Child Sister, past pupil and former Principal, Holy Child Killiney; Adrienne Lavelle, Susan McNally, Valerie, Patricia Hamilton, Tim Hannan, Dennis Reader, Molly Parkin and Barbara Taylor Bradford; Tom Dunne, Donal Falon, Rosemary de Courcy, Shane Caffrey, RTÉ Archives; John Glendon, RTÉ Radio Programme Sales; John of the Beach Guest House, Dunmore East; Gerard Walsh, *Ballybunion News*; Graham Montgomery, Dalkey Library; Nigel Curtin, Dún Laoghaire Library; Micheal O'Flaherty, Charleville Library. Finally it is with gratitude that I refer readers to the notes, which serve as a guide to the many documents I consulted in the course of my research. I would like to thank the publishers and authors of works quoted. While every effort has been made to trace copyright holders, I would be grateful to hear from any unacknowledged sources.

LIST OF ILLUSTRATIONS

First section

Market day in Charleville; Main Street, Charleville; Binchy's bakery; and Binchy Park courtesy of Charleville Library.

Maeve's father, William Binchy, flanked by two friends © Father Browne S. J. Collection, Irish Picture Library.

Mother St Dominic and the nuns of the Holy Child; and pictures of Maeve and her school friends courtesy of the Holy Child, Killiney.

Killiney Hill courtesy of National Library of Ireland.

Ballybunion in the 1950s courtesy of Tim Hannan and Clare Mulvihill.

The Mulcahy Orchestra courtesy of the Maurice Mulcahy Orchestra.

Second section

Daniel A. Binchy, Irish Minister to Germany in 1929 courtesy of Bundesarchiv.

Kevin Barry and Graduation Day at University College Dublin courtesy of the National Library of Ireland.

Gaelic Feis © Kennelly Archive.

Maeve, 'the new woman'; the Irish Women's Liberation Movement; William against divorce; Alan Gordon Walker; and Maeve's funeral © *Irish Times*.

Maeve in the landscape she loved © Ian Cook/Time Life Pictures/Getty Images.

End of Term © Fergus Bourke.

Gordon Snell, *Leap in the Dark* © BBC Photo Library.

Maeve, Anthony and Rosie; *Firefly Summer*; author and editor; and Gordon and Rosie courtesy of Rosemary de Courcy.

Maeve and Gordon at home © Ian Cook/Time Life Pictures/ Getty Images.

Maeve, St Patrick's Day float © Richard W. Baron.

All other images author's own.

INDEX

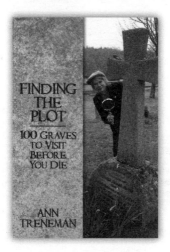

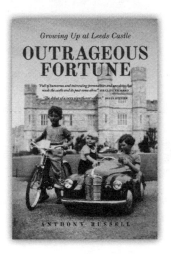